THE SEEKERS

BOOKS BY DANIEL J. BOORSTIN

The Discoverers

The Creators

The Seekers

The Americans: The Colonial Experience
The Americans: The National Experience
The Americans: The Democratic Experience

The Mysterious Science of the Law
The Lost World of Thomas Jefferson
The Genius of American Politics
America and the Image of Europe
The Image: A Guide to Pseudo-Events in America
The Decline of Radicalism
The Sociology of the Absurd
Democracy and Its Discontents
The Republic of Technology
The Exploring Spirit
The Republic of Letters
Hidden History
Cleopatra's Nose
The Daniel J. Boorstin Reader (Modern Library)

The Landmark History of the American People (with Ruth F. Boorstin)
A History of the United States (with Brooks M. Kelley)

THE
SEEKERS

THE STORY OF MAN'S CONTINUING
QUEST TO UNDERSTAND HIS WORLD

DANIEL J. BOORSTIN

The road is always better than the inn.

—CERVANTES

VINTAGE BOOKS

A DIVISION OF RANDOM HOUSE, INC.

NEW YORK

FIRST VINTAGE BOOKS EDITION, NOVEMBER 1999

Copyright © 1998 by Daniel J. Boorstin

Grateful acknowledgment is made to the following for permission
to reprint previously published material:

American Bible Society: Excerpts from the *Today's English Version (TEV) Bible,*
2nd Edition. Copyright © 1992 by American Bible Society.
Reprinted by permission of the American Bible Society.

Fourth Estate Ltd: Excerpts from *A Kierkegaard Reader,* edited by Roger Poole
and Henrik Stangerup. Copyright © 1989 by Roger Poole and Henrik Stangerup.
Reprinted by permission of Fourth Estate Ltd.

Library of Congress has cataloged the Random House edition as follows:
Boorstin, Daniel J. (Daniel Joseph), 1914–
The seekers: the story of man's continuing quest to understand his world /
Daniel J. Boorstin.
p.   cm.
Includes bibliographical references and index.
ISBN 0-679-43445-3
1. Civilization—History.   2. Meaning (Philosophy)—History.
3. Meaning (Philosophy)—Religious aspects—History.   I. Title.
CB151.B66   1998
909—dc21   98-15430

Vintage ISBN: 0-375-70475-2

www.vintagebooks.com

Printed in the United States of America
10 9 8 7 6 5 4 3 2 1

For RUTH

CONTENTS

BOOK TWO: COMMUNAL SEARCH

BOOK THREE:
PATHS TO THE FUTURE

PART VI. THE MOMENTUM OF HISTORY:
WAYS OF SOCIAL SCIENCE

PART VII. SANCTUARIES OF DOUBT

PART VIII. A WORLD IN PROCESS:
THE MEANING IN THE SEEKING

A Personal Note to the Reader

Caught between two eternities—the vanished past and the unknown future—we never cease to seek our bearings and our sense of direction. We inherit our legacy of the sciences and the arts—works of the great Discoverers and Creators, the Columbuses and Leonardos and Shakespeares—recounted in my two earlier volumes. We glory in their discoveries and creations. But we are *all* Seekers. We all want to know *why*. Man is the asking animal. And while the finding, the belief that we have found the Answer, can separate us and make us forget our humanity, it is the seeking that continues to bring us together, that makes and keeps us human. While this brief volume does not aim to survey the history of philosophy or of religion, it does sample ways of seeking by great philosophers and religious leaders in the West. This is a story not of finding but of seeking. I have chosen those Seekers who still speak most eloquently to me, and whose paths toward meaning in our lives and in our history still invite us on our personal quest.

Our Western culture has seen three grand epochs of seeking. First was the heroic Way of Prophets and Philosophers seeking salvation or truth from the God above or the reason within each of us. Then came an age of communal seeking, pursuing civilization in the liberal spirit, and then most recently an age of social sciences, when, oriented toward the future, man seems ruled by forces of history. We draw on all these ways in our personal search. They still speak to us, not so much for their answers as for their ways of asking the questions. In this long quest, Western culture has turned from seeking the end or purpose to seeking causes—from the Why to the How. Might this empty meaning from our human experience? Then how can we recapture and enrich our sense of purpose?

The plan of this volume as a whole is chronological. But in detail it has a shingle scheme. Each of the three books overlaps chronologically with its predecessor, as the story advances from antiquity to the present. This, too, is a story without end, as we continue to explore our humanity in the eternal Why. And we see how we have come from seeking meaning to finding meaning in the seeking.

BOOK ONE

AN ANCIENT HERITAGE

We have a common sky. A common firmament encompasses us.
What matters it by what kind of learned theory each man
looketh for the truth? There is no one way that will take us
to so mighty a secret.
—SYMMACHUS,
ON REPLACING THE STATUE OF VICTORY
IN THE ROMAN FORUM, A.D. 384

Great Seekers never become obsolete. Their answers may be displaced, but the questions they posed remain. We inherit and are enriched by their ways of asking. The Hebrew prophets and the ancient Greek philosophers remain alive to challenge us. Their voices resound across the millennia with a power far out of proportion to their brief lives or the small communities where they lived. Christianity brought together their appeal to the God above and the reason within—into churches, monasteries, and universities that long survived their founders. These would guide, solace, and confine Seekers for the Western centuries.

PART ONE

THE WAY OF PROPHETS: A HIGHER AUTHORITY

When we do science, we are pantheists;
when we do poetry, we are polytheists;
when we moralize we are monotheists.
—GOETHE, *MAXIMS AND REFLECTIONS*

1

From Seer to Prophet: Moses' Test
of Obedience

The future has always been the great treasure-house of meaning. People everywhere, dissatisfied with naked experience, have clothed the present with signs of things to come. They have found clues in the lives of sacrificial animals, in the flight of birds, in the movements of the planets, in their own dreams and sneezes. The saga of the prophets records efforts to cease being the victim of the gods' whims by deciphering divine intentions in advance, toward becoming an independent self-conscious self, freely choosing beliefs.

The Mesopotamians experimented with ways to force from the present the secrets of the future. Diviners watched smoke curling up from burning incense, they interpreted the figures on clay dice to give a name to the coming year. They answered questions about the future by pouring oil into a bowl of water held on their lap and noting its movement on the surface or toward the rim.

The Hebrew scriptures leave traces of how they, too, sensed the divine intention, and gave today's experience the iridescence of tomorrow. Jacob "dreamed, and behold a ladder set up on the earth, and the top of it reached to heaven; and behold the angels of God ascending and descending on it. And behold, the Lord stood above it, and said, 'I am the Lord God of Abraham thy father, and the God of Isaac; the land whereon thou liest, to thee will I give it, and to thy seed.' " And the chief priest used the *Urim* and *Thummim,* sacred stones carried in his breastplate. These gave the divine answer, by whether the "yes" or the "no" stone was first drawn out. David consulted just such an oracle, manipulated by the priest Abiathar, before going into battle against Saul. When the "yes" stone appeared, forecasting his victory over the Philistines, he advanced in battle.

"A man who is now called a 'prophet' (nabi)," we read in the Book of Samuel, "was formerly called a 'seer.' " The "seer" was one who saw the future, and his influence came from his power to predict. The priest-predictor who admitted his clients into the intentions of the gods was held in awe when his predictions came true. The prophet had a different kind of power. He was a *nabi* ("proclaimer" or "announcer") and spoke with the awesome authority of God himself. So, the ancient Hebrew prophets opened the way to belief. "I will raise them up a Prophet from among their brethren, . . ." declared the Lord, "and will put my words in his mouth; and he shall speak unto them all that I shall command him" (Deuteronomy 18:18). They used the words "mouth" and "nabi" interchangeably. Our English "prophet" (from the Greek: a speaker before, or for) carries the same message.

While the seer forecast how events would turn out, the prophet prescribed what men *should* believe, and how they *should* behave. In ancient Israel the two roles at first were not always easily distinguished. But seers, mere forecasters, came to be displaced by prophets, touched by the divinity for whom they spoke.

It was this transformed role that opened the way to the discovery of belief, toward the self-consciousness that awakened people to their freedom to choose, and their responsibilities for choice. The history of ancient Hebrew prophecy is a saga of this unfolding self. The seers, adept at interpreting signs and omens, sometimes drew on their own dreams and visions of ghosts and spirits for sights of the future. The seer could see things on earth that others could not see. But the prophet carried messages from another world. It is not surprising, then, that this "Man of the Spirit" heard his message in ecstasy and so seemed "touched" with madness. His ecstasy was commonly a group phenomenon, sometimes expressed in song.

This view of the prophet as messenger of God is distinctively biblical. With it came distrust of the techniques and tricks of the seer—the ways of the pagan Canaanite.

> When you come into the land that the Lord your God is giving you, don't follow the disgusting practices of the nations that are there. Don't sacrifice your children in the fires on your altars; and don't let your people practice divination or look for omens or use spells or charms, and don't let them consult the spirits of the dead. . . . In the land you are about to occupy, people follow the advice of those who practice divination and look for omens, but the Lord your God does not allow you to do this. Instead, he will send you a prophet like me [Moses] from among your own people, and you are to obey him. (Deuteronomy 18:9–22)

When the founding prophet, Moses, spoke to the Pharaoh he spoke for God: "Thus said Yahweh." And it was through the prophets that God governed His people. What proved crucial for the future of belief in the West was the Hebraic ideology that came with the Mosaic religion.

The single all-powerful, all-knowing, benevolent God would impose on mankind the obligation of belief—and eventually of choice. This "ethical monotheism" would create its own conundrums.

When the prophet brought no mere blueprint of the future but the commandments of God, he offered a new test of the believer, the Test of Obedience. Moses, who had seen God face-to-face, brought the Ten Commandments direct from God on Sinai. The first five commandments—prohibiting the worship of alien gods, forbidding idolatry and blasphemy, commanding observance of the Sabbath and honor to parents—affirmed the traditions of their society. But the remaining five commandments, all cast in the negative—prohibiting murder, adultery, theft, false testifying, and the coveting of neighbors' goods—emphasize the freedom of the hearer to choose a way of right belief and so avoid sin. The Ten Commandments thus made obedience the mark of the believer. This idea would become, millennia later, the very heart of Islam (from Arabic, for "resignation," surrendering to God's will).

But another distinctive element of the Mosaic religion would open the gateways of belief. The intimate God of Moses had mysteriously shared powers with his creatures. He even treated his people as his equals by covenanting with them. The supreme paradox was that this all-powerful Creator-God sought a voluntary relation with his creatures. And the relation between God and his chosen people, the Children of Israel, was to be freely chosen on both sides. "If you listen to these commands and obey them faithfully, then the Lord your God will continue to keep his covenant with you and will show you his constant love, as he promised your ancestors." This peculiar covenant relationship between God and his creatures proclaimed God's preference for a freely given obedience. This signaled the divine intention that man's life should be ruled by his choices and was the historic Hebrew affirmation of free will. As the ancient Hebrews were His chosen people, so He was their chosen God.

About the eighth century B.C. the oracles of the Hebrew prophets were written down by the prophets or their scribes. Then the prophets assumed a role beyond the community where they lived to whom God had first addressed His message. The prophet's oracles now addressed all who would know his words—even far beyond his own time and place. So the utterances of prophets became an enduring prophetic literature. And the words of the prophets became a body of divine teachings valid for people everywhere. Thus writing expanded tribal revelations into a world religion. Such a transformation had occurred before when the utterances of Zarathustra (late second millennium B.C.) became the foundations of Zoroastrianism. It would occur later, too, with the recording of the words of Jesus, and then with the utterances of Mohammed in the seventh century.

2

A Covenanting God: Isaiah's Test of Faith

The prophetic movement that set Western thought on the path of belief and of choice began around 750 B.C. and would last for about five hundred years. It brought no mere commandments but a call to faith. And the literature of prophecy, collected at various times, would give substance to the religion of Israel. The Hebrew prophets were quite different from the earlier cult prophets who had lived near the temples and joined in the rites with the priests—or the court prophets at the royal sanctuaries who predicted the desired victory for the king. Those "professionals" had included many who would be stigmatized as false prophets.

The great Hebrew prophets who opened paths to belief were a varied breed. They could be described as amateurs. For most were not priests. While their utterances had no authentic seal of a sacred profession, each had been called in his own way, and so had his own "vocation," a personal invitation to speak for God. Each directed the voice of God toward the peculiar ills of his time and place. All reminded the people of Israel of how they were failing to live up to their covenant with their chosen God.

The words of the first of this line of classical Hebrew prophets to be preserved in writing were no longer directed only to the king. They already aimed at a wider audience. Amos was an orator directly addressing a whole people. "I am not the kind of prophet who prophesies for pay," Amos explained, "I am a herdsman, and I take care of fig trees. But the Lord took me from my work as a shepherd and ordered me to come and prophesy to his people Israel" (Amos 7:14–15). He preached in a time of prosperity, when the wealthy lived in luxury and the poor were oppressed and overtaxed. Religion, he complained, had become mere ritual. He spoke for social justice and the simple faith of Yahweh. In the Book of Amos we hear God's terrifying judgment on Israel, and foresee its destruction by fire and famine if its people do not repent.

"There will be wailing and cries of sorrow in the city streets. Even farmers will be called to mourn the dead along with those who are paid to mourn.

There will be wailing in all the vineyards. All this will take place because I am coming to punish you." The Lord has spoken. . . . For you it will be a day of darkness and not of light. It will be like a man who runs from a lion and meets a bear! Or like a man who comes home and puts his hand on the wall—only to be bitten by a snake! (Amos 5:16–19)

The people of Israel must choose their way. "Make it your aim to do what is right, not what is evil, so that you may live. Then the Lord God Almighty really will be with you, as you claim he is. Hate what is evil, love what is right, and see that justice prevails in the courts." The succeeding prophets, after their fashion, carried a similar message to their times.

Hosea, following Amos, preached to the northern kingdom of Israel. He attacked their idolatry and forecast the dire consequences for Israel if the people did not mend their ways and return to their God. This prophetic lesson was allegorized in his unfaithful wife, Gomer, who had prostituted herself just as the people Israel had sold themselves to the Canaanite fertility gods. But Hosea, too, concludes with God's covenant-bound promise to give a new life to a repentant Israel.

The Book of Isaiah, the longest of the prophetic books, collects the writings of poets of several periods. The prophet now is no longer only a preacher of reform in the ways of Israel today; he also reveals God's role in history. We hear how He punishes some nations and rewards others. The southern kingdom of Judah, Isaiah warns, is threatened not only by its own sins of disobedience but by the attacks of neighboring Assyria, "the rod of God's wrath." Isaiah's next prophecies come from the time when the people of Judah, the southern kingdom, were in exile in Babylon. They have been punished enough for their sins.

> "Comfort my people," says our God. "Comfort them!
> Encourage the people of Jerusalem.
> Tell them they have suffered long enough
>   and their sins are now forgiven.
> I have punished them in full for all their sins." (Isaiah 40:1–2)

> "Arise, Jerusalem, and shine like the sun;
> The glory of the Lord is shining on you!
> Other nations will be covered by darkness,
> But on you the light of the Lord will shine. . . ." (Isaiah 60:1–2)

Now God promises victory to Israel.

> "I have trampled the nations like grapes, and no one
>   came to help me.
> I trampled them in my anger, and their blood has
>   stained all my clothing.
> I decided that the time to save my people had come; it
>   was time to punish their enemies." (Isaiah 63:3–4)

And He announces a New Creation.

> "I am making a new earth and new heavens. The events of the past will be
> completely forgotten. . . . The new Jerusalem I make will be full of joy, and
> her people will be happy." (Isaiah 65:17–18)

Isaiah's God, then, is the God not only of Israel but of all history. "Heaven is my throne, and the earth is my footstool" (Isaiah 66:1). "I am coming to gather the people of all the nations. When they come together, they will see what my power can do and will know that I am the one who punishes them" (Isaiah 66:18–19). Jeremiah's warnings (late seventh century–early sixth century B.C.) that Israel would be punished for idolatry were drastically fulfilled by the fall of Jerusalem to the Babylonian king Nebuchadnezzar, by the destruction of the Temple, and by the Babylonian exile of the people of Judah.

But a change of heart, God promises, will save the people. "I will make a new covenant with the people of Israel and with the people of Judah. It will not be like the old covenant that I made with their ancestors when I took them by the hand and led them out of Egypt. Although I was like a husband to them they did not keep that covenant. . . . I will put my law within them and write it on their hearts. I will be their God, and they will be my people. None of them will have to teach his fellow countryman to know the Lord, because all will know me, from the least to the greatest" (Jeremiah 31:31–34).

The last of the great prophets, Ezekiel, deported by the conquerors, had carried the message of faith in Yahweh and personal responsibility. The fall of Jerusalem in 587 B.C. and the destruction of the Temple were the fate of idolatry.

The Lord spoke to me and said, "What is this proverb people keep re-
peating in the land of Israel?

> 'The parents ate the sour grapes,
> But the children got the sour taste.'

"As surely as I am the living God," says the Sovereign Lord, "you will
not repeat this proverb in Israel any more. The life of every person belongs
to me, the life of the parent as well as that of the child. The person who sins
is the one who will die." (Ezekiel 18:1–4)

Only the choice of Yahweh and not the merit of the people made Israel
a special people. And since Yahweh is everywhere, the duties of the believer go with him wherever he may be.

Ezekiel, too, sees Israel redeemed in a New Covenant, a kind of new
creation. This he foresees in the famous figure of the Valley of Dry
Bones, when the Lord commands:

> "Prophesy to the bones. Tell these dry bones to listen to the word of the
> Lord. Tell them that I, the Sovereign Lord, am saying to them: I am going to
> put breath into you and bring you back to life. I will give you sinews and
> muscles, and cover you with skin. I will put breath into you and bring you
> back to life. Then you will know that I am the Lord." (Ezekiel 37:4–6)

The survival of the faith of Yahweh did not require a fixed sanctuary.
That faith could live in the heart of a believer anywhere.

3

Struggles of the Believer: Job

While Moses with his commandments posed the test of obedience and the Hebrew prophets posed the test of faith, the search for meaning was not so simple. The Seeker would not be merely a receptive audience. He would put his faith to the test of experience. The classic travail of this test is in the tale of Job. And his struggles would foreshadow the problems of all later Seekers.

The Book of Job in the Old Testament embroiders an old folktale of a just man who suffers unaccountably and seeks explanation from his God. Yahweh Himself had boasted to Satan (the Accuser) in his heavenly council. "Did you notice my servant Job? There is no one on earth as faithful and good as he is. He worships me and is careful not to do anything evil." And Satan replied, "Would Job worship you if he got nothing out of it?" Satan suggests that Job's virtue and piety are explained only by his desire for the reward of prosperity. Job has already received the reward of his virtue in a rich farm, a beautiful family, and the respect of all his neighbors. "You bless everything he does," Satan insists, "and you have given him enough cattle to fill the whole country. But now suppose you take everything he has—he will curse you to your face!"

Yahweh then allows Satan to put the man's faith to the test. Job's cattle are stolen, his sheep are struck by lightning. His children are all killed in a desert storm. And, finally, Satan covers Job's body with sores. Still Job does not curse God, but he does curse the day he was born. And he asks, "Why let men go on living in misery? Why give light to men in grief? Instead of eating, I mourn, and I can never stop groaning."

Three friends then come to Job, and each in turn gives his reasons for Job's suffering. Each has another way of saying that Job is being punished. "Can anyone be righteous in the sight of God or pure before his Creator?" asks Eliphaz. "God does not trust his heavenly servants; he finds fault even with his angels. Do you think he will trust a creature of clay, a thing of dust that can be crushed like a moth?" Bildad suggests that Job's children must have sinned and so God only punished them as they deserved. Zophar insists that Job must have sinned even when he did not know it. "God is punishing you less than you deserve." Job himself does not admit to sin, and does not curse God but only complains of God's capriciousness. There seems to be no understanding of the ways of God. In a second round of dialogues, these friends recite the punishment of the wicked, while Job retorts that on the contrary the wicked do prosper. In still another round, the friends once again accuse Job of sins he had not recognized. But Job demands an opportunity to present his case directly to God. Still Job does not curse God but extols the Wisdom "not to be found among men."

When God finally responds to Job's complaint of God's capriciousness it is not by assertions of His power, but by reminders of His glory and the wonders of His creation. He appeals not to revelation but to experience. And He reminds Job that he is addressing the Creator God.

> Who are you to question my wisdom
>   with your ignorant empty words?
> Stand up now like a man
>   and answer the questions I ask you.
> Were you there when I made the world?
>   If you know so much, tell me about it.
> Who decided how large it would be?
>   Who stretched the measuring line over it?
>   Do you know all the answers? (Job 38:2–9)

> Job, have you ever in all your life
>   commanded a day to dawn?
> Have you ordered the dawn to seize the earth
>   and shake the wicked from their hiding places? (Job 38:12–13)

Unashamedly God boasts the rhythms and glories of nature, along with the bizarre miscellany of his creatures:

> Who is it that feeds the ravens
>   when they wander about hungry
>   when their young cry to me for food?
> Do you know when mountain goats are born?
> Have you watched wild deer give birth? (Job 38:41–39:2)
> Was it you, Job, who made horses so strong
>   and gave them their flowing manes?

Did you make them leap like locusts
   and frighten men with their snorting? (Job 39:19ff.)

Look at the monster Behemoth;
   I created him and I created you.
He eats grass like a cow,
   but what strength there is in his body. (Job 40:15ff.)

Can you catch Leviathan with a fishhook
   or tie his tongue down with a rope?
Can you put a rope through his snout
   or put a hook through his jaws? (Job 41:1ff.)

Touch him once and you'll never try it again. (Job 41:18)

Finally Job confesses that the Lord is "all powerful; that you can do everything that you want . . ."

   I talked about things I did not understand,
      about marvels too great for me to know. . . .
   In the past I knew only what others had told me,
      but now I have seen you with my own eyes.
   So I am ashamed of all I have said
      and repent in dust and ashes. (Job 42:2ff.)

The Lord finally accepts Job's confession, truer than the words of his friends. And blesses Job with a greater prosperity than he had ever known before—fourteen thousand sheep, six thousand camels, two thousand head of cattle, and a thousand donkeys. Now he has seven sons and three daughters, and no other women in the world are as beautiful as Job's daughters. He lived a hundred and forty years, enjoying his grandchildren and great-grandchildren.

Why is Job not punished for questioning God's ways? Nor is he ever told why he had suffered. Was God now rewarding his faith—or only his independent spirit? Could God have admired Job's courage in challenging his maker? Or was God only reminding Job that God's ways were beyond his understanding? Did God enjoy wrestling with his creatures?

This problem that haunted Western thought—Why would a good God allow evil in the world He had created?—was one that Judeo-Christian man had made for himself. It was plainly a by-product of ethical monotheism: a "trilemma" created by the three indisputable qualities of an all-knowing, all-powerful, and all-benevolent God. "If God were good," observed C. S. Lewis, "He would wish to make His creatures perfectly happy, and if God were almighty He would be able to do what He wished. But the creatures are not happy. Therefore God lacks either goodness, or power, or both." Some have chosen a more radical solution. "The only excuse for God," said Stendhal, "is that he does not exist."

Reluctant to abandon belief in their God, Western Seekers have exercised ingenuity and imagination. Not until the seventeenth century did the philosopher Leibniz give a name to this troublesome problem. "Theodicy" (from Greek *theos,* God, and *dike,* justice) he called the study aimed to justify God's ways to man. And ever since Job, thoughtful men and women have been tantalized by the meaning of evil. They would deny neither their God nor the facts of their suffering lives. Where would they turn?

4

A World Self-Explained:
Evil in the East

But this problem of justifying God's ways to man did not haunt all the world equally. Other world religions were not especially troubled by how to account for the suffering of the innocent or the existence of evil. The Muslims (from *islam,* surrender to divine will) believed that God owed no explanations to His insignificant creature, and it was blasphemy for man Job-like to demand one. Still, Muslim thinkers volunteered explanations of their own. One was that everything was predestined by God for His own inscrutable reasons.

> Whomsoever God desires to guide,
> He expands his breast to Islam;
> Whomsoever he desires to lead astray,
> He makes his breast narrow, tight. (Koran, Sura 6:125)

So God's ways need no further gloss, for "He leads none astray save the ungodly." And "Whatever good visits thee, it is of God; whatever evil visits thee is of thyself." For the Muslim, wrong-worship, failure to surrender to the one God, was the sum of all evil, for which man alone must bear responsibility.

This was the paradox of Islam. For every man must bear the consequences of failure to surrender to "the Lord of the Lord of the worlds." Yet only an inscrutable God could guide man to the true worship. In the Koran, "the Book in which there is no doubt," Muslims dissolved the "problem of suffering" in the unchallengeable sovereignty of God. Who was man to make suffering a "problem" when it was simply a fact of Allah's creation?

Hindus and Buddhists, who had not committed themselves to a single Creator God, and so had not the burden of ethical monotheism, found their own ways of explaining evil and suffering. "For Hindu thought," Alan Watts observes, "there is no Problem of Evil. The conventional, relative world is necessarily a world of opposites. Light is inconceivable apart from darkness; order is meaningless without disorder; and, likewise, up without down, sound without silence, pleasure without pain." The fertile Indian imagination enjoyed enriching their populous celestial pantheon and embroidering their prolific mythology. They even imagined some gods who created evil against their own will.

> Prajapati created the golden egg of the universe. He created the gods, and there was daylight. Then, by his downward breathing, he created the demons, and they were darkness for him. He knew that he had created evil for himself; he struck the demons with evil and they were overcome. Therefore, the legend which tells of the battle between gods and demons is not true, for they were overcome because Prajapati struck them with evil. (Sata. 11.1.0.1–11)

Other gods created evil willingly. When a wise man asks why Brhaspati, the guru of the gods, told a lie, he replies, "All creatures, even gods, are subject to passions. Otherwise the universe, composed as it is of good and evil, could not continue to develop." The gods themselves were pleased at the variety and mixture and plenitude of the creation, which would have been incomplete without evil. This mixture was revealed in the paradoxes of good demons and evil gods. The wonderful plenitude appeared in the birth of death, in the overpopulation of the heavens with gods, in the appearance of heretical gods, and every conceivable combination of good and evil.

Still, two quite specific dogmas, shared by Hindus and Buddhists in various forms, diverted them from the problem of the origins of evil and the suffering of the innocent. First, most distinctive and ingenious—and convenient—was the idea of *karma* (from Sanskrit *karman,* "deed," fate, or work). This was a by-product of belief in the transmigration and reincarnation of souls. Karma was a name for the force of all a person's acts—good or evil—in all past incarnations shaping his destiny in the next incarnation. So karma was an ingenious way both of giving each person some responsibility for prosperity or suffering in the present life and, at the same time, of affirming a fatalism that left the person little power to change the fortunes of the present life.

A classical form of the idea imagined this *karmasaya,* an accumulation of the forces of good and evil from what a person did (or failed to do) in earlier incarnations. The suffering or good fortune in the present life, then, was a punishment or reward for earlier acts, just as suffering or good fortune in future lives would compensate for the acts in this life. Personal weaknesses like ignorance, egotism, hatred, and even the will to live all stored the seeds of punishment in the flow of karma. Writers in the Upanishads suggested that somehow the practice of yoga or the power of a god who lived outside the realm of karma might possibly help get a person off the wheel of *samsara* (life-and-death-and-life). Thus a person might avoid consequences of his acts in earlier incarnations. Otherwise, for example, by the rule of karma, a person driven by gluttony in one life might be reborn in the next life as a hog. It was conceivable that a devout ascetic, renouncing all corrupting desires, might struggle free of his karmic debts.

Some Hindu sects saw karma as physical seeds that could be passed on through the generations. A dying father, in one Upanishad text, is said to transfer his karma to his son. "Let me place my deeds on you." Then the son's acts of atonement would free the father in his later incarnation from the consequences of his own earlier misdeeds. The Jains, from the sixth century B.C., made much of these possibilities. They imagined the pure *liva,* or living spirit, in each person that could and should be kept free of the karmic pollution that might burden a person's next incarnation. The Jains' discipline aimed to keep the *liva* unpolluted, and so assure its rising toward enlightenment through rebirths. Their *ahimsa,* dogma of absolute nonviolence, made them fearful even of accidentally killing insects. As rigorous vegetarians, they applied ahimsa to plants. They refused to pick a living fruit from a tree, but waited till it fell ripe to the ground.

Followers of Buddha (who died about 480 B.C.), embroidering the Hindu notions, found their own ways of calculating the ethical balance sheet. They distinguished "deed karman" from "mental karman" (thoughts and motivations), and distinguished deeds from their results. They also attached karma to families and nations. But they kept inviolate their belief in the inevitable balancing of the karmic books. A person's present life was determined by past actions in other incarnations, but only until all those influences had been used up. Still, the chanting of sacred verses by a relative or a monk might reduce the force of evil karma. The Buddhist belief in an all-pervading flux kept them from any idea of a personal immortal soul. But they imagined a kind of karmic residue that adhered through endless incarnations.

Hindu Seekers, not believing in a single original Creation by one Creator God, unlike the West, were not so troubled by the Fall of Man. Instead, they avoided the problem by their belief in cycles—cycles of birth, death, and rebirth for the individual, and cycles for society, too. For them the problem of origins was dissolved: there was no Origin, and there never was a Beginning. Instead they dramatized the never-ending cycles in their myth of the Four Ages of Man, of deep and vague antiquity.

Similar myths in Iran, Greece, and Mesopotamia probably shaped one another from the eighth to the third century B.C. Karma was their way of saying that evil is not a single menacing overarching Sin, but an endless chain. Their culprit—if there was a culprit—was not God, Satan, or Man, but Time. They saw no single melodramatic Fall of Man, with a persuasive serpent, a tempting apple, and a seductive woman. At some remote, indefinable era they imagined that man had passed from Eternity into Time. As one of the traditional Sanskrit Puranas explains:

> In the beginning, People lived in perfect happiness, without class distinc-
> tions or property; all their needs were supplied by magic wishing-trees.
> Then because of the great power of time and the changes it wrought upon
> them, they were overcome by passion and greed. It was from the influence
> of time, and no other cause, that their perfection vanished. Because of their
> greed, the wishing-trees disappeared; the people suffered from heat and
> cold, built houses, and wore clothes. (from Vayu 1.8.77–88)

So began another cycle, when each Age of Man is less pleasant and less virtuous than the last.

> In the Golden Age, dharma was complete. There was no sorrow or delusion
> or old age or misery, no injury or quarrels or hate or famine. Man lived a
> long life. . . . in the Dvapara (the third) Age, dharma was only half left, and
> injury, hatred, falsehood, delusion, evil, disease, old age, and greed arose.
> Castes became mixed.

Civilization accumulates and creates evils—poverty, theft, murder, and falsehood. Then finally our Kali Age ends in conflagration and flood—

a "washing away" to prepare for the next Golden Age. And another cycle.

> At the end of the Age, Brahma created from his back an evil one known as Adharma. From him Kali was descended, foul-smelling and lustful, with gaping mouth and lolling tongue. He begat Fear and a daughter named Death; thus were born the many descendants of Kali, revilers of dharma. Men then became lustful, hypocritical and evil, intent upon penis and stomach, adulterers, drunkards, evil-doers. . . . The earth yielded few crops. Men abandoned the study of the Vedas and sacrifices, and they ceased to offer oblations. The gods were all without sustenance, and they sought refuge with Brahma.

Then the god Vishnu was reborn as Kalki to lead a war against the Buddhists. Kalki finally defeated Kali, but Kali "escaped to another age."

> In the Kali Age, men will be afflicted by old age, disease, and hunger, and from sorrow there will arise depression, indifference, deep thought, enlightenment, and virtuous behavior. Then the Age will change, deluding their minds like a dream, by the force of fate, and when the Golden Age begins, those left over from the Kali Age will be the progenitors of the Golden Age. All four classes will survive as seed, together with those born in the Golden Age, and the Seven Sages will teach them all dharma. Thus there is eternal continuity from Age to Age.

PART TWO

THE WAY OF PHILOSOPHERS: A WONDROUS INSTRUMENT WITHIN

We have an incapacity for proving anything which no amount of dogmatism can overcome. We have an idea of truth which no amount of skepticism can overcome.

—PASCAL

5

Socrates' Discovery of Ignorance

Just as miraculous minuscule Athens provided enduring models for Western ideals of beauty, there, too, were foreshadowed the works of Seekers for millennia to come. Their matchless trinity—Socrates, Plato, and Aristotle—revealed the powers of the courageous mind. None of the great Seekers was wholly displaced. We no longer lean on Galen and Hippocrates, but we never cease to be inspired and encouraged by the Athenian trinity. Plato was a disciple of Socrates, Aristotle a disciple of Plato. So heroic Seekers were links in an unbroken tradition, each a catalyst, an unconscious collaborator of all to follow. We are disciples of all of them. They all have become our contemporaries.

Socrates left his own account of how he was led to the questing venture of philosophy. On the final day of his trial in Athens (399 B.C.) he recalled the crisis of his intellectual life, which was reported by Plato in the *Phaedo* (translated by Benjamin Jowett). Socrates had heard a reading from a book of Anaxagoras, a leading physicist of the day, "that mind was the disposer and cause of all, and I was delighted at this notion, which appeared quite admirable, and I said to myself: If mind is the disposer, mind will dispose all for the best, and put each particular in the best place. . . . I rejoiced to find a teacher of the causes of existence such as I desired. . . . He would tell whether the earth was flat or round, and then give the reasons for it being so." And also the reasons why this was the best.

"What expectations I had formed, and how grievously was I disappointed! As I proceeded, I found my philosopher altogether forsaking mind or any other principle of order, but having recourse to air, and ether, and water, and other eccentricities." It was, he said, as if when someone asked why Socrates was in the courtroom they were told that it was because the muscles and bones of his legs had brought him there. This was only the *how* and not the *why*.

This sense of frustration convinced Socrates that while physicists might have something to say about what materials the world was made of—air, ether, or water—and how these forces moved, they could not allay his uneasiness about the meaning of it all. "I ought to be careful that I did not lose the eye of my soul. . . . I was afraid that my soul might be blinded altogether if I looked at things with my eyes or tried to apprehend them by the help of the senses. And I thought that I had better have recourse to the world of mind and seek there the truth of existence." The best scientists of the day might entertain him with their accounts of the materials of the world and of the beginnings of things, but for Socrates that was not good enough. Socrates turned inward.

Having found that he "had no head for the natural sciences," Socrates set off on his own way of Seeking—which would be the point of departure, the challenge for all Western philosophy. The miraculous ancient Greeks had already taken a long, slow journey from their glowing world of myth into the world of impersonal causes.

Socrates brought the search for meaning down from heaven to earth. While their myths still live, we also owe the Greeks our descent from Olympus. They marked our first steps on the earthly paths of science and philosophy. They led us from the affairs of Apollo and Venus to the chaste realm of elements and ideas. While Job was wrestling with the intentions of his one all-powerful God, a Greek poet, Hesiod (c. 750–675 B.C.), tending sheep on Mount Helicon, heard the Muses call him to sing of the gods. His *Theogony* (Birth of the Gods) told tales of their birth, their sexual frolics and gory battles. He told how Uranus and Gaea had emerged from the primordial Chaos, how the Titans had risen. Kronos had castrated his father, Uranus, and out of his blood came the Furies, the Giants, and the Nymphs of the Ash Trees. From his genitals arose the beautiful Aphrodite. Zeus, born of Uranus and Gaea, enlisted the hundred-handed, fifty-headed monsters to defeat the rebellious Titans, and so he ruled Olympus.

The versatile ancient Ionians, on the islands and shores of western Asia Minor around the Aegean Sea and the eastern coasts of Greece, exercise—and tax—our imagination. To their two Ionian revolutions we owe the origins both of Western science and of Western philosophy. Astonishingly, too, these successive achievements of classical Greece not only were opposite to earlier ways of Greek thought but were quite contrary to each other.

The first Ionian revolution, pioneered by Thales of Miletus (born c. 624 B.C.), boldly dethroned the gods and replaced them with impersonal elements. Instead of the erotic adventures of Kronos and Uranus, Thales sought permanent substances and general causes. "What is the world made of?" For his new question and his answer Aristotle called him "founder" of a new type of philosophy. Celebrated as the first of the "physicists" seeking the basic elements of nature (in Greek, *physis*), Thales offered a simple sensible answer—"that the principle is water . . . getting the notion perhaps from seeing that the nutriment of all things is moist and kept alive by it . . . and from the fact that the seeds of all things have a moist nature, and that water is the origin of the nature of moist things." Among other "physicists," Anaximander imagined a primal mass in everlasting motion, while Anaximenes conceived the principle to be air.

All of them imagined that the different kinds of matter were produced by heat, motion, and other natural processes. This was an epochal axiom of emerging science. Another potent and durable concept was supplied by Pythagoras, an emigrant from the Greek island of Samos to southern Italy (c. 530 B.C.). He saw a Kosmos made of number. The Pythagoreans charmed by their mystic notion of a living breathing universe, by the transmigration of souls, and their cosmology of musical harmony. They took a great leap from the mythic whimsical world of Hesiod to an orderly universe of causes. So they provided a rudimentary vocabulary for science. But only the rudiments.

In contrast to their other spectacular achievements, the ancient Greeks made remarkably little progress in the physical sciences. Though adept at the application of their knowledge to architecture, metallurgy, pottery, navigation, and astronomy, they left a legacy of obsolete theoretical sciences. Since they never divorced science from philosophy, their science remained, somehow, a search for meaning. And it never outlived its birth in philosophy—in the search for wisdom. They never recovered from their proud divorce of theory from practice. And in fact they created a grand enduring monument to that divorce. Plato's theory of ideas treated the whole world of experience as somehow unreal, by contrast to the pure and changeless ideas, according to him the only real source of knowledge. This first Ionian revolution—from mythology to "physics"—proved a dead end. The Greek physicists had demanded too much too soon. And they were not the substantial source of modern science nor the enduring catalyst of the modern scientific spirit. Instead, they produced what A. E. Taylor calls one of the periodic bankruptcies of science.

A second Ionian revolution—more momentous for the future of a seeking mankind—found Socrates as its leader and symbol. He now made philosophy more intimately personal than ever before. He asked not only what but whether man knew. Socrates left no writing and no dogma. His radically human approach to philosophy was expressed in his life. His historic influence would be not in his answers but in his questions. And he would survive in dialogues—a new literary form of questions and answers, followed by more questions and answers toward still more questions. For him it was the spoken word, the encounter between living people, with the word as the catalyst of thought, that struck sparks. And the spoken word had an enticing elusiveness, not found in writing, which always invited scrutiny. Its meaning depended on memory, which also had a special meaning for him.

The influence of Socrates, then, was not in a school of philosophy but in his person. Historians of philosophy separate the "Pre-Socratics" from the Socratics not because of a new doctrine but for a new emphasis, a new kind of seeking. His iridescence for later Seekers came from his life and the circumstances of his death. Unlike Jesus, Socrates had the misfortune to have his life reported by literary persons—Aristophanes, Xenophon, Plato, Aristotle—each with his own ax to grind.

So a halo of ambiguity surrounds the life of Socrates. And his life has become doubly intriguing, because, as Bertrand Russell observed, we really do not know how much we know about the real Socrates. Everything we know about him is reflected in the distorting mirror of another strong personality. The scholars' "Socrates Problem" allows each of us to have our own Socrates. Beside the biographical memoir Plato had to invent a new literary form—the dialogue—to communicate the meaning of Socrates. No writings of Socrates survived, and his meaning would live in reports of his spoken words.

Plato deftly revealed the suspense of the philosopher's quest. We are told that Plato began not as a philosopher but as a dramatist. He had written tragedies before he met Socrates, but, according to tradition, he burned them after he came under the influence of Socrates. Then he used his dramatic talent to interpret a philosopher whose message could be carried only in the spoken word. For a philosopher whose mission was the discovery of ignorance, the Socratic dialogues provided a convenient vehicle. The drama of the living search in Plato's Socratic dialogues was somehow not diminished by their uniformly inconclusive conclusions.

Another subtle Socratic paradox was latent in the dialogues—the idealized art of conversation. Socrates himself repeatedly denied the role of teacher, and he never bores us with the wagging didactic finger. But he did boast the role of midwife. "And like the midwives, I am barren, and the reproach which is often made against me, that I ask questions of others and have not the wit to answer them myself, is very just—the reason is, that the god compels me to be a midwife, but does not allow me to bring forth. . . . But to me and the god they owe their delivery. . . . many of them in their ignorance . . . have gone away too soon; and have not only lost the children of whom I had previously delivered them by an ill bringing up, but have stifled whatever else they had in them by evil communications." The very midwifely ("maieutic") technique by which Socrates revealed the general ignorance suggested that truths lay undiscovered within each person being questioned. So the Socratic technique implied a latent wisdom in everyone.

There was a real Socrates, born in Athens about 469 B.C. His father probably was a prosperous stonemason or sculptor, and Socrates himself may have begun learning the sculptor's craft. His early years seem to have been conventional enough. He served as a hoplite, or member of the heavy-armed infantry. These were citizens not wealthy enough to provide themselves with cavalry horses, but able to afford the heavy body armor that we associate with the Greek warrior—a helmet with nasal and cheek pieces, a breastplate and greaves (for the leg below the knee). His chief defense was a heavy bronze shield, circular or elliptical, attached to the left arm. For weapons he carried a short straight iron sword and a nine-foot spear ready for thrusting. Burdened with this heavy armor, well-drilled hoplites in proper formation could resist archers or cavalry. Fighting for Athens in the Great Peloponnesian War, Socrates acquired a reputation for endurance and courage.

It is hard to imagine the squat and diffident Socrates known to historians of philosophy in this belligerent macho role. But it was his feats on the battlefield that first brought him a citywide reputation. "I was with him in the retreat," his companion Laches reported of him at Delium in Boeotia in 424, "and if everyone were like Socrates, our city would never have come to disaster." During the expedition to Potidea he saved the life of Alcibiades, who would play a troublesome role for Socrates in the chaotic politics of his maturity. Socrates reputedly refused to take part in politics, for holding office, he said, would require sacrifice of his principles.

As a citizen he showed conspicuous courage. In 406, as a member of the Boule, or legislative council, he alone stood out against popular demand that some accused generals be tried en masse instead of individually, as the law required. Membership on this council was not a political office but only a routine citizens' duty. Again two years later, when the oligarchy of the Thirty Tyrants tried to implicate Socrates in their acts of judicial murder, his friends went along, but at risk of his life Socrates stood firm. His independence then would have been fatal if there had not been a counterrevolution the next year restoring the democracy. And this same independence of spirit would lead to his trial in 399 B.C. for introducing strange gods and corrupting youth.

How did the city's admired model soldier become its insufferable gadfly—and martyr to the independent mind? To answer this interesting question we have no solid autobiographical evidence, and only the tendentious accounts of envious or adoring philosophers and historians. Still, despite the confusing evidence, there is incandescent coherence to the legendary Socrates. We, lay newcomers to the "Problem of Socrates," must marvel at how the disparate rays of contradictory testimony collect into a brilliant beacon illuminating the philosopher's endless quest.

If there ever was a man with a vocation, it was surely Socrates, yet how or when he heard the call we do not know. There is no evidence of his being a member of any unorthodox religious sect. But there were legends of his occasionally sensing a divine sign (what he called "the customary sign") of his daimonion. There is ample evidence that he was not governed only by the prosaic syllogism. When it might have incriminated him, in his final speech to the court, Socrates recalled his periodic mystic experience.

I experience a certain divine or daemonic something, which in fact Meletus has caricatured in the indictment. It began in childhood and has been with me ever since, a kind of voice, which whenever I hear it always turns me back from something I was going to do, but never urges me to act. This is what has prevented me from taking part in politics. (Plato, *Apology,* Jowett trans.)

Among the remarkable qualities of Socrates, Alcibiades recalled that Socrates was never seen drunk, that he had an astonishing fortitude and endurance.

> One morning he was thinking about something which he could not resolve; he would not give it up, but continued thinking from early dawn until noon—there he stood fixed in thought; and at noon attention was drawn to him, and the rumour ran through the wondering crowd that Socrates had been standing and thinking about something ever since the break of day. At last, in the evening after supper, some Ionians out of curiosity . . . brought out their mats and slept in the open air that they might watch him and see whether he would stand all night. There he stood until the following morning; and with the return of light he offered up a prayer to the sun, and went his way. (Plato, *The Symposium,* Jowett trans.)

Socrates himself seems to have put great store by this divine inner voice. For at the end of the *Apology,* after his condemnation and his refusal to request a change in the penalty or be smuggled out of the country, he reassures his friends. "Hitherto, the divine faculty of which the internal oracle is the source has constantly been in the habit of opposing me even about trifles. . . . But the oracle made no sign of opposition, either when I was leaving my house in the morning, or when I was on my way to the court, or while I was speaking, at anything I was going to say. . . . It is an intimation that what has happened to me is a good, and that those who think that death is an evil are in error."

By the time Socrates was in his late thirties he seems to have gathered a following of young Athenians intrigued by his person and his quizzical view of life. They were so impressed that one of them, the impetuous young Chaerephon, actually went to Delphi (as Plato and Xenophon report) to ask the oracle, "Is anyone wiser than Socrates?" Pythia, the priestess of Apollo, responded that no one was. The Greek oracles, like the Hebrew prophets, spoke for the god. But, unlike the Hebrew prophets, the Delphic oracle—the Pythian priestess speaking for Apollo—had a reputation for wanting to please its clients. It would leave the suppliant to riddle out his own preferred meaning. The wise worshipper would not jump to conclusions. So, when the Athenians asked how to find safety against an impending Persian invasion, they were advised to seek the safety of a "wooden wall." After the meaning was debated at length, Themistocles' interpretation was accepted—that the god meant the bulwark of a strong navy. In Socrates' case, too, the oracle might have meant the obvious—that Socrates was indeed the wisest of men. Or it might have carried the god's message that no one was wiser than Socrates simply because wisdom was not to be found among men.

In any event, Socrates called the oracle's message the turning point in his life. As Plato reports Socrates' words in the *Apology:*

> When I heard the answer, I said to myself, What can the god mean? and what is the interpretation of his riddle? for I know that I have no wisdom, small or great. What then can he mean when he says that I am the wisest of men? And yet he is a god, and cannot lie; that would be against his nature. After long consideration, I thought of a method of trying the question. I reflected that if I could only find a man wiser than myself, then I might go to the god with a refutation in my hand. I should say to him, "Here is a man who is wiser than I am; but you said that I was the wisest." (*Apology,* Jowett trans.)

Literal-minded historians have doubted that Socrates could have reacted in this way, for he hardly showed the respect he professed for the god if he obeyed the god by trying to prove him a liar.

In fact, as Socrates himself explained, it was his effort to disprove the oracle that made him the host of enemies who eventually brought on his fatal trial. He went about interviewing Athenians in all walks of life. He first interviewed a politician who had a reputation for wisdom.

> When I began to talk to him, I could not help thinking that he was not really wise, although he was thought wise by many, and still wiser by himself; and thereupon I tried to explain to him that he thought himself wise, but was not really wise; and the consequence was that he hated me, and his enmity was shared by several who were present and heard me. So I left him, saying to myself, as I went away: Well, although I do not suppose that either of us knows anything really beautiful and good, I am better off than he is—for he knows nothing, and thinks that he knows; I neither know nor think that I know. In this latter particular, then, I seem to have the slight advantage of him. Then I went to another who had still higher pretensions to wisdom, and

my conclusion was exactly the same. Whereupon I made another enemy of him, and of many others besides him. (*Apology*, Jowett trans.)

Socrates went to the poets. To his astonishment he found "that there is hardly a person present who would not have talked better about their poetry than they did themselves. Then I knew that not by wisdom do poets write poetry, but by a sort of genius and inspiration; they are like diviners or soothsayers who also say many fine things, but do not understand the meaning of them." When he consulted the artisans he found that they did know many fine things of which he was ignorant. But they fell into the same error as the poets: "because they were good workmen they thought that they also knew all sorts of high matters, and this defect in them overshadowed their wisdom." So his inquisitions multiplied his enemies.

But even some of his devoted disciples questioned the effectiveness of his educational technique. An ardent admirer, Antisthenes (c. 445–360 B.C.), founder of the Cynic school of philosophy, embarrassed Socrates. He asked why, if Socrates really believed women to be just as educable as men, he was unable to improve the temperament of his wife, Xanthippe, reputedly "the most troublesome woman of all time." By this woman whose name would become a byword for the shrew, Socrates had had three sons. Through the wine haze of the symposium, Socrates good-naturedly retorted that it was precisely because of her reputation that he had married her—to test his educative talents. Just as a horse trainer shows his mettle not by handling a docile animal, so, he said, if he could tame Xanthippe he would have proved there was no one he could not mollify.

These interviews persuaded Socrates that he had found the true meaning of the Delphic oracle: "He [the Delphic oracle] is not speaking of Socrates, he is only using my name by way of illustration, as if he said, He, O men, is the wisest, who, like Socrates knows that his wisdom is in truth worth nothing" (*Apology*). So it became his vocation to vindicate the oracle by quizzing people of all sorts, and showing them that they were not as wise as they thought they were. And he explained that he had no time for public affairs or for any concern of his own, and remained in poverty by his devotion to the god. Aristotle, perhaps deliberately to discredit Plato's dramatic tale in the *Apology*, was reported to offer a much simpler explanation. He suggested it was Socrates' own visit to Delphi, where he was impressed by the inscription "Know Thyself" carved on the temple there, that inspired him to pursue his studies of the nature of man.

Whatever may have been the impulse, Socrates' historic mission was the discovery of ignorance. As a young man he seems to have shared the physicists' interest in nature. But this interest dimmed as he saw that their cosmologies spawned a chaos of contradictory oversimplifications. And meanwhile the Sophists—like Protagoras and Gorgias and others—prospered not as a school of philosophy but as teachers of the arts of persuasion and the way to success. Protagoras said he taught "virtue," by which he meant the arts of succeeding in his conventional world. His famous motto "Man is the measure of all things," which has become a slogan of latter-day humanism, seems to have carried a different message for him. It then expressed his doubts of the authority of the gods, and affirmed a relativism that made it man's highest duty to obey the prevailing rules of his community. Gorgias was celebrated for developing the arts of rhetoric and persuasive oratory, which burgeoned with the rise of the democratic party in Athens. In these unhappy years of the Peloponnesian War (431–404 B.C.), the people of Athens suffered a disastrous plague (430–429 B.C.) along with military defeat and the treachery of trusted leaders. With Athens' decline from the self-confident age of Pericles (c. 460–429 B.C.), the Sophists were only another symptom of cynicism and the distrust of absolutes. The god of success could not satisfy a society that had so conspicuously failed in its long battle for empire. Was there, perhaps, some way of thought, some instrument, some resource, that transcended the whims of the populace or the conceit of politicians? Could the questing mind, cleansed of pride, at least find a way to knowledge that might be the highest, permanent good? Meanwhile, could the seeking itself be a solace?

In later years a number of doctrines were fathered on Socrates. One was the doctrine of forms (or ideas), which Plato attributed to him and on which Plato built his own philosophy. This was the notion that behind every term like beauty or goodness lay the pure and changeless form of an idea, accessible not to the senses but only to the mind. What the senses perceived, then, seemed real only because they somehow participated in that ideal form. Aristotle also made Socrates the founder of logic. "For two things may be fairly ascribed to Socrates—inductive arguments and universal definition, both of which are concerned with the starting point of science." Still Aristotle himself doubted the applicability of scientific method to ethics. And competing schools of philosophy would grow out of both the doctrine of forms and the methods of Socratic logic. Socrates' own contribution to these ideas would be long debated and disputed. But Socrates would survive as the discoverer of ignorance, the patron saint of self-scrutiny.

Despite the sanctity of the Word, the Seekers who left the most durable imprint on Western history are those who embodied the mystery of their achievement in their lives—and their deaths. The message of Jesus was less in what he said than in his life and Crucifixion, his martyrdom for human "salvation." The words of sacred Scripture would be endlessly debated. What preserved a single Christian tradition was a Man on the Cross. Similarly, the message of Socrates was not in what he taught, but in how he urged men to seek, dramatized in his life and martyrdom. Plato was astonished at Socrates' "absolute unlikeness to any human being that is or ever has been." His final affirmation at his trial was "that the unexamined life is not worth living." So he set us on a philosophic path where the effort of thought was justified not by the finding but by the seeking.

This elusiveness justified Socrates' repeated claim that he, one of history's most influential teachers, was not a teacher at all but only a kind of midwife. "I have never been the teacher of anyone whatsoever." The ambiguity of his martyrdom becomes more tantalizing with the centuries. Precisely why was he sentenced to death, and why did he choose death over flight?

The trial of Socrates was embodied in the turbulent Athens of the fifth century. We have already seen enough of Socrates' life to explain the hostility of powerful Athenians. Socrates was a friend of Critias, the unscrupulous leader of the Thirty Tyrants who brought a reign of terror in 404, the year of Athens' surrender to Sparta. But Socrates had earned the enmity of the Thirty Tyrants by refusing to go along with their acts of judicial murder. He was also a friend of the traitor Alcibiades, who was thought responsible for the fall of Athens. But he had also been a critic of the democratic constitution, which had now taken over.

Socrates was caught in the crossfire. "It was not surprising," Plato reported, "that in a period of revolution excessive penalties were inflicted by some persons on political opponents. . . . some of those in power brought my friend Socrates . . . to trial before a court of law, laying a most iniquitous charge against him and one most inappropriate in his case; for it was on a charge of impiety that some of them prosecuted and others condemned and executed the very man who would not participate in the iniquitous arrest of one of the friends of the party then in exile, at the time when they themselves were in exile and misfortune."

The indictment, as Xenophon reports, declared Socrates "guilty of refusing to recognize the gods recognized by the State and introducing other, new divinities. He is also guilty of corrupting the youth. The penalty demanded is death." The chief accuser, Meletus, was, according to Socrates, "an unknown young man with straight hair and a skimpy beard," who seems to have been used by Anytus, a powerful democratic politician. But the recent democratic amnesty forbade political charges. Meletus was probably chosen by Anytus for his conspicuous religious enthusiasm. In that same year Meletus initiated another "religious" prosecution with a speech that survives as a rare voice from antiquity of religious fanaticism.

Since Socrates was no enthusiast for democracy, he was a natural enemy of the party in power in 399 B.C., the year of his trial. He denied that he had taught strange gods. But his own speech at the trial explained why he could have been called the "corrupter of youth."

> Young men of the richer classes, who have not much to do, come about me of their own accord; they like to hear the pretenders examined, and they often imitate me, and proceed to examine others; there are plenty of persons, as they quickly discover, who think that they know something, but really know little or nothing; and then those who are examined by them instead of being angry with themselves are angry with me: This confounded Socrates, they say; this villainous misleader of youth! . . . for they do not like to confess that their pretence of knowledge has been detected—which is the truth. (*Apology*)

After conviction, the court did not have to accept the penalty prescribed by the prosecutor. The accused himself could suggest a lighter penalty. And the prosecutors seem to have expected or even hoped that Socrates would propose banishment, which the court would have accepted, and so relieved them of the guilt of murder.

Socrates would have none of this, as Plato reports. Instead of asking for mercy, Socrates flaunted his uncanny talent for irritating. Which helps us understand the impatience with his character expressed by acute historians. "The more I read about him," Lord Macaulay declared, "the less I wonder why they poisoned him." Socrates demanded a reward for all he had done for Athens. Like the Olympic winners and others who had brought glory to the city, should not he, too, be given free meals in the Town Hall? Still he would not refuse to pay a fine, which his supporters had already agreed to raise for him. By Xenophon's different account Socrates showed his contempt by not offering any alternative to execution. He also refused the offer of his friend Crito to help him escape prison and leave the country. He would not think of his own life or his children first, and justice afterward. He would not violate the laws of the city that had nurtured him. "Now you depart in innocence," Socrates reported hearing the voice of the laws of Athens, "a sufferer and not a doer of evil; a victim, not of the laws but of men. But if you go forth, returning evil for evil, and injury for injury, breaking the covenants and agreements which you have made with us, and wronging those whom you ought least of all to wrong, that is to say, yourself, your friends, your country and us, we shall be angry with you while you live, and our brethren, the laws in the world below, will receive you as an enemy" (*Crito,* Jowett trans.).

The inner voice on which he finally relied reassured Socrates in his submission to the death penalty. "This, dear Crito, is the voice which I seem to hear murmuring in my ears, like the sound of the flute in the ears of the mystic; that voice, I say, is humming in my ears, and prevents me from hearing any other. . . . Leave me then, Crito, to fulfil the will of God, and to follow whither he leads" (*Crito*).

In this court of random Athenians of all stations, a shift of only thirty votes (Socrates observed) might have brought acquittal. After Socrates' own statement, reported in Plato's *Apology,* the court voted the death penalty by an even larger majority.

The irony of the trial and death of Socrates still challenges us. The gadfly of the state, who had repeatedly risked his life in battle for his city and then outraged citizens by asserting the superiority of individual reason over the conventional wisdom, finally gave his life in deference to the laws of his little community. It is no wonder that the trial of Socrates has become a trial of historians demanding answers where Socrates himself saw only questions. To this sanctuary of doubt, Socrates testified in his last words, reported by Plato, which could be an invocation to Western philosophy:

> Still I have a favour to ask of the judges. When my sons are grown up, I would ask you, O my friends, to punish them; and I would have you trouble them, as I have troubled you, if they seem to care about riches, or anything, more than about virtue; or if they pretend to be something when they are really nothing—then reprove them, as I have reproved you, for not caring about that for which they ought to care, and thinking that they are something when they are really nothing. And if you do this, both I and my sons will have received justice at your hands.
>
> The hour of departure has arrived, and we go our ways—I to die, and you to live. Which is better, God only knows. (*Apology,* Jowett trans.)

6

The Life in the Spoken Word

The grand concepts that for the Western world would define morals, create communities, cement nations, and build empires would be the product of a small city-state. Ten men are too few for a city, Aristotle would say, "and if there are a hundred thousand it is a city no longer." The great Athenian Empire hardly had the population of a modern city. In Pericles' day, the whole of Attica had some 250,000 people, and Athens had about 80,000, who were reduced by the Great Peloponnesian War and the plague to as few as 21,000. That so many of the ideas that ruled the Western world should have come from so few is another miracle of classic Greece. Alfred North Whitehead is not alone in describing the tradition of European philosophy as "a series of footnotes to Plato."

And Plato's work bore the indelible mark of this small Athenian community. The Way of Dialogue was a special way of seeking. It was the style of the Seeker in a community of the *spoken* word. We miss its meaning unless we grasp this peculiarly fertile role of the spoken word in classic Greece, which left the secondary role to writing. For us the thinker is a writer; for them the thinker was a speaker. As Socrates explained (in Plato's *Phaedrus*), just as the painting, unlike the living person, cannot respond to questions, so, too, the written word is lifeless. But the spoken word, "an intelligent word graven in the soul of the learner . . . can defend itself, and knows when to speak and when to be silent." "The living word of knowledge has a soul . . . of which the written word is properly no more than an image." So the thinker "will not seriously incline to 'write' his thoughts 'in water' with pen and ink, sowing words which can neither speak for themselves nor teach the truth adequately to others" (*Phaedrus*).

A thinking person, then, must not take the written word too seriously, for he knows that the true life of ideas is not there. "In the garden of letters he will sow and plant, but only for the sake of recreation and amusement; he will write them down as memorials to be treasured against the forgetfulness of old age, by himself, or by any other man who is treading the same path. He will rejoice in beholding their tender growth; and while others are refreshing their souls with banqueting and the like, this will be the pastime in which his days are spent."

> *Phaedrus.* A pastime, Socrates, as noble as the other is ignoble, the pastime of a man who can be amused by serious talk, and can discourse merrily about justice and the like.
> *Socrates.* True, Phaedrus. But nobler by far is the serious pursuit of the dialectician, who, finding a congenial soul, by the help of science sows and plants therein words which are able to help themselves and him who planted them, and are not unfruitful, but have in them a seed which others brought up in different soils render immortal, making the possessors of it happy to the utmost extent of human happiness.

If Plato believed what he put in the mouth of Socrates, he must have felt embarrassment at having burdened later generations with a score of written dialogues besides more than a dozen Letters. Perhaps Plato saw his writings as a harmless pastime.

In his own person, in the Seventh Letter, Plato disowned any who would claim to have written down his teachings.

> Thus much, at least, I can say about all writers, past or future, who say they know the things to which I devote myself, whether by hearing the teaching of me or of others, or by their own discoveries—that according to my view it is not possible for them to have any real skill in the matter. There neither is nor ever will be a treatise of mine on the subject. For it does not admit of exposition like other branches of knowledge; but after much converse about the matter itself and a life lived together, suddenly a light, as it were, is kindled in one soul by a flame that leaps to it from another, and thereafter sustains itself. (Seventh Letter, J. Harward trans.)

Plato lived in an age of transition in Athens when the written word was invading the world of learning. And this seems to confirm the warnings (reported by Plato) of the Egyptian god-king Thamus to Thoth, the inventor of writing. "This discovery of yours will create forgetfulness in the learners' souls, because they will not use their memories; they will trust to the external written characters and not remember of themselves. The specific which you have discovered is an aid not to memory, but to reminiscence, and you give your disciples not truth, but only the semblance of truth . . ." (*Phaedrus*).

In the earlier great age of ancient Greek literature, writing had been mainly an aid to speaking. The *Iliad* and the *Odyssey* were written down to be memorized for singing or speaking. The "works" of the great tragedians—Aeschylus, Sophocles, Euripides—were dramas written to be witnessed in ritual competition. A pitifully small sample in writing survives of even the three great tragedians. Most of the Greek tragedians survive only in their names. We are misled because the "literature" that makes the ancient Greeks great for *us* survives as the written Word. So we *read* the words of Demosthenes that were intended to be *heard*.

In Plato's time the relative merits of the written and the spoken word were being debated. Herodotus and Thucydides had produced written histories, and Anaxagoras and Democritus had written works of philosophy. Thucydides apologizes and explains at the outset of his history that his written account can only approximate the evanescent spoken word. But he aims to provide "a possession for all time," which he describes as if it were a new literary form. Reading aloud was still the common way of enjoying literature. The crucial event in Socrates' intellectual life (reported by Plato in *Phaedo*), which we have noted, was not his own reading from a book of Anaxagoras, but hearing someone read the book. The rhetorician and Sophist Alcidamas (fourth century B.C.), champion of Gorgias and the old school of Sophists, was still arguing that speeches should never be written down, even for delivery, but should always be improvised. We can better understand the Athenians' impatience with the written word when we recall the cumbersome form of the written word in their time. The reader had to unroll the papyrus, seeking passages without aid of an index—in an unpunctuated text, without paragraphs or even spaces between words.

Athens, we must remember, was not governed by pieces of paper shuffled among bureaucrats. Government was by a live assembly of citizens, each of whom served as soldier and, in the democratic interludes, as judge and member of the governing body, all in his own person. The idea of *representative* government did not occur to them. In the sovereign assembly the citizens could debate, offer proposals, decide on war or peace, on taxation or other government measures. A smaller body of some five hundred, the *boule,* prepared for these meetings, controlled foreign policy, supervised administration, and sat as a judicial body (as in Socrates' case). These five hundred were chosen by lot for one year, but no one could serve more than twice in his lifetime. Most officials, too, were chosen by lot, and all were directly responsible to the Assembly or the Council (Boule). Participation in Athenian democracy meant being physically present, and saying your piece in your own voice. Being a citizen meant going frequently to the center of government, an automatic limitation on the size of the city-state.

Since political wisdom was assumed to emerge from these encounters of the spoken word, it is not surprising that Athenians thought the fires of philosophic wisdom might be ignited in the same way. "After much converse about the matter itself and a life lived together, suddenly a light, as it were, is kindled in one soul by a flame that leaps to it from another, and thereafter sustains itself" (Seventh Letter). What the Assembly and the Boule were to Athenian politics, the Dialogue would be to Athenian philosophy.

It is significant but not surprising that none of Socrates' writing has survived, since his way of seeking was in the living words. Yet all of Plato's dialogues that we know about have survived in writing. And nothing is more revealing of Plato's way of seeking than his chosen vehicle, the dialogue. Just as the exchanges of the living words of citizens would ensure the health of the city-state, so the converse of citizens in dialogue could promote the health of their souls. Socrates, a man of notable physical vigor, and an admirer of medical science, considered himself a doctor of the soul. His conversations were not in a lecture hall, but in an open-air Athenian athletic center. To the gymnasium (from the Greek word meaning "place to exercise naked") Athenians came for the vigor of their bodies, filling rest periods with conversation. An ancient Greek gymnasium was usually an open court surrounded by columns, with places for running and jumping and a covered hall for wrestling and bathing. This legacy—athletics for body and mind—survived in the names of two great Athenian schools of philosophy, Plato's "Academy" and Aristotle's "Lyceum." Both were names of gymnasium groves near Athens.

The playful interludes and interruptions in Plato's dialogues remind us that the Way of Dialogue was exercising the mind at play. Plato believed that learning could not be forced, and that to be remembered, lessons should take the form of play. Man must be wary of taking himself too seriously. "May we not conceive each of us living beings to be a puppet of the Gods," observes Plato's Athenian Stranger in *The Laws,* "either their plaything only, or created with a purpose—which of the two we cannot certainly know."

Far from being a textual exercise, the pursuit of philosophy, the love of wisdom—for Plato as for his teacher Socrates—was an athletic activity of minds in converse. The Dialogue as a written work seems to have been an invention of Plato, in whose hands this new literary form flourished. Plato is reputed to have written dramas, which he destroyed. And his dialogues are full of drama. His Socratic dialogues, as Werner Jaeger has observed, revealed "his desire to show the philosopher in the dramatic instant of seeking and finding, and to make the doubt and the conflict visible." And the dialogue survived as a literary form for Seekers. Though less appropriate to Aristotle's way of seeking, Aristotle's own dialogues (most written before the death of Plato) were applauded. They survive only in fragments. The form was to be exploited by Plutarch and Lucian, and the Latin dialogue provided Cicero with the vehicle for some of his most durable ideas.

Plato is rare among the great figures of ancient Greek thought in that the whole of his works seem to have been preserved. Socrates (in Plato's *Phaedrus*) explained that "lovers of wisdom, or philosophers" were worthy of their name only if they were able to defend their ideas "by spoken arguments, which leave their writings poor in comparison." "He who cannot rise above his own compilations and compositions, which he has been long patching and piecing, adding some and taking away some, may be justly called poet or speechmaker or law-maker." But not a philosopher.

7

Plato's Other-World of Ideas

In early life Plato had fancied himself in a political career, but he was turned off by the sordid politics of Athens in the era of the Peloponnesian Wars. He saw the Thirty Tyrants, including his relatives, try to involve his friend, the aged Socrates, in their crimes. When Socrates, "the most upright man of that day," was sent to his death on fabricated charges, Plato determined to "withdraw from any connection with the abuses of the time." And so he stifled his "strong impulse towards political life."

What we know of Plato's sallies into politics leaves us doubly glad that he saved himself from a longer career of frustration. His naive Sicilian adventure proved him a poor judge of people and of political opportunities. Still, he was not pipe-dreaming when he had thought of a political career. For his distinguished family and the Athenian tradition of civic participation would easily have offered him opportunities for leadership. But we have little reason to believe that he could have been another Pericles, or that he had the conspiratorial talents even to be an Alcibiades.

Plato claimed to trace his ancestry back to the old kings of Athens, to friends of the legendary Solon, and finally to the god Poseidon. His stepfather, in whose house he was raised, was a prominent supporter of Pericles. But Plato himself had seen more than enough of Athenian politics to make him critical of "democratic" ways. When only eighteen he seems to have been a listener, if not actually a disciple, of Socrates.

After Socrates was put to death, his friends, under suspicion by the regime, may have moved for a while to nearby Megara. At this time Plato may have taken something like a grand tour of southern Italy, Cyrene, neighboring Africa and Egypt. Some of his remarks in *The Laws* on Egyptian customs, games, art, and music have the authentic ring of the observer. Before he first visited Sicily, he had already arrived at his familiar axiom that "there will be no cessation of evils for the sons of men, till either those who are pursuing a right and true philosophy receive sovereign power in the States, or those in power in the States by some dispensation of providence become true philosophers."

What Plato, now in his forties, found in southern Italy and Sicily excited his "strong disapproval of the kind of life which was there called the life of happiness, stuffed full as it was with the banquets of the Italian Greeks and Syracusans, who ate to repletion twice every day, and were never without a partner for the night. . . . For with these habits formed early in life, no man under heaven could possibly attain to wisdom—human nature is not capable of such an extraordinary combination."

The fateful event of this first visit to Syracuse was meeting an attractive and impressionable young man, whose fortunes and misfortunes would draw Plato into Sicilian politics for the rest of his life. Dion became his eager disciple. At first Plato did not realize that Dion, son-in-law of the reigning "tyrant," Dionysius I, was contriving the overthrow of the ruling tyranny. Could this be a time and a place for testing Plato's vision of the philosopher-king? "For Dion, who rapidly assimilated my teaching as he did all forms of knowledge, listened to me with an eagerness which I had never seen equalled in any young man, and resolved to live for the future in a better way than the majority of Italian and Sicilian Greeks." Dion's reformed ways made him unpopular among his contemporaries. Numerous stories recount the efforts of Dionysius I to be rid of Plato. One tells that Dionysius I had Plato kidnapped and handed over to a Spartan admiral, who exposed him for sale as a slave at Aegina, but Plato was luckily ransomed by an acquaintance from Cyrene.

It was probably on his return to Athens (about 388 B.C.) that Plato founded his famous Academy. Some would call Plato's Academy the ancestor of the modern university, and so have distinguished Plato as "the first president of a permanent institution for the prosecution of science by original research." But it could not have been more Athenian. The site he chose—about a mile out of Athens—was a garden next to a grove sacred to the Hero Hekademus or Akademus, from whom it took the name "Academy." It was reputed to be a delightful, quiet place with shaded walks and a gymnasium. Plato had a small house of his own nearby. He soon acquired fame as a lecturer and attracted pupils from other Greek cities. There was no admission or tuition fee, but he did receive handsome presents from the pupils and their rich families. The comedies of the time ridicule the students for their fine and delicate garments and their elegant affectations. This was a far cry from the atmosphere surrounding Socrates' conversations, open to the public as he passed his days in the marketplace or in the public porticoes. The rural atmosphere of the Academy attracted and held students for three or four years. Athens' fame as the school of Hellas was gained and sustained here in Plato's Academy.

Isocrates' competing institution was a school for practical success in the Athens of the day; Plato believed in the pursuit of truth for its own sake. And while Isocrates taught rhetoric and the arts of persuasion, Plato focused on mathematics.

Exactly how, when, or why Plato *wrote* the dialogues that became the foundation of Western philosophy remains a mystery. Perhaps his most famous Socratic dialogues were written before he was forty, and so before he founded his Academy. A few works, including his *Laws,* are usually ascribed to his old age. What might have been the course of Western philosophy if Socrates had never had a disciple in Plato?

Plato at the Academy—from the age of sixty till his death at eighty—busied himself organizing the school and lecturing. What Plato wanted was not written "works" of philosophy but active "discovery" in the company of other discovering minds. Aristotle describes Plato's teachings at the Academy as "unwritten doctrine," and he observes that Plato himself did not "lecture" from a manuscript. Plato's famous lecture on "the Good," supposed to be the best summary of his own philosophy, survives in diverse versions by hearers—Aristotle, Xenocrates, and Heraclides of Ponticus, who published their notes. But no manuscript by Plato himself has survived.

What might Plato have done with the last twenty years of his life if he had not been seduced into a Sicilian adventure? The death of Dionysius I of Syracuse in 367 gave Plato his tempting opportunity. As annually elected dictator and generalissimo, Dionysius I had ruled Syracuse for thirty-eight years. Plato's first visit to Sicily had introduced him to the Pythagorean communities that flourished there, pursuing a tradition quite different from that of the pioneer Ionian scientists. A charismatic personality, Pythagoras (born about 580 B.C.) of Samos had settled in southern Italy about 525 B.C. There he founded a school that had the appeal of a religion. Among other mystic dogmas he taught the transmigration of souls, and even claimed to remember his own earlier incarnations. Pythagoras saw the world organized around the aesthetic of numbers—for him the only reality. Having discovered the mathematical basis of musical intervals, Pythagoras had elaborated a cosmology of mathematical order. None of Pythagoras' writings survived and, unlike Socrates, he never had the good luck to attract a recording disciple. But some of his themes lived on in Plato's dialogues. And the overseas communities in Magna Graecia in southern Italy and Sicily tempted Plato with the opportunity he never had in Athens.

When Dionysius I died in 367 B.C. he was succeeded by his son, Dionysius II. This young man of weak character and little education was not up to the challenge of the expanding Carthaginians. Plato's favorite pupil, the young man's uncle Dion, now became ruling regent. "He thought it essential," Plato records, "that I should come to Syracuse by all manner of means and with the utmost possible speed to be his partner in these plans, remembering in his own case how readily intercourse with me had produced in him a longing for the noblest and best life." But Dion's party of young men fed Plato's misgivings, "for young men are quick in forming desires which often take directions conflicting with one another." "Lest I might some day appear to myself wholly and solely a mere man of words," Plato decided to dare the Syracusan morass. "If ever anyone was to try to carry out in practice my ideas about laws and constitutions, now was the time." With the enthusiastic aid of Dion, he needed only to persuade the new dictator of Syracuse.

Dionysius II proved even weaker than Plato had feared. After Plato had been in Syracuse only four months, intriguers at the court persuaded the insecure young tyrant that Dion was plotting to seize the throne. Dion was put out to sea in a small boat. Dionysius II feared being discredited by the departure of Plato and imprisoned him in the Syracusan acropolis. The young tyrant, though he became attached to Plato, refused to learn the lessons that might have made him a successful philosopher-king. Still Plato's influence at court appeared when the study of geometry became fashionable. Defeated by court intrigues and Dionysius II's weakness, Plato finally gave up his effort to educate the young ruler and was allowed to return to Athens.

This was not yet the end of the Sicilian adventure. Dionysius II kept in touch with Plato. Even after the young tyrant seized Dion's property and forced his wife to make a dynastic marriage, Plato did not give up hope. Surprisingly, he responded to still another invitation, and returned again to advise Dionysius in 361 B.C. This trip was not entirely fruitless, for Plato did actually make a draft of a constitution for a federation of overseas Greek cities. A year later, when his life was threatened by Dion's enemies, Plato returned to Athens, and never again played a role in Syracusan politics. Dion himself kept trying. He returned to Syracuse hoping to take over the government, but was murdered by one of his own officers. Perhaps the finest fruit of all these Sicilian adventures was Plato's vivid autobiographical letter.

Could someone of Plato's intelligence and his chastening experience of political intrigue in Athens and Syracuse ever really have hoped to test his utopian vision in the profligate city-state of Syracuse? May he not at least have welcomed the opportunity, not available in Athens, to see what good could be done by one properly instructed dictator? Or perhaps he thought that his improved constitutions could help the Greek communities in Sicily resist the invading Carthaginians.

The Way of Dialogue, with its idealization of the spoken word—the sparks that fly in living conversation—makes it difficult to define the doctrines of particular philosophers. It is risky to turn Socrates' questions into answers. Of all literary forms, then, dialogues are least suited to summary. Still, one idea more than others that have emerged from Plato's works has become a symbol of "Platonism" and a clue to Plato's own way of seeking. This was his Theory of Ideas (or Forms). We cannot know how much of it was owed to Socrates, but the historic influence of the theory is plainly due to Plato and his disciples.

One impulse to the theory must have been the malaise in Athens in the lifetimes of Socrates and Plato. Thucydides in his *History of the Peloponnesian Wars* gave a classic description of that malaise:

> . . . the whole Hellenic world was convulsed. . . . The sufferings which revolution entailed upon the cities were many and terrible, such as have occurred and always will occur, as long as the nature of mankind remains the same. . . . Revolution thus ran its course from city to city. . . . Words had to change their ordinary meaning and to take that which was now given them. Reckless audacity came to be considered the courage of a loyal ally; prudent hesitation, specious cowardice, moderation was held to be a cloak for unmanliness; ability to see all sides of a question, inaptness to act on any. Frantic violence became the attribute of manliness; cautious plotting, a jus-

tifiable means of self-defence. . . . Thus religion was in honour with neither party; but the use of fair phrases to arrive at guilty ends was in high reputation. . . . Thus every form of iniquity took root in the Hellenic countries by reason of the troubles. The ancient simplicity into which honour so largely entered was laughed down and disappeared; and society became divided into camps in which no man trusted his fellow.

To confront this impermanence, the Sophist teachers had prepared their own paradoxical response: "Man is the measure of all things." Protagoras' maxim was a way of seeking solace from the evanescence of everything else in the permanence of Man himself. At the same time they expressed the relativity of all other standards. So they taught rhetoric and the arts of persuasion, how to get on in the world where you happened to find yourself. Socrates, on the other hand, had sought to unmask the false contemporary certitudes, and to provide a technique of universal definition.

Plato, moving along Socrates' path, came up with a dazzling idea, to which he gave unforgettable form in his myth of the cave in *The Republic:*

> Behold! human beings living in an underground den, which has a mouth open towards the light and reaching all along the den; here they have been from their childhood, and have their legs and necks chained so that they cannot move, and can only see before them, being prevented by the chains from turning round their heads. Above and behind them a fire is blazing at a distance, and between the fire and the prisoners there is a raised way; and you will see, if you look, a low wall built along the way, like the screen which marionette players have in front of them, over which they show the puppets. (Jowett trans.)

The cave becomes Plato's stage for revealing the difference between his "real" world and the world of shadows which others have mistaken for reality. If anyone is "liberated and compelled suddenly to stand up and turn his neck around and walk and look towards the light, he will suffer sharp pains; the glare will distress him, and he will be unable to see the realities of which in his former state he had seen only the shadows; and then conceive someone saying to him, that what he saw before was an illusion, but that now, when he is approaching nearer to being and his eye is turned towards more real existence, he has a clearer vision. . . .

will he not be perplexed? Will he not fancy that the shadows which he formerly saw are truer than the objects which are now shown to him?"

So Plato urges us, too, to seek the changeless forms only crudely sensed in our shadowy sense experience. To describe objects in this changeless world, our English word "idea" is misleading. The Greek word *ideai* connotes "forms." But, while we think of "ideas" as somehow fleeting and unreal, for Plato the Idea was fully and permanently real. At the head of the hierarchy of ideas stands the Good, which plays the same role in the intelligible world that the sun plays in the visible. And it is not only grand ideas like the Good that have a static eternal reality. Even a humble object like a bed is a shadow of some static eternal Form.

> Well then, here are three beds: one existing in nature, which is made by God, as I think that we may say—for no one else can be the maker?
> No.
> There is another which is the work of the carpenter?
> Yes.
> And the work of the painter is a third?
> Yes.
> Beds, then, are of three kinds, and there are three artists who superintend them: God, the maker of the bed, and the painter?
> Yes, there are three of them.
> God, whether from choice or from necessity, made one bed in nature and one only; two or more such ideal beds neither ever have been nor ever will be made by God.
> Why is that?
> Because even if He had made but two, a third would still appear behind them which both of them would have for their idea, and that would be the ideal bed and not the two others.
> Very true, he said.
> God knew this, and He desired to be the real maker of a real bed, not a particular maker of a particular bed, and therefore He created a bed which is essentially and by nature one only.

What better refuge from the transient world of the senses?

Plato had created a new cosmology of Ideas, a secret universe of the mind. And so he gave absolute reality—in fact, the only reality—to the pure models. Taking off from the Socratic motto "Know thyself," Plato had surprisingly led Seekers into another Other-World. But he had also set philosophers on a newly fertile path. While the physicists, the early Ionian philosophers, had looked only for beginnings, Plato, with his Theory of Ideas, set philosophers on a search for ends. And so he would show the way for his brilliant pupil Aristotle into vast new realms for Seekers of the following millennia.

8

Paths to Utopia: Virtues Writ Large

The Other-World of Ideas was not much everyday help to the citizen or the practical politician. But Plato found another way of seeking that might provide earthly models as guides to virtue. In his longest and most influential dialogue, *The Republic,* Plato offered some specific this-worldly guidance. At the same time he created still another new literary form, the Utopia, depicting the ideal commonwealth. And just as homely analogies helped him explain his Theory of Ideas with his "three-tiered ontology" of the bed, he now made another simple analogy in search of the Good Society.

The English title of this dialogue, based on the Latin *res publica,* is incomplete. The Greek title—*The State, or On Justice*—makes it clear that the focus is on moral philosophy. Near the beginning, Plato explains this way of seeking.

> . . . suppose that a short-sighted person had been asked by some one to read small letters from a distance, and it occurred to some one else that they might be found in another place which was larger and in which the letters were larger— if they were the same and he could read the larger letters first, and then proceed to the lesser—this would have been thought a rare piece of good fortune.
>
> Very true, said Adeimantus; but how does the illustration apply to our enquiry?
>
> I will tell you, I replied; justice, which is the subject of our enquiry, is, as you know, sometimes spoken of as the virtue of an individual, and sometimes as the virtue of a State.
>
> True, he replied.
>
> And is not a State larger than an individual?
>
> It is.
>
> Then in the larger the quantity of justice is likely to be larger and more easily discernible. I propose therefore that we enquire into the nature of justice and injustice, first as they appear in the State, and secondly in the individual, proceeding from the greater to the lesser and comparing them.
>
> That, he said, is an excellent proposal. (*The Republic,* Bk. II, Jowett trans.)

In his way of seeking, Plato thus had made two crucial assumptions. One was the unity of the virtues, which we meet in other dialogues; the other, that there are as many forms of the state as there are forms of the soul. The character of a government expresses the character of its citizens. "Do you know, I said, that governments vary as the dispositions of men vary, and that there must be as many of the one as there are of the other? For we cannot suppose that States are made of 'oak and rock,' and not out of the human natures which are in them, and which in a figure turn the scale and draw other things after them?" "Yes, he said, the States are as the men are; they grow out of human characters."

Plato's notion of the identity of the virtues of the individual and of the state had momentous implications, to be revealed with the passing centuries. A beneficent implication was that "reasons of state" could not defy personal morality. But it implied, too, that the state, like the individual, required a coherent and orthodox set of beliefs. Morality for the individual meant ideology for the state. But the modern social sciences would discover crucial differences between the ways of groups and those of individuals.

The whole *Republic* is thus one grand metaphor reminding us of the identity of seer and poet in ancient Greece. Great philosophers before Plato (Xenophanes and Empedocles, for example) had actually written in verse. Much of the charm and unforgettableness of *The Republic* remains in its myths and metaphors, of which the myth of the cave is only the most famous. As we shall see, the Utopia as a literary form would be wonderfully fertile, serving some of the most eloquent and passionate Seekers in the West. Though it would help open paths to change in the real world, a Utopian ideal sometimes would also breed despair, frustration, and violence.

The metaphor of virtues writ large, which Plato so beautifully pursues in *The Republic,* attracted later generations precisely because it was a metaphor. Historians and philosophers would never cease to debate whether and to what extent Plato intended his grandest work to be a blueprint for the ideal community, or only another sally in his experiments of the intelligence. But whatever Plato may have intended for this work, it left a potent legacy as a metaphor. Later generations of Seekers would, after their different fashions, cast their own efforts to give meaning to their society in Utopian form. Myth and metaphor would be invitations to Utopia, with results that were not always happy. We can sense the spirit of later Seekers by their reactions to Plato's *Republic*.

It is not surprising that the mythic charms of Plato's work were quite lost on Thomas Jefferson, a Seeker in a more prosaic age. "I amused myself with reading seriously Plato's republic," in 1814, in his mellow seventieth year, he wrote from Monticello to his friend John Adams. "I am wrong in calling it amusement, for it was the heaviest task-work I ever went through. I had occasionally before taken up some of his other works, but scarcely ever had patience to go through a whole dialogue. While wading thro' the whimsies, the puerilities, and unintelligible jargon of this work, I laid it down often to ask myself how it could have been that the world should have so long consented to give reputation to such nonsense as this?" Adams responded gladly that Jefferson's reflections "so perfectly harmonize with mine." Despite Plato's "bitter Satyre upon all Republican Government," Adams reported that he had learned two things from Plato: where Benjamin Franklin had "borrowed" one of his popular ideas, and "that Sneezing is a cure for the Hickups. Accordingly I have cured myself and all my Friends of that provoking disorder, for thirty years with a Pinch of Snuff."

Modern critics, after the rise of fascism, imperial communism, and Nazism, have found Plato's ideas less amusing than menacing. *The Republic,* according to the eloquent Karl R. Popper, reveals Plato as the historic enemy of the "open society" and a kind of anti-Christ of democracy. Plato's idea of destiny and the inevitable decay of political forms makes him for Popper the patron saint of "historicism," the destructive belief that history is governed by its own iron rules and man is not free to shape his own experience. Our somber retrospect from the totalitarian governments of the twentieth century has made it hard for us to enjoy Plato's playful speculative spirit.

Yet the speculative spirit of the dialogue is stifled in *The Republic* itself—Plato's grandest dialogue and his most un-Socratic. Here Plato offers insistent answers to the problems that Socrates preferred to leave as questions. En route the dialogue offers conversational byplay on the meaning of Justice and the Good, and the relation of sensible experience to reality. Now Socrates himself is the narrator, recounting to his friend Timaeus on the next day the offerings of the participants.

What most troubles modern liberal critics are two features of Plato's ideal community: its absolute and static character and its hierarchical class structure. "Although all the rulers are to be philosophers,"

Bertrand Russell objects, "there are to be no innovations; a philosopher is to be, for all time, a man who understands and agrees with Plato." The state arises, Socrates explains, "out of the needs of mankind; no one is self-sufficing, but all of us have many wants." Division of labor then provides the needed services, while allowing each person to do what he is best fitted for. So the community has farmers, weavers, builders, merchants, shoemakers, and all the rest. And as the state expands to meet multiplying wants, it must have a standing army. Yet, until the refinements of culture have been added, this is no better than a "city of pigs."

In another of his great myths, adapted, Plato says, from an old Phoenician tale, he offers one of those "necessary falsehoods" that hold the community together—"just one royal lie which may deceive the rulers, if that be possible, and at any rate the rest of the city."

> Citizens, we shall say to them in our tale, you are brothers, yet God has framed you differently. Some of you have the power of command, and in the composition of these he has mingled gold, therefore they have the greatest honour; others he has made of silver, to be auxiliaries; others again who are to be husbandmen and craftsmen he has composed of brass and iron; and the species will generally be preserved in the children. But as all are of the same original stock, a golden parent will sometimes have a silver son, or a silver parent a golden son. And God proclaims as a first principle to the rulers, and above all else, that there is nothing which they should so anxiously guard, or of which they are to be such good guardians, as of the purity of the race. (*The Republic,* Jowett trans.)

Athenians took such pride in being sprung from the soil of the city where they lived that until the mid-fifth century B.C. they wore golden cicadas in their hair as the symbol of their local origin.

Just as the role of each individual was fixed in the materials of his being, so the society as a whole had its destiny fixed in rigid cycles of history. In contrast to the unchanging Other-World of Ideas, Plato saw a universal earthly law of decay. Aristocracy (rule of the best) degenerates into Timocracy (the rule of honor), which degenerates into Oligarchy (the rule of the wealthy), which in turn degenerates into Democracy (the rule of the people). The chaos of Democracy finally produces Tyranny. Procreation at the wrong seasons accelerates this process by intermingling the races of gold, silver, brass, and iron. Incidentally Plato offers a whimsical Pythagorean formula, improved by the Muses, for finding the best seasons of procreation.

The Republic was not the last step in Plato's move from the Socratic Way of Dialogue to the way of dogma. After *The Republic,* and probably after his last Sicilian venture in 360, Plato wrote another work of similar length, *The Laws.* Ostensibly this, too, is in the form of a dialogue. But long monologues fill whole Books offering Plato's views as those of "an Athenian Stranger." Here dialogue ceases to be a lively intellectual encounter and becomes a mere frame for the Athenian Stranger's opinion. *The Laws'* Twelve Books begin with still another exposition of the origins of government and the lessons of history, the kinds of constitutions, schemes of education, and the nature of virtue. Along the way are sententious observations on the pleasures and perils of strong drink, on crime and punishment, sex, slavery, property, and the family. While *The Republic* was for a community "of a size to which it can grow without losing its unity," the Laws are designed for a community of 5,040 households. To ensure that the Laws will be "irreversible," Plato prescribes a Nocturnal Council of specially educated Guardians. Most of the ideas in *The Laws* are better explained in other dialogues. But the hopes for the rule of the wise found in *The Republic,* a city "laid up in the heavens," have become demands for the rule of earthly laws. And so Plato has displaced the question by the answer.

9

Aristotle: An Outsider in Athens

Who would have guessed that Plato's most famous disciple would be (in words attributed to Plato) "the foal that kicks its mother"? Or that the inheritor of the mantle of the man sent to his death for exposing the pretensions of his time would be the West's first encyclopedist? Or that it was possible to build a philosophy on a faith that "What everyone believes is true" (*Consensus omnium*)? Or that this Aristotle, a prize pupil in Plato's Academy for twenty years, instructed in the Theory of Forms denying the reality of the sensible world, would produce a grand omnium-gatherum of facts on everything in the heavens and on the earth—from the ways of bees and horses to the form of the human heart and brain and the laws of nations civilized and barbaric?

Yet precisely such a prodigy emerged from classical Athens. Seekers found clues in the successes, failures, and confusions of predecessors, who became their inspiration, their targets, their resource. From Socrates, Plato learned both caution and the need for bold patterns of meaning of his own. From Plato, Aristotle learned the perils of deserting the world of the senses. Still the later somehow did not make the earlier irrelevant. Seekers, like artists, never wholly displaced those who had tried before. They all enlarged and enriched the menu.

Aristotle is the colossus whose works both illuminate and cast a shadow on European thought in the next two thousand years. Though thoroughly immersed in fourth century B.C. Athens, he was an outsider. "The Stagirite," his nickname in the Middle Ages, underlined his non-Athenian origins. Born in Stagira, a town in northeastern Greece, in 384 B.C., he did not come to Athens until he was seventeen. His father, Nicomachus, was the personal physician to the king of Macedonia, Amyntas, who was the father of Philip of Macedon and grandfather of Alexander the Great. Aristotle's family had a long tradition in the practice of medicine, then the most practically minded of the Greek sciences. After he was left an orphan, he was sent to Athens for his education. There he joined Plato's Academy, as a student. But he never ceased to be a stranger. As a "metic"—a resident foreigner—he could not own real estate in Athens.

"In Athens," Aristotle recalled in a letter written just before his death, "the same things are not proper for a stranger as for a citizen; it is difficult to stay in Athens." He is reported to have observed acidly that the only honor the city of Athens ever gave him was the accusation of impiety, in 323 B.C. Plato was away on his second Sicilian frolic when Aristotle first came to Athens. But despite Plato's occasional absences Plato's spirit dominated the Academy.

The impressionable young Aristotle was only one among many foreigners attracted to the Academy by Plato's fame in northern Greece. He seems to have read Plato's dialogues during these years. And he was especially impressed by the *Phaedo,* which became his model for his own commemoration of a friend many years later. Even his works attacking Plato's theory of ideas reveal how deeply Plato had influenced him. But he was not sympathetic to the emphasis on mathematics in the Academy, signaled by the legendary inscription over the entrance: "Only geometers may enter." "The moderns have turned philosophy into mathematics," Aristotle would later complain in the *Metaphysics,* "though they pretend that one should study them for further ends." Plato provided a shining target for the young and increasingly independent outsider. Plato's grand otherworldly theme that denied the reality of the sensible world proved the perfect challenge, for Aristotle's practical spirit was obsessed with the range and variety of experience. Still, he was sympathetic enough to Plato's intellectual sallies to remain in the Academy for twenty years. He did not leave the Academy until Plato's death in 347 B.C., and even then went to join another circle of Plato's followers.

In retrospect we might wonder why Aristotle, reputedly Plato's most brilliant pupil, was not then named head of the Academy. But he had probably already spoken out against Plato's theory of forms. A more eligible candidate was Speusippus, son of Plato's sister. As a "metic"—a resident alien—Aristotle could not have inherited the property without a special dispensation. The rising Demosthenes was at this very time stirring Athenian fears of the perils from Macedonia, where Aristotle had been born and raised. Nor could Aristotle return to Stagira. It had just been destroyed (348 B.C.) by Philip as one of the last obstacles to his expansion of his Macedonian empire, and the Athenians had not been able to rescue it.

All this provided the opportunity for Aristotle to set out on his own version of Plato's Sicilian adventure. Joined by Xenocrates, a friend from the Academy, he went in search of a site for a new academy, and was attracted by an adventurous king, Hermias, of a small kingdom in Asia Minor, whose capital was Atarneus. Hermias may have visited the Academy in Athens, and seems to have welcomed the enlightened guidance of Platonic philosophers. He assigned a city, Assos, for their new Academy, and gave his niece and adopted daughter to Aristotle in marriage. At Assos the philosophers met and conversed in a *peripatos,* a covered walk, the prototype of Aristotle's later more famous academy. And there Aristotle pursued his lifelong interest in nature, recorded in numerous references in his *Natural History* to places and creatures in this part of Asia Minor. But Hermias met a violent death at the hands of the Persians before he could become a Platonic philosopher-king. Aristotle would praise his lost patron in a eulogy to *Arete,* Virtue. After only three years at Hermias' academy, Aristotle moved to the nearby island of Mytelene, where he was when Philip of Macedon went seeking a tutor for his son Alexander.

In a historic coincidence the West's most influential philosopher was instructing the future conqueror of the most far-flung empire of the West before Roman times. Plutarch reports on Philip's search for the world's greatest philosopher to tutor his thirteen-year-old son. The reasons for Philip's choice of Aristotle are not clear, for Aristotle had not yet a grand reputation. Perhaps Aristotle himself had sought the post to ensure the rebuilding of his hometown of Stagira. We do know that Aristotle was handsomely rewarded for his tutorial services, and that he died a rich man. It also appears that Philip and Alexander subsidized Aristotle's research in natural history by assigning gamekeepers to tag the wild animals of Macedonia. Unfortunately, the drama ends in anticlimax, for there is little evidence of Aristotle's lasting influence on Alexander the Great. Aristotle never mentions Alexander in his surviving works, nor refers directly to his time as tutor in Macedonia. Nor do we have a report from Alexander himself of his impressions of the world's greatest philosopher. Bertrand Russell uncharitably speculates that the ambitious young Alexander must have been bored by "the prosy old pedant set over him by his father to keep him out of mischief."

"The young man is not a proper audience for political science," Aristotle complained, "he has no experience of life, and because he still follows his emotions, he will only listen to no purpose, uselessly." Still, Aristotle seems to have written some pamphlets especially for the young Alexander, among them *On Kingship, In Praise of Colonies,* and possibly *The Glories of Riches.* For the practical-minded Aristotle the Platonic philosopher-king ideal must have seemed pure fantasy. He was more impressed by the possibilities that resided in the actual character of "the Hellenic race," which was intermediate between the Europeans, who were "full of spirit, but wanting in intelligence and skill; and therefore they retain comparative freedom, but have no political organization, and are incapable of ruling over others," and "the natives of Asia . . . intelligent and inventive, but . . . wanting in spirit, and therefore they are always in a state of subjection and slavery." By happy chance, the Hellenic race, situated between them, was "intermediate in character, being high-spirited and also intelligent. Hence it continues free, and is the best governed of any nation, and, if it could be formed into one state, would be able to rule the world." But by including barbarians with Greeks, Alexander's grandiose scheme failed to reap the special benefits of the Hellenic character.

After three years, when Alexander was only sixteen, his father, Philip, went on a campaign against Byzantium and left his son as regent. This ended Aristotle's term as tutor but was only the beginning of a Macedonian friendship with the general Antipater that would shape his life. When the twenty-year-old Alexander came to the throne in 336 and set out on his ambitious Asian campaign, he left Antipater as his regent for Greece. Aristotle benefited from his developing friendship, and he named Antipater as the executor of his will. All this helps explain Aristotle's paean to friendship in his *Ethics.* "Without friends no one would choose to go on living, though he possessed every other good thing." Macedonia was dominating Greece, and the Macedonian power over the peninsula would be helpful to Aristotle on his return to Athens. But the Macedonian connection would eventually be his doom.

10

On Paths of Common Sense

Returning to Athens and finding the Academy under less friendly auspices, Aristotle set up his own teaching center in the Lyceum, a grove and gymnasium near Athens, which Socrates himself had enjoyed. There Aristotle would stroll on the public walk (*peripatos*) talking philosophy with his students until it was time for their rubbing with oil. Following the plan of the Academy, the Lyceum, too, was a cult of the Muses along with lecture rooms and a library. Legend credits Aristotle with collecting here the first extensive systematically arranged library. *Symposia,* or festive meals, were conducted by rules that Aristotle himself composed.

At the Lyceum, Aristotle lectured, pursued scientific research, supervised and collated the research of disciples. The mornings he gave to lectures for serious scholars, his evenings to any who wanted to come. He walked as he talked and so became the "peripatetic" philosopher. The atmosphere was quite different from that of Plato's Academy with its Way of the Dialogue, where the light came from sparks struck by conversing minds. Here Aristotle sought the light of experience of the sensible world, to which Plato gave no dignity. Aristotle was closer to the pre-Socratic Ionian philosopher-scientists who asked what the world was made of and how it worked. He collected his own notebooks on all subjects, and made them available to students. Assigning each student a different topic, he encouraged students to make their own observations and draw conclusions from what they found. When pupils found the odorous dissection of some of Nature's minor works repulsive, Aristotle replied, "The consideration of the lower forms of life ought not to excite a childish repugnance. In all natural things there is something to move wonder."

The most conspicuous contrast to Plato's Way was in politics. While Plato's *Republic* painted a glowing picture of an ideal commonwealth, Aristotle's speculations were solidly based on his assistants' descriptions of 158 different operating Greek political systems. A surviving example is the recently discovered *Constitution of Athens,* the first book

of the series, perhaps written by Aristotle himself. The lost 157, probably by his students, covered the Mediterranean world from Marseilles
in the west to Crete, Rhodes, and Cyprus, communities on the Aegean,
Ionian, and Tyrrhenian seas, elsewhere in Europe, and in Asia and
Africa. Yet Aristotle sensibly cautioned that in political science we
should be content with "the truth roughly and in outline." "It is the mark
of an educated man to look for precision in each class of things just as
far as the nature of the subject admits; it is evidently equally foolish to
accept probable reasoning from a mathematician and to demand from a
rhetorician scientific proofs."

During these twelve years at his Lyceum, Aristotle rounded off the
works that made him our first encyclopedist and the shaper of the Western vocabulary on all subjects from logic and poetry to politics and biology. We cannot know for sure how much of this legacy was
influenced by Plato, and how much was a reaction against Plato. Nor do
we know for sure the order of his surviving works. The very "writings"
of Aristotle—which in the late Middle Ages became a kind of sacred
scripture for Western Christianity and the basis of "Scholasticism," and
interpreted with relentless textual pedantry by modern historians—are
shrouded in mists of uncertainty.

Surprisingly, the works of Aristotle that have survived are not the
works that he had "published." It is not his afternoon and evening talks
to all comers, his popular or literary works, but his morning lectures to
serious scholars at the Lyceum that remain for us. With his fellow
philosophers at the Lyceum he was continually revising these "lecture-
manuscripts." The surviving "works" of Aristotle, then, probably include some of Aristotle's own notes, amplified or explained by the notes
of his students or his fellow teachers. Besides, there are research reports
compiling facts gathered by members of the Lyceum on every conceivable subject—from the shape of animals' limbs to the laws and constitutions of every known state. His work *On the Parts of Animals* and the
rediscovered *Constitution of Athens* are samples. Aristotle's boundless
curiosity and his effectiveness as a teacher appear in his collections of
questions arranged by subject, each beginning with a "Why . . . ?" and
then offering alternative answers, "It is because . . ."

Oddly enough, it was this collection of notes from many hands that
became the revered "works" of Aristotle in later centuries. And while

the writings of other great thinkers have commonly been designed for an audience—learned or popular—the surviving works of Aristotle are different. They record work in progress, the Seeker at work with himself, reflecting and emending as he went along. While they lack the wit and poetry of Plato's dialogues, they have a pedestrian momentum of their own. Reading Aristotle, we join a mind trying to sort out the trivia of experience and relate them to the grandest questions.

The selective survival of Aristotle's encyclopedic miscellany is itself a saga. The pioneer Greek geographer Strabo (c. 63 B.C.–A.D. 19), who had settled in Rome (c. 20 B.C.), tells the story. At his death Aristotle left his library and writings—along with the directorship of the Lyceum—to his versatile friend and colleague Theophrastus (c. 371–c. 287 B.C.), who had earned his leadership of the Peripatetic School by his writings on botany and his *Metaphysics,* and marked new paths for essays by his witty "Characters." At Theophrastus' death he left Aristotle's literary remains to a younger philosopher Neleus, whom he expected to be his successor at the Lyceum. Neleus came from a town called Skepsis in Anatolia, in the area where Aristotle had enjoyed the patronage of Hermias. Neleus then left them to his own heirs who were not philosophers. When the Attalid kings of Pergamum invaded Skepsis seeking works for their library, these heirs had buried the books in an underground cellar, where they were left to mold and moth. Still, they eventually found a buyer for the disintegrating books and papers.

The bibliophile Apellicon made and published new, careless copies. The next chapter in the Aristotelian saga is reported by Plutarch. When Sulla (138–78 B.C.), the Roman general, captured Athens in 86 B.C. in his campaign against Mithridates, he seized Apellicon's library, including the books and papers of Aristotle, and brought it to Rome. There, luckily, a disciple and admirer of Aristotle, the grammarian Tyrannio, friend of Cicero and Caesar, secured the confidence of the librarian, worked on the books, organized the papers, and made new copies. Cicero himself so admired Aristotle's "golden flow of speech" (in his dialogues now lost) that he said he had tried to write "in the Aristotelian manner." Happily, Tyrannio supplied his copies to Andronicus of Rhodes, also an admirer of Aristotle.

And it was this Andronicus who opened a newly informed era in the fame of Aristotle. About 40 B.C. he arranged the works in the order in which they have survived, and on which later lists rely. He wrote his own treatise on the works, wrote a life of Aristotle, and provided a transcript of Aristotle's will. Before Andronicus, Plutarch observes, "the earlier Peripatetics were clearly clever and scholarly men in themselves, but had no extensive or accurate acquaintance with the writings of Aristotle and Theophrastus." Andronicus had unwittingly given shape to the philosophic and scientific vocabulary of Christian Europe.

The fate of Aristotle's works again dramatized the difference between his way of seeking and Plato's, for the influence of Plato's Way was continuous, through small groups of friends and disciples. The dialogues that Plato himself had written and recited in the Academy were soon collected. By contrast Aristotle's influence was interrupted or perhaps not fully launched until three centuries after his death, when finally some coherent version of his writings became available. Plato's Academy, formally organized as a religious guild, had the aura of a great spirit reaching out to all listeners. But Aristotle's legacy was a body of knowledge, marking the path of modern learning—accumulating the facts of the world and human experience with an explanation of causes. Aristotle's legacy, then, was not the power of a charismatic personality of grand poetic gifts, but rather the accumulation of a lifetime of scholarly observation. And before Aristotle's writings were recovered by Andronicus, there were centuries of opportunity for his ideas to be distorted. Plato's was an unbroken tradition, Aristotle's was a series of renaissances.

Aristotle was in Athens in the summer of 323 B.C. when news came of the death of the Macedonian conqueror Alexander the Great. Alexander was only thirty-two, and many doubted that he could be dead. This was the signal for the Athenian Assembly to declare war against Antipater, Aristotle's patron, who held the garrisons for Macedonia. The Macedonian prodigy Aristotle, Antipater's friend, was also naturally suspect. He became another victim of the familiar charge of "impiety." The trumped-up charge was based now on an accusation that Aristotle had written a paean to his old patron, the pro-Macedonian Hermias, as if he were a god. He fled to Chalcis, a Macedonian stronghold, to prevent the Athenians from "sinning twice against philosophy." Aristotle died in Chalcis in 322, at sixty-three years of age. His will made generous provisions for his family and for emancipating some of his slaves.

The philosopher Aristotle, Bertrand Russell observes, was "the first to write like a professor . . . a professional teacher, not an inspired prophet"—"Plato diluted by common sense." Aristotle's success as a professional teacher is nowhere better proven than by the decisive and enduring shape he has given to every subject he interpreted. Yet he avoided the narrowness of the pedant. There was no subject, question, or field of knowledge that this Seeker failed to encompass. The amazing scope of his curiosity and knowledge would never be matched in Western thought. The next such effort we shall see was Diderot's *Encyclopédie* (1751–1756), which required the collaboration of the great thinkers of the age in thirty-five volumes. In retrospect, as amazing as the scope of Aristotle's writings was their succinctness, for he managed to compress his universal survey into only fifteen hundred pages. Later encyclopedias have used the crutch of alphabetical arrangement of articles to give an appearance of order. But Aristotle created an order that derived from the subjects themselves. While the obviousness of some of these ideas might embarrass the subtle philosopher, it is this common-sense view of experience that has given Aristotle his perennial appeal.

For the heart of Aristotle's seeking is the way of common sense. By starting philosophic treatises with common sense, Aristotle gives his ideas a plausibility that puts opponents—especially subtle philosophers—on the defensive. The order that he finds then does not seem imposed by the philosopher, but seems rather a progressive classification of everyone's experience.

Aristotle's treatises commonly begin with what everyone seems to agree on. And he is not afraid of appearing banal. "Every art and every inquiry, and similarly every action and pursuit," his *Ethics* begins, "is thought to aim at some good. . . ." "Every state is a community of some kind," opens the *Politics,* "and every community is established with a view to some good." Even the *Metaphysics* takes off from a commonplace: "All men by nature desire to know. An indication of this is the delight we take in our senses." Aristotle sets out from the assumption "that what everyone believes is true. Whoever destroys this faith will hardly find a more credible one." And he follows Hesiod (eighth century B.C.), the father of Greek didactic poetry, who said that "No word is ever lost that many peoples speak."

Aristotle's deference to common sense, the common opinion, would help give him the insight to his God and served him in other areas, too. The general experience made his *Nicomachean Ethics,* with its emphasis on the mean, seem eminently sensible. And he commonsensically insisted (against Plato) that the virtues are multiple, that they are fostered less by contemplation of some changeless Idea than by a "habit of choice." And his *Politics,* too, as we have seen, rests on the common political experience of his time.

But Aristotle's deference to the institutions of his own time also channeled and confined his social ideas and explains the obsolescence of some of his works in modern times. The conspicuous example is his view of slavery. Nowhere does he more clearly reveal his immersion in the customs of his age or his reluctance to defy what "everyone" believed. At the beginning of his *Politics,* he explains that the state is made up of households "and the first and fewest possible parts of a family are master and slave, husband and wife, father and children." "He who is by nature not his own but another's man, is by nature a slave; and he may be said to be another's man who, being a human being, is also a possession." He concedes that some deny such a natural distinction and insist "that the distinction between slave and freeman exists by law only, and not by nature; and being an interference with nature is therefore unjust." He concedes, too, that slavery by mere right of conquest is unjust. The child of a "natural slave," he says, may not always be a natural slave, and Greeks should not enslave Greeks. He argues, too, that master and slave share the same interests. The master should reason with his slave, and "it is expedient that liberty should be always held out to them as the reward of their services."

So he aims to justify slavery as a reflection of the unity of nature. "For in all things which form a composite whole and which are made up of parts . . . a distinction between the ruling and the subject element comes to light. Such a duality exists in living creatures, but not in them only; it originates in the constitution of the universe." Having freed himself from Platonic abstractions, he still has confined his thinking in forms of his (and his community's) making. The broad empirical spirit that governed his comparison of alien constitutions somehow did not liberate him from the habits of his own household.

Starting from the wholesale—the gross common experience—Aristotle then proceeds to the retail, breaking down experience into many classes. As Aristotle is a master of the unities of experience, so he is a master—and a pioneer—in sensing the diversities and classifying experience into manageable parts. The *Metaphysics* begins by distinguishing man from the other animals, the *Ethics* by distinguishing the ends of different actions, the *Politics* by classifying the different communities and kinds of governments. The *Poetics,* starting from "the primary facts," then distinguishes the different forms of imitation—Epic Poetry and Tragedy from Comedy and Dithyrambic Poetry. Different kinds of tragic plots are described and the kinds of characters defined. Whether or not the reader agrees with Aristotle, he has from the outset a feeling of grasp on the subject, its extent and varieties.

Aristotle's bent for classifying would have a lasting, and also inhibiting, influence on biological thought for following centuries. He was so dominated by the reality and distinctiveness of every individual in nature that he gave currency and authority to the idea of species, the existing forms of nature. In a revised, empirical version of Plato's forms or ideas, Aristotle saw the species in nature as fixed and unalterable, each reproducing after its kind. Then there could be no such thing as a new species. Thus the idea of original and unchanging species was his way of showing the constancy and uniformity of nature, and its constant, challenging variety.

Aristotle explained the intriguing *scala naturae* (ladder of nature) with a sophistication that engages the modern biologist:

> Nature advances from the inanimate to animals with such unbroken continuity that there are borderline cases and intermediate forms of which one cannot say to which class they belong. First after the inanimate come plants. These differ from each other in the degree to which they appear to have life, and in comparison with other bodies appear animate but in comparison with animals inanimate. And the transition from them to animals . . . is continuous, there are creatures in the sea about which one might well be in doubt whether they are animals or plants. (*Historia Animalium*)

The medical tradition in his family and his interest in the specifics of experience made Aristotle an industrious and scrupulous observer of plants and animals and their parts and functions. What Aristotle's "ladder of nature" lacked in order to become a theory of evolution was the dimension of time. If he had seen the ladder in time as well as in space he might have glimpsed the possibility of emerging and disappearing species. Perhaps he was discouraged from this by a notion inherited from Plato that Forms were permanent and preceded matter. And Aristotle's obsession with the vivid and specific units in the cosmic order encouraged him to believe that the species had always existed and were indestructible. Every place in the ladder had been filled in nature and the loss of any species would leave an unnatural gap.

11

Aristotle's God for a Changeful World

Only the simplest explanation can account for the uncanny commanding appeal of Aristotle's works in the Western centuries. For he was a Seeker who had a wondrous capacity to see the contrary and contradictory features of experience without giving in to the temptation to philosophical oversimplification. Yet he was not afraid of seeming obvious. To attempt to summarize his work would be no more useful than to summarize an encyclopedia. We can only hope to capture his spirit. He believed in the unity and continuity of nature and at the same time in the primacy of the particular in human experience: "The observed facts show that nature is not a series of episodes, like a bad tragedy. As for believers in the Ideas, this difficulty misses them; for they construct spatial magnitudes out of matter and number" (*Metaphysics*).

Nature, to Aristotle, showed continual motion and change—"So, goodbye to the Forms. They are idle prattle, and if they do exist are wholly irrelevant." No Platonic simplicities! For Plato sensible objects existed only as they were related to changeless intelligible objects. Not for Aristotle, for whom the particular sensible object—example of a species—was the only real existence. Thus the reality of musicians did not depend on some Idea called Music. The very existence of the abstraction depended on the individuals: "Musicianship cannot exist unless there are musicians." Musicalness cannot exist unless there is someone who is musical.

Everywhere Aristotle saw purpose, and every species in nature was the fulfillment of a unique potentiality. And potentiality meant growth and motion within the limits of the species. His powers of observation, and even his teleology, led him to some insights. Charles Darwin, whose "two gods" were Linnaeus and Cuvier, found them "mere schoolboys to old Aristotle." In the troubled field of embryology, the leading modern historian Joseph Needham finds "the depth of Aristotle's insights into the generation of animals" unsurpassed by any later embryologist and never equaled. For teleology, Needham shrewdly observed, "is, like other varieties of common sense, useful from time to time." Aristotle's powers of observation and his talent at recording made him the giant of ancient biology. Neoplatonist philosophers criticized him for neglecting theology and paying too much attention to physical matters. But Aristotle preferred the insights of "those who have spent more time among physical phenomena." They are "better able to posit the kind of principles which can hold together over a wide area," while "those who through much abstract discussion have lost sight of the facts are more likely to dogmatize on the basis of few observations."

It is surprising, in view of Aristotle's commonsense preference for observation and not "losing sight of the facts," that he spread himself across the whole world of experience and aspiration. But for Aristotle the meaning was hidden in the particulars of experience. The scope of his work was itself witness to his belief in the unity of experience and his confidence that it could somehow be encompassed by the human mind. And so he confirms his axiom that "the actuality of thought is life." He divides all knowledge into practical, productive, or theoretical. And the theoretical sciences are three: Physics (the science of nature), Mathematics (the science of the quantitative aspect of things), and Theology ("first philosophy" or the science of being).

Another study, preliminary and basic to all the others, is Logic. Aristotle calls it Analytics. It is not itself a science but an essential tool to all the sciences. Analytics is a suggestive name for it, for it is devoted to analyzing the processes of thought. The need for this science is plain, since knowledge is of the universal. But the realities that need explaining are only of individuals, of which, strictly speaking, there can be no "knowledge." How, then, make the leap from the specific experience to the general truth? Logic (for Aristotle, Analytics) was the science of that leap.

Aristotle pioneered in making the ways of expressing our thoughts into the subject of a science—which meant dealing with the forms of thought apart from subject matter. So Aristotle is commonly said to be the founder of logic. And his vocabulary and his framework for this science have dominated the West until the last century. The syllogism with its three parts (major premise, minor premise, conclusion) was Aristotle's idea. For him it described the technique of drawing conclusions from premises, or deductive reasoning. His logic included not only the technique of drawing conclusions from premises (the formal syllogism), but also the science of demonstration (how to use reason to serve science) and "dialectic," the technique of using reason to win a debate. His several treatises on logic came to be called the *Organon* (or Instrument), which he considered necessary for understanding any subject.

Some see Aristotle as a pioneer not only in philosophic self-consciousness but in historical self-consciousness. He was, according to Werner Jaeger, the first thinker to set up along with his own philosophy a conception of his own place in history. He presents his own ideas as coming from his criticism of Plato and others before him. So Jaeger would make him "the inventor of the notion of intellectual development in time."

In the customary arrangement of the two-hundred-odd titles attributed to Aristotle in ancient catalogs, first come the treatises on logic, the *Organon,* followed by the physical treatises (*Physics, On the Heavens, On Generation and Corruption, Meteorology*), the *Metaphysics, On Psychology (On the Soul),* short physical treatises (*On the Sensible, On Memory, On Sleep and Sleeplessness, On Dreams, On Prophesying, Longevity, Youth and Age*), biological treatises (*On the History and Parts of Animals, On the Motion, On the Gait, and On the Generation of Animals*), *Ethics, Politics, The Athenian Constitution, Rhetoric,* and *Poetics.* Of this staggering encyclopedic array of treatises none was without influence on Western thought, and several (for example, the *Organon,* the *Ethics,* the *Politics,* and *Poetics*) provided the dominant Western framework and vocabulary until recent times.

Aristotle's overwhelming influence was due not only to the amazing inclusiveness of his surviving works but also to his emphasis. While Plato had first put him on the paths of philosophy, it was his reaction against Plato that gave him his distinctive appeal and explained how he suited the future of the West. Plato's appeal had been the charm of the ideal, the enduring, and the changeless. But Aristotle's interest in nature and experience led him to focus on a world of motion, change, and time. It was the changeful variety of nature that fascinated Aristotle the biologist. For Aristotle, then, there was no real world of the static. When he saw the chicken, he imagined its coming from the egg. When he saw an egg he imagined a chicken.

Nature for him was a realm of unfolding purposes. He repeatedly said that nature does nothing in vain. Which led him to his teleology, his emphasis on ends. The biologist in him also encouraged his search for purpose, which has never ceased to obsess biologists. Why is the plant or animal shaped as it is? Which means, for what purpose? The search for the rationale of living plants and animals, their generation and their motion, dominated his thinking about nature and led him, too, to the idea of potentiality, the power to become the fulfilled individual of the species—which awed and fascinated him.

This obsession with the changeful world of motion also drew him to the idea that gave him his potent role in Christian Europe. He, too, was unable to escape the yearning for changelessness in a world of change, which Plato had so elegantly embodied in his theory of forms. The concluding Book of his *Physics* aims to show that motion, like time, "always was and always will be"—"an immortal never-failing property of things that are, a sort of life as it were to all naturally constituted things." Which set the stage for Aristotle's God—the Unmoved Mover. This may have been as much a deference to common sense—the prevalent views of his community—as to logic or evidence. The Unmoved Mover was his name for the most divine being accessible to man. Since the activity of God was thought, it was also man's highest faculty.

> That which is capable of receiving the object of thought, is mind, and it is active when it possesses it. This activity therefore rather than the capability appears as the divine element in mind, and contemplation the pleasantest and best activity. If then God is for ever in that good state which we reach occasionally it is a wonderful thing—if in a better state, more wonderful still. Yet it is so. Life too he has, for the activity of the mind is life, and he is that activity. His essential activity is his life, the best life and eternal. We say then that God is an eternal living being, the best of all, attributing to him continuous and eternal life. That is God.

Even in describing the Unmoved Mover, Aristotle makes activity his ideal.

PART THREE

THE CHRISTIAN WAY: EXPERIMENTS IN COMMUNITY

These two ways of seeking—from a higher authority and from the reason within—were brought together by the Christians in a new harmony of the voices of Hebrew prophets and Greek philosophers. The Old Testament had been written in Hebrew, the New Testament would be written in Greek. One chronicled history since the Creation, the other brought Gospel words—"Good News"—and a new beginning that fixed the calendar for the West. Christians together created new institutions—the church, the monastic orders, and the university—destined to become bastions of orthodoxy, fortresses of protest and reform. An inspiration to Creators in great works of architecture, sculpture, painting, literature, and music. And a justification of dogma and persecution.

12

Fellowship of the Faithful: The Church

Western history would be dominated by the birth and life of a Galilean Jew, who died before the age of thirty-five. Son of a woman married to an obscure carpenter, this overwhelming figure was not a political leader nor a warrior nor an explorer nor an artist. He left no writing. His life and teachings were eventually reported by disciples in the four Gospels of Matthew, Mark, Luke, and John. The first Christians had no written Gospels, but were held together by oral tradition, the Holy Spirit, and faith in their Savior. Written Gospels responded to the needs of a growing community of disciples. This widening circle would create a fellowship of the faithful and a momentous new institution of Seekers, the Church.

The special appeal of Christianity came from the fact that it was a voluntary religion of those who adored its founder, Jesus of Nazareth. Grand consequences followed from being a "founded" religion, whose members had chosen to put their faith in a new Savior. By contrast, Judaism was the religion of a Chosen People, and the Hebrew Prophets spoke for God. After the destruction of the Temple in Jerusalem (587 B.C.) and the Babylonian exile, Jewish communities were organized around synagogues, where rabbis expounded and interpreted the law that had been given to this people. Hinduism, too, was an ethnic religion among people not free to reject its claims, and the priesthood was inherited by a Brahmin caste. While Judaism was the religion of a Chosen People, Christianity would be a chosen religion. Since there were no barriers of birth, caste, or blood to joining the faith, Christianity could hope to become universal. And the rule of celibacy for the Christian priesthood, in addition to its other benefits, would assure the voluntary non-hereditary priestly commitment.

All these features that made Christianity preeminently a religion of choice—a religion of Seekers—were the seeds of another uncelebrated innovation of the new religion—the creation of a Church. Ironically, the religion that had advanced as the way of faith and choice for the poor and the oppressed would become the core of a powerful new institution.

The Church would become an independent corporation organized in a hierarchy with its own professional priesthood. And in turn it, too, would become an instrument for imposing belief and ritual on the unwilling. Other religious institutions, like Hinduism or Judaism, with an ethnic base either were diffused throughout the society or were auxiliary to the state.

In the Athens of the great age of Socrates and Plato, the citadel of the city faith, the Parthenon, was built for the cult of Athena Parthenos (Athena the Virgin). The city-goddess was the goddess of all Athenians. Similarly, the religion of Rome was only the religious aspect of the empire. At the height of the Roman Empire the state religion was supervised and its rites conducted by a college of pontifices (priests of the state cult), headed by the pontifex maximus. "Judge and arbiter of things divine and human," he survived as the religious spokesman of the ancient kings of Rome. In the Republic he sat in the Regia, the royal palace of the ancient kings near the Forum. He supervised the sacrifices and named the Vestal Virgins. For many years the college of pontifices also fixed the state calendar, oversaw rituals, and kept the official records of the state cult. Emperor Augustus, following the example of Julius Caesar, declared himself pontifex maximus in 12 B.C. and the succeeding emperors did not give up the title.

The fervent Catholic emperor Gratian (367–383), under the influence of Saint Ambrose, was the first to abandon the title. The rise of Christianity in the West, then, is a saga of how an unpretentious and persecuted fellowship of the faithful followers of Jesus of Nazareth became transformed in three centuries into an autonomous institution challenging the ancient imperial power. It is not surprising that the fellowship that accomplished this feat claimed and was credited with miracles.

The Church, the fellowship of the faithful, was made theologically real by Saint Augustine of Hippo (354–430) as it had been made politically real by Emperor Constantine the Great (c. 285–337). Saint Augustine's *City of God* (written 413–426) defended the new religion from responsibility for the fall of Rome to the barbarians. His figure of "two cities," the "city of God" (*civitas Dei*) and the "earthly city" (*civitas terrena*), had been familiar in both Hebrew biblical and Greek philosophical wisdom. Now he brought them together in his Christian classic in the

Latin language of Europe that dominated learning for the next centuries. The Psalms had spoken of a city of God and Plato's *Republic* made a similar division. Saint Augustine now provided a theological base for the dogma of predestination. And his *Confessions* recounted the painful stages by which he personally was overcome by the revelation of a heavenly city.

The making of a Church, the transformation of Christianity from a persecuted sect into the dominant force in a Christianized empire, was to be the work of a troubled and ambivalent emperor in one of the empire's most turbulent eras. It was an age of civil war, of endless battles between Eastern and Western emperors and among claimants for the throne. Constantine the Great was no saint, but a master of military strategy and command, unbeaten in provincial battles, conqueror of the Franks and the Goths. A vigorous and effective administrator, reforming the coinage and the tax system, he made Byzantium into a "Second Rome," to be called Constantinople. He earned his title of Constantine the Great by his secular achievements. The Christianizing of the empire was accomplished not by crusading zeal but by gradual stages of depaganizing. Perhaps the spectacle and frustration of the Roman emperor Diocletian's terrible ten-year persecution of the Christians (303–313) had inoculated Constantine against draconian measures in religion.

Born into the military governing class, the son of Constantius, who was appointed Caesar, or deputy emperor, under Diocletian, Constantine served in the army against Persia. Raised in the Eastern Empire at the court of Diocletian at Nicomedia (modern Izmit in Turkey), he was a brilliant soldier in Egypt. His own military career spanned the empire—from Sarmatia near the Black Sea to the northern reaches of the British Isles. He joined his father, who had assumed the titles of Caesar and Augustus on an expedition to pacify the barbarians of Scotland. When his father died at York, Constantine succeeded to his father's titles by the acclaim of the army. And when his rival emperor Galerius allowed him only the title of Caesar, Constantine fabricated a claim to the imperial throne, marched across Gaul in 312, won victories in northern Italy and marched on Rome. There Maxentius, son of the old Western emperor Maximian, had rebelled. At the Milvian Bridge, in 312, Constantine won his imperial power in the name of the Christian God. The

Christian apologist Lactantius reports that Constantine had been instructed in a dream to paint the Christian monogram on the shields of his troops. According to Eusebius of Caesarea (?260–?340), "the father of ecclesiastical history," Constantine had seen in the sky a cross with the words "In hoc signo vinces" (In this sign you will conquer). Constantine claimed that God had brought him from remote Britain across Gaul to overcome impiety and bring peace.

Did Constantine become a Christian only to secure the support of the Christian God in battle? If so, he was in a well-established tradition. The ancient Greeks and Romans had assumed that piety would be rewarded by success in battle. It is no wonder, then, that Constantine should have engaged the power of the new Christian God in battle, nor that he should have been grateful to the God in whose name he had won the decisive battle at the Milvian Bridge. What requires explaining is that Constantine should have become committed to the new religion and have used the imperial power to suppress the strong pagan opposition.

The public stages are clear in Constantine's movement from pious follower of the old Roman gods to a pious Christian banning paganism. The personal stages in his movement of conscience are not so clear. And the mystery of Constantine's motives has made him a favorite figure for either the admiration or the malice of historians. After the Christian God had helped him to victory in 312, he ceased to take part in pagan ceremonies, but retained the title of pontifex maximus. The triumphal arch erected in his honor after his defeat of Maxentius, which we can still see in Rome, shows Constantine holding a cross with the legend "By this saving sign I have delivered your city from the tyrant and restored liberty to the Senate and people of Rome." He had the name of Jupiter erased from the arch—a hodgepodge of earlier Roman sculpture and (in Gibbon's words) "a melancholy proof of the decline of the arts and of the meanest vanity." Still Constantine kept the old gods on his new gold coin, the solidus, which would survive for centuries as the unit of Byzantine currency. And he continued to associate himself with the Roman sun-god. His political adeptness was proved by his ability for many years to give guarantees to both of the conflicting religions.

After the Battle of Milvian Bridge, Constantine still tolerated paganism. But he restored the confiscated property of Christian communities,

Christians were favored for public positions and their proselytizing was supported. By 320 Constantine was openly attacking polytheism. Perhaps, as Jacob Burckhardt suggests, Constantine himself was simply a deist hoping to enlist the common devotion of all religions, including even the ancient sun-god and Mithras. So he proposed rituals that both pagans and Christians could conscientiously observe. One was his prayer for the armies "to honor the Lord's Day, which is also called the day of light and of the sun."

Constantine brought an epochal change in the relation of religion to the state. A new institution—the Church—was conjured up by his acts of toleration, the Edicts of Milan (313). The first edict recognized the Christian clergy as a class or corporation (*clerici*). He granted equal rights to all religions at the same time that he restored the confiscated property of the Christians. What was implied was even more significant than what was declared. For the very idea of a state religion, which had dominated ancient Greece and Rome, was abolished, "until Christianity clothed itself with the shell that paganism had discarded," as Jacob Burckhardt elegantly observes.

As Constantine's support of Christianity solidified, and his opposition to paganism grew, he was increasingly concerned by divisions within the Church and took measures to heal them. He tried to suppress the "Donatist" schism in North Africa over whether priests and bishops who had lapsed from the Church could be readmitted.

Then he intervened to settle the division over the two natures of Jesus, which would long trouble the fellowship of the faithful. The Christian Gospel in the West had responded both to the need for a superhuman authority, in the tradition of the Hebrew prophets, and to the need of each believer to reach within himself, in the tradition of the Greek philosophers. This dual appeal was expressed in the two titles of Jesus—Son of God, Son of Man. And the Gospels tell how the Son of God brought salvation to the world by the sacrifice of the Son of Man. But what was the relation between these two natures of Jesus? Disciples of Jesus, from the earliest time, were troubled and divided by efforts to define this duality. If Jesus had been *created* by God, then he was not of the same substance as God, but if he was *begotten* by God, then he must be of God's same substance. Constantine saw Christian unity threatened by bitter exchanges on this theological issue. The followers of Arius (born c. 250) believed that Christ, being the most perfect creature in the material world, had been "adopted" by God as a son. And the view had been spread by Arius' popular poetic work, *Thalia* ("Banquet"), which led to Arius' condemnation by the bishops as a heretic, and his exile from his post as priest in Alexandria. Constantine betrayed his own theological innocence when he called this dispute "a fight over trifling and foolish verbal differences."

Without calculating the consequences of this act of theological goodwill, Constantine unwittingly gave a new independent reality to the Church—and a new institutional reality to the fellowship of the faithful that would enable it to challenge the age-old imperial authority. Before this time there had been synod meetings of representatives of local churches. But the Council of Nicaea that Constantine convened would be something new, and newly menacing to the secular power. For the first time this council would be ecumenical (from the Greek *oikoumene,* the inhabited world)—and hence speak for a universal church. Such a community of all believers could hardly have seemed feasible before there was a Christian empire of the Roman world. The Church would speak for a new power in the world—a fellowship of the faithful, which before long would consider itself the equal or superior of the imperial power that convened it.

Constantine himself opened this first Ecumenical Council at Nicaea in Asia Minor in May 325, with an address. He had already written to Arius observing that the dispute Arius had fostered was a product of too much leisure and worried a trivial issue that could easily be settled. For this council, Constantine had brought together some 318 bishops, including delegates even from Armenia and Scythia outside the empire. But he did not sense the theological hatred (*odium theologicum*) he had roiled, nor did he imagine the Frankenstein he had created.

After three months' discussion, the assembled bishops agreed upon a creed—the Nicene Creed—which would become the dogma of Christian orthodoxy for succeeding centuries. Was Jesus the Son of God identical in substance with God or merely a demigod? The Council declared that Jesus was "begotten not created, one in being (*homoousios*) with the Father." Eusebius of Caesarea was there and reported the decisive intervention by Emperor Constantine himself. "Our emperor, most beloved by God, began to reason [in Latin, with a Greek translation supplied by an interpreter] concerning [Christ's] divine origin, and His existence before all ages: He was virtually in the Father without generation, even before he was actually begotten, the Father having always been the Father, just as [the Son] has always been a King and a Savior." To enforce this dogma, all books by Arius or his followers were to be burned "that not a single record of it should be left to posterity," and anyone who possessed such a work and refused to burn it should be put to death.

This search for agreement on the two natures of Jesus the Christ did not succeed in enforcing orthodoxy. For forty years after Constantine, Arianism remained the doctrine of the Eastern Empire. But it had drawn Christians together and brought an ominous new institution into being. The Church would be governed by the bishops of the whole Christian world. By 324 Constantine had seen himself, he explained to the bishops, as "a bishop established by God of those outside [the Church]," even as a "thirteenth apostle." The seeking would unite, while the finding and defining would divide. Succeeding Church councils would elaborate the dogma as they continued to redefine the nature, or two natures, of the Christ. Each new definition provided new targets for objection, more ammunition for dissent.

Battles between Church and state would punctuate all Western history and leave fertile ambiguities even in the New World. But Constantine had created a new relation between the state and religion. The religion of the state would no longer be a state religion. Yet Constantine's name would be given to the policy of establishing a Christian Church as the religion of the state, signaling a special close alliance between the state and a particular Christian Church. "Constantinism" troubled Europe for centuries.

Ironically, too, this close association of the state with the independent Christian forces of virtue provided a classic example of the historic powers of forgery. The so-called Donation of Constantine was a supposed grant by Emperor Constantine to Pope Sylvester I (314–335) in Rome of spiritual sovereignty over all the other great patriarchs and over all matters of faith and worship, as well as temporal sovereignty over Rome and the entire Western Empire. This was said to have been Constantine's thank-you gift to Sylvester for miraculously healing his leprosy and converting him to Christianity. A brilliant example of the independent Renaissance spirit was the demonstration in 1440 by the vigorous Italian humanist Lorenzo Valla (1407–1457) that the "donation" was only a forgery designed to empower the papacy. This was a foretaste, too, of the spirit of the Protestant Reformation. For centuries Constantine's supposed Donation remained the basis for the expansive powers of medieval popes over kings, princes, bishops, and patriarchs.

Christianity, we must not forget, did not come into a religious vacuum. It came on a Roman scene adorned by a vivid and sumptuous state religion, headed, as we have seen, by the college of pontiffs and a pontifex maximus, now the emperor himself. Even when Gratian became emperor in 375, six decades after Constantine's victory at the Milvian Bridge, most senators were pagans—still being sworn into office on the altar of the ancient Roman goddess of Victory in the Senate Hall, with libations of wine and incense. This was only one sign of a still-powerful pagan religion that commanded the loyalty of most of the ruling nobles of Rome. Edward Gibbon's famous "Five Causes of the Growth of Christianity," which aroused the ire of faithful and credulous Christians, is not often enough seen as a catalog also of the powers of the dying but still-prevalent and revered pagan religion. "While that great body [of the Roman Empire] was invaded by open violence, or undermined by slow decay, a pure and humble religion gently insinuated itself into the minds of men, grew up in silence and obscurity, derived new vigour from opposition, and finally erected the triumphant banner of the cross on the ruins of the Capitol."

The affair of the Altar of Victory in 382 dramatized the power of the ancient Roman religion. Fortunately, the words of the heroes on both sides have been preserved. This affair actually offers us one of the most vivid and eloquent dramas of appeal to the spirit of tolerance and the force of tradition. The fortunes of the Altar of the ancient goddess of Victory in the Senate Hall had varied with the tastes of the emperors. Constantius had removed it, Julian the Apostate had restored it, but the Christian zealot Gratian removed it again in 382. In Rome at the time there were some 424 pagan temples, so that, as Gibbon observes, "in every quarter of Rome the delicacy of the Christians was offended by the fumes of idolatrous sacrifice."

Four respectable pagan deputations begged Gratian's successor, Emperor Valentinian II, to restore the Altar of Victory, symbol of the gods under whom Rome had flourished. They set the stage for a classic confrontation between the old religion of the greatness of Rome and the new religion of Christ and Constantine. Spokesman for restoring the pagan altar was the eloquent Symmachus, a wealthy and noble senator, prefect of the city, a pontiff and augur, and proconsul of Africa, who reported on the affair to Emperor Valentinian II. His moving plea for tradition was also a surprisingly liberal diatribe against ideology. "Grant, I implore you," urged Symmachus, "that we who are old men may leave to posterity that which we received as boys." The ancestral Roman polytheism had kept people honest, and would continue to do so. "All things," he declared, "are full of God, and no place is safe for perjurers, but the fear of transgression is greatly spurred by the consciousness of the very presence of deity." Then Symmachus quoted the Eternal City herself (*aeterna Roma*) begging the emperors:

> Let me use my ancestral ceremonies, she says, for I do not repent me of them. Let me live after my own way; for I am free. This was the cult that drove Hannibal from the walls of Rome and the Gauls from the Capitolium. Am I kept for this, to be chastised in my old age? . . . I do but ask peace for the gods of our fathers, the native gods of Rome. It is right that what all adore should be deemed one. We all look up at the same stars. We have a common sky. A common firmament encompasses us. What matters it by what kind of learned theory each man looketh for the truth? There is no one way that will take us to so mighty a secret. All this is matter of discussion for men of leisure. We offer your majesties not a debate but a plea.

The answer to Symmachus is also eloquent, but more surprising. It is given by Saint Ambrose (340–397), who had brought Saint Augustine to Christianity. Apologizing for his homely words, Ambrose deals respectfully with Symmachus' arguments in a simple paean to progress, a translation of the Gospel message of Good News to the people of Rome:

> Why cite me the examples of the ancient? It is no disgrace to pass on to better things (*nullus pudor est ad meliora transire*). Take the ancient days of chaos when elements were flying about in an unorganized mass. Think how that turmoil settled into the new order of a world and how the world has de-

veloped since then, with the gradual invention of the arts and the advances of human history. I suppose that back in the good old times of chaos, the conservative particles objected to the advent of the novel and vulgar sunlight which accompanied the introduction of order. But for all that, the world moved. And we Christians too have grown. Through wrongs, through poverty, through persecution, we have grown; and the great difference between us and you is that what you seek in surmises, we know. How can I put faith in you when you confess that you do not know what you worship?

13

Islands of Faith: Monasteries

Of all the institutions created by Christian Seekers, none was more influential in its time nor more obscured in the currents of later history than the monasteries. All the great world religions have found a place for the monk. Monasticism is generally based on a belief that the world is evil and that withdrawal will somehow open the way to higher truth. Withdrawal has commonly included celibacy (escape from physical passions and family ties), obedience to a superior (escape from the selfish will), and poverty (escape from the material world). The Hindus from earliest times had monasteries where monks shared a life of mortification and study of sacred texts. The Gautama Buddha elevated the Hindu doctrine of deliverance and withdrawal into the only path to Nirvana, and provided more than two hundred rules for his monks. In Tibet after the seventeenth century Buddhist monasteries became major state institutions. Before the Communist conquest there, monks were said to form a fifth of the population and the government was controlled by the chief abbot, the Dalai Lama.

The Old Testament religions—Judaism, Christianity, and Islam—give monasticism a lesser role. In Judaism, withdrawal from the world to seek union with Jehovah would be blasphemous. Still, the Dead Sea Scrolls seem to record rules for the monastic life of the Essenes. Mohammed declared that there were no monks in Islam, and did not mention them in the Koran. Nor does monasticism seem to have been essential to Christian practice. We know of no Christian monks until at least two centuries after the death of Jesus. And withdrawal never became as integral to Christianity as it was to Buddhism. But Christianity developed its own fertile monastic institutions. Although only one form of Christian life, the monastic way attracted some of the most eloquent, persuasive, and constructive of the faithful, and it became a vehicle and catalyst of Western culture.

The story of Christian efforts at withdrawal dramatizes the problems man makes for himself by efforts to separate the quest for meaning from experience of the world. The monasteries that would shape Christian life in Europe in the Middle Ages found their unlikely origins in the Egyptian desert. The Church, which, as we have seen, organized and had given power to the faithful, created a new need for escape. Escape from the oppressive powers of the community into the sacrificing Christ-like self, and from the burdens of the material world. And the ascetic spirit took the form of monasticism.

The ironies of this monastic search for meaning have made monks in the West an attractive target for criticism. They provided Edward Gibbon with the subject for one of his most vivid and acerbic chapters. "The Ascetics fled from a profane and degenerate world, to perpetual solitude, or religious society" but "soon acquired the respect of the world, which they despised." The monks with poverty and self-denial "trod the steep and thorny path of eternal happiness. . . . Time continually increased, and accidents could seldom diminish, the estates of the popular monasteries . . . and in the first century of their institution, the infidel Zosimus has maliciously observed that, for the benefit of the poor, the Christian monks had reduced a great part of mankind to a state of beggary." For the worldly, Gibbon's monastic history revealed the futility of the effort to flee from the community and the material world into the security of the self.

The legendary founder of Christian monasticism, usually called the first Christian monk, was a Coptic Christian, Saint Anthony of Egypt (c. 250–355), who had inherited wealth. He became an ascetic at the age of twenty and at thirty-five retired to solitude in the desert. For the next twenty years he remained in retreat in a ruined fortress, then instructed others who followed his example. So he set the style and suggested the name "hermit" (from the Greek word for desert) for those who (in Gibbon's phrase) sought "lonely retreat in a natural or artificial desert."

Saint Anthony's own career was a parable of the impossibility of retreat. Athanasius' classic life of Anthony recounted how he had read Jesus' command to the rich young man to "go and sell that thou hast, and give to the poor and thou shalt have treasure in heaven: and come and follow me." Son of a wealthy landed peasant, Anthony had chosen the desert for his experiment because it was the proverbial habitat of the demons against whom the hermits would wage war. The "Demonology" of the New Testament was a rich and vivid inheritance from Jewish apocalyptic literature, recounting the many forms that Satan took to seduce mankind. Athanasius reported how Satan, having failed to tempt Anthony by the joys of the family he had given up, then took ingenious guises—monks with bread when he was fasting, women, beasts. All these Anthony repelled with prayer and the sign of the cross. These Christian efforts to ward off evil spirits led the emperor Julian the Apostate (331–363) to declare that "the quintessence of their theology [was] to hiss at demons and make the sign of the cross on their foreheads." The struggles of Saint Anthony would enrich Western art with the visions of Hieronymus Bosch, Matthias Grünewald, and Max Ernst.

Anthony's fame attracted visitors and disciples. During his lifetime others made their retreats into the desert, where they followed the tenets of Egyptian monasticism—manual labor, prayer, and reading Scripture. They favored the region around Luxor in Upper Egypt and areas west of the Nile Delta in Lower Egypt. Commonly they settled in huts near the cell of a seasoned saintly hermit. Many were illiterate peasants who had to memorize passages of Psalms and the New Testament for recitation and meditation. But they managed somehow, assisted by their literate fellows.

The fourth century saw a wide variety of ascetic experiments from Egypt and neighboring regions. The monk (from *monachos,* Greek for one who lives alone) sought isolation from ordinary social relations, but not necessarily from other ascetics. The retreating monk imposed chastity on himself along with a strict routine of prayer and Scripture reading. Scholars speculate that in the year 1000, when the population of the Byzantine Empire was about 15 million, the empire may have held more than 150,000 monks and some seven thousand monastic establishments. Emperors aiming to prohibit new monasteries recited the excessive numbers already in existence.

The two different styles of asceticism that appeared in late-third-century Egypt would mark the traditions of Western monasteries for following centuries. One was the individualist, the tradition of the hermit, or anchorite (from the Greek for withdrawal), of which Saint Anthony was the founder and patron. The other was the communal, or cenobitic (from Greek *koinos bios* for living a common life), of which Saint Pachomius was the father. Pachomius, born in Upper Egypt about 287, when in his twenties was guided by an older man to try the solitary life. After seven years as a hermit, he had discovered the trials of the solitary life and he founded a community of monks on the right bank of the Nile north of Thebes. There the monks lived a "cenobitic" life grouped in houses (each holding thirty to forty men) within a circling wall. They gathered for prayer and meals and followed a rule of 194 chapters devised by Pachomius. At his death in 346 there were nine of his monasteries for men with several thousand monks and two for women. Then there developed the laura (or *lavra*), combining features of the hermitage and the monastery in a collection of the cells of individual hermits who gathered on regular occasions.

Enthusiastic ascetic Seekers exhausted their imaginations in quest of personal ways up "the steep and thorny path of eternal happiness." With diabolical ingenuity they devised obstacles on the angelic path. The most famous of these was Saint Simeon Stylites, a passionate shepherd born about 390 near modern Aleppo in Syria and who died in 459. When his strict ascetic habits made him unwelcome in his monastery, he became a hermit and was soon venerated for his miracles. Then what Gibbon called his "singular invention of an aerial penance" helped him escape people demanding his blessing, and punished him at the same time that it separated him from importunate admirers. To pursue his divine meditations without interruption, he began living on top of a single column, and so acquired the name of "Stylites" (from the Greek for pillar dweller). At first the column was only six feet high but was gradually extended till it reached about fifty feet. There, beginning about 420, he is said to have remained day and night until his death in 459. The narrow platform surrounded by a railing was exposed to the elements and too small for him to do anything but stand or sit. While the railing prevented him from falling, a ladder communicated with the ground where acolytes brought small gifts of food. Only occasionally would he descend to give pilgrims his blessing or his counsel. Awe at his performance converted many visitors to Christianity and was said to have persuaded the Eastern Roman Emperor Leo I to the orthodox view of the dual nature of Christ. Simeon's example inspired other ascetics.

Simeon Stylites was only the most ingenious and conspicuous of the self-mortifying hermits, Seekers desperate to separate themselves from the common life. The Dendrites lived in trees or in hollow tree trunks. The "Browsers" subsisted on roots and grass. Some dwelt in tombs or in huts with roofs so low that it was impossible to stand inside. Others loaded themselves with chains.

The later history of monasticism reminds us again and again of the moderating influence of community on the excesses of self-regarding virtue. Saint Basil of Caesarea (329–379), rare among the Church Fathers in doubting the possibility of a good solitary life, insisted that only in community could fallen mankind repair human weakness by the works of charity. His "Rules" declared "That it is necessary with a view to pleasing God to live with like-minded persons, and that solitude is difficult and dangerous."

Quest for the good monastic life produced Saint Benedict's *Rule,* one of the most remarkable documents of Seekers in Western Christendom and one of the most durable institutions of Western communal life. The leader and creator of the movement of moderate communal asceticism, Saint Benedict, came from Umbria, northeast of Rome. Here was another story, like that of Saint Anthony and Saint Thomas Aquinas, of a rich man's son seeking through Christian withdrawal to escape the meaningless world of dissipation. The transformation of Western monasticism was a legacy of this Saint Benedict of Nursia (c. 480–547).

Most of what we know of Benedict's life comes from the *Dialogues* of his admiring disciple Saint Gregory the Great (540–604; pope, 590–604). Gregory, himself a rich man's son, had given away his landed inheritance to establish a half-dozen monasteries and fled into the retreat of a monastery. In 590 he was reluctantly summoned by acclamation of the people of Rome from his monastic cell to the throne of Saint Peter. Architect of the medieval papacy, he also left the Gregorian chant as his legacy. His *Dialogues* report the life and miracles of Saint Benedict, which would endure in Christian tradition.

Benedict lived when Theodoric and his Ostrogoths were conquering the cities of northern Italy. Totila, king of the Goths, repeatedly besieged Rome and finally took the city in 549. Sent to Rome for a liberal education, Benedict was repelled by the dissipation and decadence he saw. "He withdrew the foot he had just placed in the entry to the world; and despising the pursuit of letters, and abandoning his father's home and property, desiring to please God alone, he determined to become a monk." Benedict tried living in a village (Enfide) about thirty miles from Rome. There, when one day by earnest prayer he miraculously mended an earthenware tray that had been shattered, he attracted a throng of visitors. To find a more secure retreat, Benedict, under the influence of a holy man nearby, settled into a desolate cave in a rocky cliff, where he remained isolated for three years. He was fed only the bread that the holy man drew up in a basket and let down in a rope over the rock. When shepherds discovered him, clothed in the skin of beasts, they first took him for a wild animal. As his reputation spread people brought him food and asked his blessing and his advice.

In these years, Gregory reports, Benedict was repeatedly besieged by Satan. "The tempter came in the form of a little blackbird, which began to flutter in front of his face. It kept so close that he could easily have caught it with his hand. Instead he made the sign of the Cross and the bird flew away. . . . The evil spirit recalled to his mind a woman he had once seen, and before he realized it his emotions were carrying him away. . . . Almost overcome in the struggle, he was on the point of abandoning the lonely wilderness when suddenly with the help of God's grace he came to himself." To defeat temptation he suddenly threw off his clothes and flung himself into a nearby patch of nettles and briars. "There he rolled and tossed till his whole body was in pain and covered with blood. Yet once he had conquered pleasure through suffering, his torn and bleeding skin served to drain off the poison of temptation from his body." He never again suffered a temptation of this kind.

Benedict's reputation for holiness brought him the invitation to become abbot of a nearby rock-hewn monastery. But when the monks found his discipline too strict, they tried to get rid of him by poisoning his wine. "A glass pitcher containing this poisoned drink," Saint Gregory reports, "was presented to the man of God for customary blessing. As he made the sign of the Cross over it with his hand, the pitcher was shattered even though it was well beyond his reach at the time. It broke at his blessing as if he had struck it with a stone." He organized the disciples attracted by his "signs and wonders" into twelve monasteries with an abbot and twelve monks in each in the neighborhood of Subiaco about fifty miles east of Rome.

In 529, when a jealous local priest drove him away, he moved eighty miles south of Rome to Monte Cassino, where he built his famous monastery on the site of a pagan temple he destroyed. (Menaced by

Lombards and Saracens, and shaken by earthquakes, this was the key point in the German defensive line in World War II, blocking the Allied advance on Rome, but it was destroyed by Allied bombing in 1944. It has since been rebuilt.) At first Benedict seems to have lived at Monte Cassino as a hermit. Later he no longer put his disciples in separate houses but collected them under his supervision. And here he wrote his famous *Rule,* his prescription for the communal monastic life, initially for the monks of Monte Cassino but eventually to become a norm for monasteries in the West. So Benedict's good sense attracted many into Christian faith and opened the gates of the Western Heritage to other Seekers. His Benedictine *Rule* was an inspired treaty of otherworldly faith with the demands of this world. A pact between asceticism and common sense, it was the farthest cry from the self-flagellating hermits of the Egyptian desert.

Benedict's "little Rule for beginners" we can read today in a pamphlet of seventy-three chapters, less than a hundred pages. "We are about to open a school for God's service," the Prologue announces, "in which we hope nothing harsh or oppressive will be directed." He opposes all self-inflicted pain, assuming that the world itself will provide enough. Having heard that a monk in a cave near Monte Cassino had chained his foot to the rock, Benedict sent him a message, "If you are truly a servant of God, chain not yourself with a chain of iron but with the chain of Christ."

Benedictine asceticism was moderate. Except, perhaps, for the classic monastic rules of poverty, chastity, and obedience, it was not an unsuitable life for the devout layman. The Fathers of the Egyptian desert who made sleeplessness a virtue took their rest on bare ground with rocks for pillows. But Benedict's *Rule* allowed eight hours of uninterrupted sleep for most of the year, with "mattress, coverlet, blanket and pillow." There was no fetish of bare feet. Shoes were to be provided and "suitable clothing . . . dependent on the climate." Not starvation but frugality was the dietary rule, and wine was drunk sparingly. "Idleness is an enemy of the soul," prescribed Chapter 48. "Therefore the brothers should be occupied according to schedule in either manual labor or holy reading."

The schedule depended on the season and the hours of daylight, of course limited by the crudity of their timepieces and the problems of the water clock. The twenty-four hours of a normal Benedictine day in summer would include about four hours for the Divine Office (*Opus Dei*), including eight periods of communal prayer throughout day and night; four hours for reading (all were expected to be or become literate and to read); six and a half hours for work (which helped make the monasteries self-sufficient); eight and a half hours for sleep; and one hour for meals. All were to read in the Bible and the writings of the Fathers, whose Latin was no obstacle, since it was the monastery vernacular.

There was no privacy in the monastery. Nor was there any oppressive rule of silence. Again moderation was the rule—not *silentium* but *taciturnitas*. The vice was not talking but talkativeness, with a ban only on "all small talk and jokes."

The Benedictine community, or community of communities, made a model of autonomy and self-regulation. There is no evidence that Benedict himself was ever ordained as a priest. It seems, too, that he never intended to found an "order" aimed at one special kind of work. The only preparation, the Benedictines said, was for Heaven. Unlike the Franciscans and others with a centralized international authority, each Benedictine monastery was independent, electing its own abbot (from Aramaic *Abba,* "Father"), who stood in Christ's place and governed the community for life.

Another distinctive Benedictine contribution to monastic life was stability. Benedict's *Rule* begins by distinguishing the kinds of monks. Best were "the Cenobites . . . who live in a monastery waging their war under a rule and an abbot." The Anchorites by living in a monastery "learn to fight against the devil," preparing themselves "for the single combat of the hermit." "The Sarabaites (the worst kind), unschooled by any rule," lie to the world by their tonsured heads, live together in twos and threes, and whatever they wish they call holy. Finally, there are "the gyratory monks," who wander about staying in various monasteries three or four days at a time.

To Benedict's community, no one was to be admitted lightly—only after a year of probation. Stability meant that once a novice had taken his vows he was committed until death to the house that had accepted his profession. This was wholesome insurance against the tendency, among Egyptian ascetics and others, to make the monastery only a way station toward the life of a hermit. And it gave each monk his own Benedictine family to replace what he had left outside. If members of one monastery were commanded by their abbot to found a new house, their vows of stability were transferred.

Saint Benedict's legacy has survived for fifteen hundred years as a norm for the monastic life of Western Christendom. The era from the sixth to the twelfth centuries in Europe was christened "The Benedictine Centuries" by Cardinal Newman. During these years the Benedictines were the chief religious, civilizing, and educating influence in the Western Church. Others have called this the Golden Age of Monasteries. In 817 at the Synod of Aachen, the city that Charlemagne (742–814) had made the capital of Western culture, Benedict's *Rule* was adopted as the basic text for all Western monks.

A tradition of Benedictine mysticism—Benedict's way of seeking union with God—inspired Western Christendom in the Middle Ages. His most influential disciples were Saint Gregory the Great and Saint Bernard of Clairvaux (1091–1153), who fought against the rationalist philosophy of Abelard. Thus Benedict had nourished two disparate tendencies—the inward-reaching upward-reaching and the love of learning and the book. In the libraries of the Benedictines the literary treasures of antiquity and of Christianity were preserved throughout the Middle Ages, and Benedict became the patron saint of the manuscript book. The Benedictines spread the belief that "A monastery without a library is like a castle without an armory," and none were more effective than the Benedictines in preserving and strengthening that armory. The alliance of the monasteries with learning under the patronage of the Frankish, Visigothic, and Anglo-Saxon kings kept Western culture alive through turbulent times.

Benedictine scholars also left their indelible marks on the vocabulary of Western learning, especially on the study of history. The Venerable Bede (672–735), sometimes called the first Benedictine scholar, "the pattern of a Benedictine as is St. Thomas of a Dominican" (in Cardinal Newman's phrase), set a pioneer standard of laborious accuracy in his *Historia Ecclesiastica gentis Anglorum* (Ecclesiastical History of the English People). His method of dating events from the birth of Jesus Christ is said to have come into general use through the popularity of his *History* and his two works of chronology. A later French Benedictine scholar, Jean Mabillon (1632–1707), wrote *De Re Diplomatica*

(1681), founding the modern science of diplomatics—the critical study of ancient official manuscripts and other formal sources of history.

Benedict's *Rule* also surprisingly provided a physical model for Western communities. The plan for the Benedictine monastery of St. Gall in Switzerland, drawn by a German cleric about 820, may be the earliest document of Western urban planning. It displaced the haphazard scheme of Eastern monasteries by a functional plan. Its axial design conveniently met the needs of a self-contained monastic community—including an infirmary, guest house, kitchens, bakehouse, privies, workshops, housing for lay workers, stables for livestock, and a cemetery. This would become a norm for Western monastic architecture and also suggested the grid scheme of later urban planners. Incidentally, too, monastic libraries provided models for modern public and university libraries.

The tenth-century Burgundian monastery of Cluny founded a centralized movement for return to the *Rule* of Benedict. The Cistercians, also reformers, founded in 1098 at Citeaux near Dijon, flourished under the influence of Bernard of Clairvaux and had founded 338 Cistercian abbeys by the time of Bernard's death.

The late Middle Ages saw some paradoxical forms and reforms of the Christian ascetic spirit, of monasteries and the monastic movement. None was more fertile or more contradictory of the tenets of primitive monasticism than knighthood and the orders of chivalry. The Christian knight had found his own way of seeking. Like the desert hermit, he was devoted to fighting the devil—whom he saw in the infidel and the heretic. With his vow of knighthood, the knight took up the Cross. From the Christian canon, then, he adopted humility and obedience, and to the familiar Christian virtues he added valor and largess. Knights were commonly lovers of women or were married men, and the monkish virtue of chastity was astonishingly displaced by the ideal of "courtly love." In the King Arthur legends, Galahad could have "the strength of ten" because his heart was pure. Sinful knights ended as monks. Yet the Knights Templars and the Knights Hospitalers did take the vow of celibacy.

The transmutation of the monastic, ascetic spirit was revealed in the most famous of the knightly orders, the Knights Templars. These have become known to English readers through the villainous Sir Brian de Bois-Guilbert of Sir Walter Scott's *Ivanhoe*. About 1119, eight or nine French knights placed their hands within those of the Patriarch of Jerusalem and vowed to devote themselves to protect pilgrims to the Holy Land. The few strongholds in the hands of Crusaders and pilgrims in those days were being harassed by Muslim bands. To the knights who formed a religious community for this purpose the Crusader Baldwin II, king of Jerusalem, gave a wing of the royal palace in the area of the former Jewish Temple. From this they were called Templars. They attracted followers with the aid of a *Rule* of seventy-two chapters that had been inspired and probably mostly written by Saint Bernard of Clairvaux. This "Thaumaturgus of the West," as we shall see, was a bitter opponent of the way of disputation—the dialectical scholasticism of the universities. He abhorred "scandalous curiosity"—the way of Abelard—and favored prayer and the fighting faith of the ill-fated Second Crusade (1147–49).

Except for the vow of chastity, other monastic vows were part of the knight's faith. This included the vow of obedience—the denial of self-interest in favor of God's will expressed by the master of the order. Under Bernard's *Rule,* knights had no privacy. They were not to receive letters from parents or friends without the master's permission, nor were they even allowed locks on their chests. The monastic ideal proved remarkably adaptable to holy warfare. The Knights Templars had adopted a *religio militaris,* and according to Bernard's *Rule:*

> This new *genus religionis,* as we believe, by divine providence began with you in the Holy Land, a *religio* in which you mingle chivalry (*milicia*). Thus the armed religion may advance through chivalry, and smite the enemy without incurring sin. Rightfully then we decree that you shall be called knights of the Temple and may hold houses, lands and men, and possess serfs and justly rule them.
>
> Our word is directed primarily to all who despise their own wills, and with purity of mind desire to serve under the supreme and veritable King; and with minds intent choose the noble warfare of obedience, and persevere therein.

The growth of cities in twelfth-century Europe—the century of the flourishing monastery and the fervent Crusade—provided centers for new communities of education and learning. The universities—new institutions born here—would have some of the stability of the Benedictine monastery and some of the cosmopolitanism of the adventuring Crusaders.

The quest of spiritual Seekers that began with Saint Anthony's lonely retreat into the desert had become an outreaching enterprise of institutions and communities. The search for self-perfection and union with God was a venture of inescapable paradox. "A monk is a man who is separated from all, and who is in harmony with all," the Byzantine historian Evagrios observed. "When the mind raises itself up to heavenly things," Saint Gregory insisted, "when it fixes its attention on spiritual things, when it tries to pass over all that is outwardly seen . . . it narrows itself that it may be enlarged." The universities would offer their own enduring compromise.

14

The Way of Disputation: Universities

The Church and the monasteries set the stage for universities. Just as they had known no Church, so the ancients knew no universities. Students of Socrates, Plato, or Aristotle, however much they learned or were inspired, did not face examinations or receive degrees. Our university, like the Church, is a legacy of the Middle Ages, and few modern institutions have so clear a genealogy. When the contrary seeking traditions of Athens and Jerusalem confronted, confuted, and enriched one another, the product of their reaching was the university.

The word *universitas* in the twelfth and thirteenth centuries, when the new institution was taking shape, did not describe the scope of knowledge to be explored. It did describe the people who came together in search. Then *universitas* was a general name for a corporation, a group that had a legal existence. At the two original European universities, in Paris *universitas* was the group of masters, while in Bologna it meant the whole body of students. From them the university emerges more plainly into the light of history.

By the thirteenth century the rise of European cities had led to the forming of guilds. Now scholars would have their own. Attached to the great cathedrals were schools where, before the rise of universities, the body of knowledge consisted of the *trivium* (grammar, rhetoric, logic, or dialectic), and the *quadrivium* (arithmetic, geometry, astronomy, music). These narrowly defined Seven Liberal Arts (*artes liberales*) were the disciplines appropriate for training a gentleman, a *homo liber*. Centuries passed before the universities would go far beyond—with advanced studies of theology, law, and medicine—and become centers of intellectual creativity.

In 529 the Christian emperor Justinian finally closed the ancient philosophical school of Athens, the last pagan academy. It was in the same year that Saint Benedict founded the monastery of Monte Cassino as a refuge of Christian faith. And in the next centuries "university" came to mean a guild of masters and students, *universitas societas magistrorum discipulorumque*. In Paris the university grew out of the Cathedral School. And the transfer of educational activity from monks to the "secular" clergy (who did not belong to a religious order) opened the way to a new cosmopolitanism. The curriculum was liberated from the Seven Liberal Arts. At the same time the universities themselves grew into a third power besides salvation and government—between Church and Empire. Speaking for "wisdom," they commanded the interest and favors of popes and princes. Which explained the privileges that shrewd rulers like Frederick Barbarossa, in 1158, and Philip Augustus, in 1200, showered on scholars, freeing them from the secular authorities.

Paris—the Rome of the university world—revealed this new energy of the world of learning. The first papal recognition of the university there was a bull of Innocent III about 1210, followed by other grants of authority to the guild of masters and students. And the welcoming outreach of the university, in splendid contrast to the inwardness of the new world of monasteries, created a kind of pedagogical United Nations. At Paris the student body and the administration were divided into four "Nations," according to the places from which the students came: the French, the Normans, the Picards, and the English. In fact the student body came from all over Europe. For this purpose the "Nation" of Picardy included all the Low Countries, while the French embraced all the Latin countries, and with the English were the Germans and others from the north and east of Europe. Teachers had to be Masters of Arts in order to be members of their "Nation," headed by a proctor. The university claimed the right to grant licenses for teaching in any part of the world.

In the early thirteenth century, when the population of Paris was about 150,000, the academic population of the city may have been around 3,500. Students became important to the economic life of the city. The students at Bologna organized against gouging by landlords and food vendors. In the beginning the "universitas" had no buildings, which left disgruntled students free to move (or threaten to move) away in a body. On several occasions they actually migrated, to the despair of local businessmen. These threats gave them power to fix the price of books and lodgings. Masters, like the local businessmen, lived on the fees of students and in fear of their displeasure. The earliest statutes in Bologna aiming to guarantee students their money's worth forbade professors to be absent without leave, and required that a master who departed the city should give a deposit to ensure his return. It was an age of famous and popular professors, when scholars would cross the continent to study with an Abelard or a Thomas.

The University of Paris had three faculties—theology, law, and arts—but the Faculty of Arts considered itself the mother of the others. There most of the reading was in Aristotle, with an emphasis that varied with the changing dogmas of the Church. Surprisingly, there were relatively few students in theology, since theological training for the priesthood did not come until the Counter-Reformation in the sixteenth century.

In the thirteenth century the University of Paris was a lively and often turbulent place. Since texts were scarce and costly to rent, a distinctive technique of interactive teaching developed, with lectures and disputations. Lectures (from Latin *legere,* "to read") were readings from the prescribed text with commentary by the lecturer and, often, opportunity for questions. The increasingly important disputations became the distinctive feature of the medieval university, and gave a special character to scholastic thought. Founded in Aristotle's logic, dialectics was a way of subjecting the propositions of Christian belief to rigorous objections in search of satisfying answers.

For a formal disputation, the master offered a thesis. Objections would then be raised by the master, by students, or by anyone else present. A younger teacher (*baccalarius*) would uphold the thesis and answer the question. At the next lecture the master would resume the subject, restate the thesis, select the arguments against it, and offer his own decision, while refuting objections. Saint Thomas Aquinas' *Summa theologiae,* a model of the disputatious technique, was not a set of dogmatic assertions but a series of questions with objections and answers. He began by asking, "Whether, besides the philosophical sciences, any further doctrine is required?" Two well-stated objections are posed against the necessity of "sacred doctrine," then each is refuted in turn. Then the next question, "Whether Sacred Doctrine is a Science?" More than a hundred questions, each with objections and answers, proceed in rigorous order—from God and the Order of Creation through the whole of Christian doctrine. In addition to disputations held by each master for his students, there were public disputations during the second week of Advent and the third or fourth week of Lent, when anybody could submit a question on any subject. To become a master, a typical career at Paris required six years of study and twenty-one years of age for the liberal arts and eight years of study and thirty-four years of age for a master of theology. Scholasticism—the name for the writing and teaching that grew out of this technique of questioning (and answering)—produced a "scholastic philosophy" in the Faculty of Arts and a "scholastic theology" in the Faculty of Theology.

The lectures—which would begin around six or seven A.M. when the clergy recited the Divine Office and lasted till about nine—were relieved by questions. But the disputations were especially lively. After the master offered the topic to be disputed and opened the discussion, anyone present, in order of seniority, could raise an argument for or against. After the last objection, the master gave his own solution (*determinatio*) on the morning following. For the *quodlibet* (from *quodlibetum,* "whatever you wish") disputations of the faculty of theology, while the master was free to reject politically dangerous questions, there were no other restrictions and anyone could propose a subject. Thomas Aquinas would be known for specially favoring these "quodlibetal" exercises.

By contrast with its modern successor, the medieval university was a loosely organized society where control was seized by teachers and students, depending on local opportunities. There were generally no endowments, no officials to fill an "administration" building, nor any board of trustees, nor state control. Flowing in and out, students created a varied and colorful community. The *goliardi,* or wandering scholars, not always welcomed by the masters, sang their own scurrilous anticlerical songs. On more than one occasion members of the University of Paris appealed to the king to restore order:

> Priests and clerks . . . dance in the choir dressed as women, or disreputable men, or minstrels. They sing wanton songs. They eat black-puddings at the altar itself, while the celebrant is saying Mass. They play at dice on the altar. They cense with stinking smoke from the soles of old shoes. They run and leap throughout the church, without a blush at their own shame. Finally they drive about the town and its theatres on shabby carriages and carts, and rouse the laughter of their fellows and the bystanders in infamous performances, with indecent gestures and with scurrilous and unchaste words.

It was not easy to discipline so volatile a body of masters and scholars. Only in the later, humanistic age did these wanderers become respectable. Erasmus was one of them.

The truths of medieval scholars, we must remember, were not to be found by freely searching. These had already been revealed by authority, and Seekers could only grasp, reflect on, and confirm the beauties of revelation. "I believe in order that I may know," explained Anselm, "I do not know in order to believe."

It is remarkable to the modern unbelieving mind how much intellectual vigor and vitality, how much delight in discovery could be found within the revealed limits. In the thirteenth century masters were condemned, and even imprisoned, for errors of theology. The most notorious was the Condemnation of 1277, when the University of Paris was notified of thirty errors in arts. Though these were not quite heretical, they were evil enough to require the deposing of anyone who taught them. They even included condemnation of certain forms of Latin nouns and verbs. Dare we agree with C. H. Haskins and other charitable medievalists who insist that "a fence is no obstacle to those who do not desire to go outside. . . . He is free who feels himself free"?

The medieval university grew and flourished with the rise of scholasticism, the discipline of reasoning within the limits of revealed faith. It is remarkable how lively were these intellectual exercises, how relentless were the masters in challenging the propositions of faith with the faculties of reason, and how grand and elegant were the intellectual structures they erected. Despite the grandeur of these structures, we may share Bertrand Russell's misgivings:

> There is little of the true philosophic spirit in Aquinas. He does not, like the Platonic Socrates, set out to follow wherever the argument may lead. He is not engaged in an inquiry, the result of which it is impossible to know in advance. Before he begins to philosophize, he already knows the truth; it is declared in the Catholic faith. If he can find apparently rational arguments for some parts of the faith, so much the better; if he cannot, he need only fall back on revelation. The finding of arguments for a conclusion given in advance is not philosophy, but special pleading.

Russell therefore would not rank the great scholastics with the best philosophers of Greece or of modern times.

The great scholastics plainly distinguished theology from philosophy. But they had made the trouble for themselves by insisting on applying the tests of philosophy to the truths of revelation. A pioneer was Peter Abelard (1079–1142), notorious for his ill-starred love affair with Héloïse. In the book entitled *Yes and No* (*Sic et Non*) that he compiled at the Benedictine monastery of St. Denis outside Paris, he gave a perilous new direction to Christian theology. "By doubting we come to questioning," he declared, "and by questioning we learn truth." Following this axiom, he answered one after another the 158 key questions in Christian theology.

Like other Seekers' problems ever since Job, the scholastics' problems were self-created, from their faith. If Job had not believed in a single omnipotent, omniscient, omnibenevolent God, the sufferings of the innocent (including his own) might have posed no problem for his faith. Now the Christian scholastics, too, started with their faith and challenged philosophy to find reasons for it. Abelard's *Sic et Non* steadily followed Aristotelian logic. As Abelard, one of the Peripatetics, wandered from school to school, he developed his own philosophy of language and immortalized his suffering by his *Historia calamitatum* (History of My Troubles). In *Sic et Non* he expounded the conflicting opinions of the Church Fathers on Church doctrine, then offered ways of resolving them, using the changing meanings of words to aid his explanation.

While only Scripture, Abelard argued, was infallible, apart from Scripture, dialectic was the sole road to truth. Yet his readiness to test the axioms of faith by the instruments of philosophy did not go unchallenged. The most powerful challenge came from the contemporary mystic Saint Bernard of Clairvaux. Bernard became his archenemy, denouncing the scholastics' "scandalous curiosity" that degraded God's mysteries to the level of human reason. Bernard insisted that "We discover with greater facility through prayer than through disputation." But the mystic champions of prayer lacked a feeling both for the real world and for the needs of the speculative mind. Bernard's sponsorship of the Second Crusade failed from his political ineptitude. And despite his affable reputation (*doctor mellifluus*) for "sweet as honey" teachings, his influence on the wide community of Christian thought was not comparable with the catalytic appeal of Abelard's *Sic et Non*.

Abelard's rational Aristotelian instruments would be monumentally productive in the hands of Saint Thomas Aquinas (1224–1275). In this greatest of Catholic theologians we see both the possibilities and the limits of human reason in support of divine revelation. Saint Thomas's first essential task was to mark the distinction between philosophy and theology and so show how reason could serve Christian revelation, yet not menace it. His work was the enduring product of the new cosmopolitan community of Seekers in universities. New institutions (the Church, the monasteries, and the universities) nurtured a Christian synthesis—of the Hebrew prophetic tradition and the Greek philosophic tradition—defined by revelation and defended by reason. It is remarkable that a work of Saint Thomas's vast reach could arise from his narrowly academic experience. His achievement demonstrated the distinctive productivity of the new community of universities.

Thomas was born at Roccasecca near Aquino on the road from Rome to Naples. From boyhood he experienced the battle between the pope and the emperor, for his family, of the minor nobility, had served under Emperor Frederick II against the pope, and held a small feudal domain on the boundary between the two powers. When Thomas was only five, his family deposited him as an oblate at the nearby Benedictine monastery of Monte Cassino "therein to be instructed in holy matters and to prepare himself for God's illumination." His family had more worldly motives. They hoped that Thomas might someday become abbot, and so give the family a share in the revenues of the monastery, besides the power of an additional feudal lordship. After nine years, when Thomas was only fourteen, the emperor expelled the monks for their loyalty to the pope and the family hopes were frustrated.

Meanwhile, Thomas had begun his education and made his first acquaintance with the *Rule* of Saint Benedict. At Monte Cassino he learned calligraphy and grammar and read works in Italian (the *volgare*) as well as Latin. Devout biographers note his progress "in logicalibus et naturalibus." At the early age of fourteen Thomas was sent to Naples to study at the university recently (1224) founded by Emperor Frederick II, king of Jerusalem, to keep his intellectuals from going abroad. There he studied philosophy, which the emperor had ordered to be based on the texts of Aristotle and his commentators, many newly available in translations from Greek and Arabic.

At Naples, Thomas was attracted to the Dominican order, founded only thirty years before. In the rising cities the Dominican Seekers pursued a path different from that of the old monastic orders. Retreating into the hills (as at Monte Cassino) the monks had pursued personal salvation and perfection in obedience to their abbot. And some of these monasteries had accumulated great wealth. It was in protest against their worldliness that Saint Dominic (1170–1221) founded his order of preaching friars (later indicated by "O.P."). Their mission to preach Christian doctrine was formerly assigned to bishops and their delegates. To accomplish their preaching mission, unlike the Benedictines, they were not a collection of autonomous houses, but went wherever they were needed, preaching the true doctrine and pursuing their studies. Dominican friars were encouraged to be scholars. Dominic established houses in large cities, favoring those with universities. They became relentless champions of orthodoxy, and would eventually administer the Inquisition. Required to renounce all personal or community property, they took vows of poverty and had to beg to support themselves. So they came to be called mendicant friars (from *mendicare,* "to beg").

Thomas's Dominican superiors, assuming that his family would oppose his new interests, assigned him at once to Paris to put him out of the family's reach. There, in the university center of Europe, he could pursue his Dominican studies. Thomas's ambitious mother, Theodora, not so easily outwitted, enlisted her other sons and soldiers of the emperor to capture the fugitive Thomas. Trying to strip him of his Dominican habit, they imprisoned him under strong guard at a family castle near Aquino, where the family used all their wiles to dissuade him from his Dominican vows. When they attacked his chastity by sending a girl into his cell, the steadfast Thomas seized a firebrand from the hearth and put her to flight. Then reportedly he used the same firebrand to trace a large cross on the wall, before falling to the floor in prayer. The family's two-year effort (1244–45) to break his faith was unsuccessful. His fellow Dominicans, according to his first biographer and adoring disciple, aided his midnight escape, like Saint Paul's flight from Damascus, by letting him down from a window by a rope.

Now Thomas began his academic odyssey. The master of his order, John the Teutonic, took him to Paris in October 1245 to the priory of Saint-Jacques, the great university center for Dominicans. There he became the disciple of Albertus Magnus (c. 1200–1280), with whom he had a natural kinship. For Albert, too, had fought his own family to join the Dominicans. After three years Thomas accompanied Albertus to Cologne, where a new Dominican university community (*studium generale*) was being founded for students from all over. At Cologne he remained Albertus' disciple for four years.

Never was there a happier coincidence than that which brought Thomas from southern Italy to be the disciple of Albert. Their works would be an enduring monument to the medieval university—a forum for the best restless minds. The temperaments and interests of Albert and Thomas proved wonderfully complementary. With different emphasis, they explored the same rich resources that the twelfth-century renaissance had providentially offered them. The rediscovered prodigious works of Aristotle and of Greek and Arabic philosophy and science provided materials for both these giants of scholasticism. Albertus Magnus aimed to make all Aristotle's encyclopedic works "intelligible to the Latins" by paraphrase and explanation. After twenty years he completed the work that survives in forty edited volumes.

Thus Albert brought the study of nature (through Aristotelian texts) into the Christian universities. He introduced his own notion of "experiment" and insisted on the value of observation as a source of knowledge, for he believed reason and faith were inevitably in harmony. Albert made his own observations on the causes of sound and light and on the thermal effects of the sun. Correcting Aristotle's statement that the lunar rainbow occurs only twice in fifty years, he noted that he had observed two in a single year. Even without a telescope, he suggested that the Milky Way might be composed of stars and that the dark spots on the moon might be features of its surface. He pioneered ways of classifying plants and animals and even hinted at the mutability of species.

In 1252 Thomas was sent to Paris, where he became a Master of Theology in 1256 and was appointed to a chair reserved for mendicant friars. During these years he began his own great work, more original and destined to be more influential than that of his teacher. Aristotle's work had made the achievement of both of them possible. Albert provided for the Latin Middle Ages a complete paraphrase of Aristotle's encyclopedic works. He was so eager that no part of nature remain uncovered that he even filled out a botanical work of dubious authorship to ensure that this aspect of the Aristotelian world was fully treated. Albert has been praised as the greatest "purveyor of a knowledge not his own," but Thomas made Aristotle his own. Thomas did more than simply "baptize" Aristotle. He assimilated Aristotle's work into the Christian arsenal, and for future generations would make Aristotle a prop of Christian faith. Albert was an acolyte of Aristotle. Thomas made Aristotle into an acolyte of Christianity.

During these years in Paris (1252–59) Thomas began his two great summaries of Catholic theology, first his *Summa contra gentiles,* followed by his *Summa theologiae.* If it was an age of faith, it was also an age of lively controversy that stimulated the great systematic works of theology. Believers became alert to the arguments that menaced their doctrine and ingenious at making works of pagan philosophy and science serve their faith. Thomas's lifetime was a simmering crucible. With solvent ideas came a new threat to newly established Christian institutions. Thomas enlisted both to give a new life to Christian doctrine. In the early Middle Ages, Aristotle was known as the author of works on logic translated by Boethius. Surprisingly, Plato was then the most cited ancient authority on nature. The Church Fathers had drawn heavily on Platonic ideas. But the renaissance of the twelfth century had brought new manuscripts of Aristotle and his Arab commentators, with the spread of Islam into Spain. For the first time the Church seemed threatened by a body of scientific learning, fathered by Aristotle. The study of nature and the instruments of reason challenged the articles of faith, which led the Church authorities to try to stem the Aristotelian tide. Albert tried to encompass the newfound treasures of Aristotelian thought. Thomas went further, using Aristotle's emphasis on reason to make his works the ally of revelation.

Institutions, too, seemed threatened by new forces. The old monastic orders withdrawn into their monasteries were being challenged by the new orders of mendicant friars. Now Francis of Assisi (1182–1226) and Dominic sought holiness in the world. And their attack did not go unchallenged. At the University of Paris the aggressive William of Saint-Amour (c. 1200–1272), dean of the theology masters, led the attack. His *Liber de Antichristo et ejusdum ministris* (Book of Antichrist and His Ministers, 1255) cast the Dominicans as the vanguard of the catastrophic age to come. Though Popes Alexander IV and Clement IV both defended the new orders, these remained centers of controversy—for their implied criticism of the Church hierarchy and their insistence on preaching and hearing confessions without episcopal consent. Thomas Aquinas, vigorous Aristotelian and leading Dominican, stood for the new.

It is not surprising then, that in a disputatious age, in new university communities which lived by the arts of disputation, the monumental works of theology should take the form that Thomas gave to his two Summae: Questions, Objections, and Replies to the objections. Taking nothing for granted, as we have seen, Thomas opens his *Summa theologiae* with the question "Whether, besides the philosophical sciences, any further doctrine is required." The whole relevance of philosophy (including Aristotle, "The Philosopher") to Christian doctrine depends on the distinction between philosophy and theology, at which Thomas is the master. He warns against trying to use philosophy (the agent of reason) to play the role of faith, and against testing faith by the rigors of reason. "In arguing with nonbelievers about articles of faith, you should not try to devise necessary arguments in behalf of faith, since this would derogate from the sublimity of faith, whose truth exceeds the capacity not only of human but also of angelic minds." The ancient Greeks had assumed that philosophy included all knowledge—even knowledge of God. If theology must always govern the Christian mind, what then is the use of philosophy? The human mind needed faith, Thomas answers, even in things that could be discovered by reason "because only a few men come to rationally acquired truth about God, and this after a long time and with the admixture of error."

We need theology, Thomas argues, because revelation gives us truths that cannot be arrived at by reason. To define the role of theology, Thomas draws also on Aristotle's distinction between the practical and the speculative sciences. He assigns three roles to philosophy. First, to demonstrate "the preambles of faith, . . . (what things in faith it is necessary to know), those things about God which can be proved by natural argument, such as that God exists, that God is one, and the like." Second, to find similarities among the articles of faith. And third, to combat objections to faith by showing them either false or unnecessary. Since religious belief concerns matters not accessible to natural reason, it cannot be replaced by knowledge. Since, for a Christian, philosophy and theology are necessarily compatible, he need not fear using philosophy to explain and reinforce articles of belief. And the study of philosophy (by which Thomas means Aristotle) must precede theology.

Thomas's *Summa theologiae*—organized in its Questions, Objections, and Replies—was, of course, not intended to be an alternative to the Bible. It was only an aid to beginners, making clear, explicit, and defensible the doctrines implicit in Scripture. The First Part concerns God and the order of Creation, the Second and Third Parts concern the goal of human life in beatitude and the return of all things to God. What is generally considered Thomas's most original contribution to theology is his exposition of the virtues and vices. The Third Part deals with Christ and the Sacraments as means to salvation. All along the way Thomas draws on Scripture, the Church Fathers, and Saint Augustine and Aristotle, among others. References to specific works of Aristotle provide a framework for his ideas. On some points, like Aristotle's view that the world is eternal, Thomas takes issue with The Philosopher, while still insisting that the matter could not be decided by philosophy. And he freely disagrees with commentators. He defends Aristotle's belief in the survival of individual souls after death against the "unicity" of intellect, the argument of the Spanish-Arabic Averroës, the Muslim interpreter, that there is only a single mind in which all souls participate.

Thomas had begun his first introduction to theology, his *Summa contra gentiles* (1258–64), in Paris. Then, after 1259, he spent some peripatetic years in Italy, first at the papal court, then in several Dominican houses, and there he began his *Summa theologiae,* which he continued on his return to Paris in 1269. After Thomas's death in 1274, Albert returned to Paris to defend his disciples' teachings, which were under attack. The defense was surely needed. The 219 propositions condemned by the theology masters of Paris in 1277 included at least twelve of Thomas's own. But after Thomas's canonization in 1323, the condemnation was canceled, and as new generations of Thomists arose his influence increased with the years. By the time of the Council of Trent (1545–63) the leading Catholic theologians were Thomists. The twentieth century has seen another revival of Thomist thought wittily espoused by G. K. Chesterton's praise of the "dumb ox." Thomas has become the pope's exemplar of Catholic openness to truths from any source. The first monument of the modern university, our self-styled institution of "free enquiry," was a defense of Catholic doctrine. Perhaps, as Bertrand Russell suggests, the systematic wholeness of Thomist theology meant that "the yoke of orthodoxy was not so severe as is sometimes supposed; a man could always write his book, and then, if necessary, withdraw its heretical portions after full public discussion."

15

Varieties of the Protestant Way:
Erasmus, Luther, Calvin

As they succeeded, the three thriving institutions—the Church, the monasteries, and the universities—that emerged from the European Middle Ages became not only communities of Seekers but targets for Christians seeking control of their own lives and thought. The Church, no longer a mere agent of the state, became a competitor for worldly power and for the treasure of believers. Monasteries, while claiming the moral superiority of withdrawal from the world and from the burdens of wealth, prospered, acquired the odium of riches, and flouted their vows of poverty, chastity, and obedience. And universities, elaborating the ways of disputation, developed a pedantic arrogance that overshadowed the simple messages of faith and Scriptures.

It is not surprising that the passions of Christian Seekers could not remain confined and channeled in these institutions. Their ardor would be expressed in countless independent ways. Three enduring spokesmen give us clues to their range and variety: Desiderius Erasmus (c. 1466–1536), the Dutch apostle of moderation, spokesman of Christian humanism; Martin Luther (1483–1546), outspoken German advocate of "justification by faith" alone, founder of the Protestant Reformation; and John Calvin (1509–1564), French creator of a Reformed Church. They followed divergent paths of classical scholarship, biblical exegesis, dogmatic theology, and reforming zeal toward conflicting views of the higher truths and how to reach them. Fueled by the passions and resentments of others less eloquent and more violent, their dissension would make Western Europe a battleground and cemetery of contesting Christians. How they disagreed over the meaning and contours of Christianity and ways of seeking salvation is not impossible to recount. What remains puzzling is why so many acolytes of a reputed God of Love should have been willing to kill—or be killed—over a theological nuance. Europe in the sixteenth and seventeenth centuries became a chaos of faith and persecution.

A Protestant Humanism: Erasmus

Moderation, praised by moralists, has seldom had its due from history. But if the spirit of Erasmus had prevailed, the history of Europe in the early modern era would have been quite different. "Prince of humanists" and godfather of the Protestant reformation, he remains a subject for scholars, historians, and novelists. His contemporaries, Luther and Calvin, would be founders of thriving sects and become household names in the Christian West.

The birth of Erasmus in Rotterdam about 1466 was clouded by mystery and the stigma of illegitimacy. Erasmus himself reported that his father, Gerard, had had a secret affair with his mother, Margaret, "in the expectation of marriage." When Gerard's parents opposed the marriage, he fled, leaving Margaret to bear his child. Later in Rome, where Gerard was employed as a copyist, he received word from his family that Margaret was dead. Out of grief he became a priest. When Gerard returned home he discovered the deception, but he still did not marry her, and stayed by his priestly vows. This saga became the basis of Charles Reade's popular historical romance, *The Cloister and the Hearth* (1861). The cloud of illegitimacy haunted Erasmus all his life.

His mother sent him as a boy with his brother to a school in Deventer in eastern Netherlands dominated by a "Modern Piety" movement of the Brethren of the Common Life. The most famous of these brethren, Thomas à Kempis (1380–1471), had expressed their spirit in his *Imitation of Christ* when he urged, "Trinity is better pleased by adoration than by speculation." The sect's founder, Gerard Groote, had urged study of the ancient classics, such as Seneca and Cicero, as pagan preparations for the Gospel, but his movement emphasized inwardness. The lack of printed texts still encouraged memorizing as the avenue to literature, and Erasmus learned Horace and Terence by heart. "An occult force of nature drove me to the humanities," he wrote. At sixteen, apparently attracted by their library, Erasmus joined the Augustinian Canons at Steyn, and at the end of his novitiate year, he took the vows of the strict order.

There Erasmus wrote *On Contempt of the World,* a rhetorical exercise on the virtues of monastery life. Then, before he was twenty, he wrote his *Antibarbari* (Against the Barbarians) defending the value of pagan learning. Just as the Church had not rejected the Old Testament despite its plea for obedience to laws that Christians had discarded, so, Erasmus said, the Church should not abandon the classics because they celebrated pagan gods. "You tell me that we should not read Virgil because he is in hell. Do you think that many Christians are not in hell whose works we read? It is not for us to discuss whether the pagans before Christ were damned. . . . either they are saved or no one is saved. If you want to give up everything pagan you will have to give up the alphabet and the Latin language, and all the arts and crafts." So he began his lifelong championing of the ancient classics. He was ordained a priest in 1492.

The bishop of Cambrai sent Erasmus to Paris to study theology at the Collegia Pauperum of the Collège de Montaigu. This was the Paris of "Stygian darkness" that Rabelais ridiculed, and Erasmus, too, was troubled by the scholastic dogmas, quibbles, and intolerance. The masters of theology were fiercely quarreling. "You say you do not want to be called a Platonist or a Ciceronian," he had argued, "but you do not mind being called an Albertist or a Thomist." To support himself as a scholar, Erasmus sought pensions, gifts, and pay for the flattering dedications in his books. Despite his love of classical moderation in philosophy and theology, he was an extravagant sycophant where it brought him the money he needed. To draw on the wisdom of the ancients, he made a collection of proverbs from the Bible and Greek and Latin authors. His first edition of *Adagia* in 1500 offered some eight hundred proverbs, but later editions exceeded five thousand. These included many expressions that would become familiar in the West—"Leave no stone unturned," "Where there is smoke there is fire," "A necessary evil," "The mountain labors and brings forth a mouse." His *Colloquies* used the ancient dialogue form for models of Latin conversational style, spiced with Erasmus's own wit.

First Speaker: From what coop or cave did you come?

Second: From the Collège de Montaigu.

First: Then I suppose you are full of learning.

Second: No, lice.

Invited to England in 1499 by the young and charming Lord Mountjoy, Erasmus formed friendships with aristocrats and leading philosophers and clerics of the age, especially John Colet and Thomas More. To his own surprise he was captivated by the English delights of hunting, and "that most admirable custom of kissing at every turn." He had some knowledge of Greek before going to England, but English scholars persuaded him to master the language. While the philosophers were enthusiastic Neoplatonists, Erasmus was wary of obscurantism. He never claimed a religious ecstasy, and remained the steadfast advocate of classical humanism.

On leaving England to return to France, Erasmus was stripped of his meager funds by Henry VII's agents at Dover enforcing the ban on exporting currency. He fled from the plague in Paris and at Orléans, then in the Netherlands he immersed himself in studying Greek until 1505. He had started on an edition of Saint Jerome for which he needed Greek. And he was also editing Cicero. When Erasmus discovered a manuscript of Lorenzo Valla that annotated the New Testament as if it were by some classical author, it reminded him that Holy Scriptures, like other ancient books, could be given textual scrutiny. This suggested, of course, that Saint Jerome's translation of the New Testament into Latin might require revision.

Appealing to Pope Clement V's earlier directive to study the ancient languages, Erasmus opened the path of modern biblical scholarship. He had found the perfect convergence of his classical and his Christian interests. Then, with his *Enchiridion Militis Christiani* (Handbook of the Christian Soldier), he became a spokesman for Catholic reform. Cautioning against the mere externals of religion, he praised the spirit of Saint Paul and "a warm love for the scriptures." And by discounting the outward forms of religion, Erasmus invited the suspicion of both Catholics and Reformers.

In his *Enchiridion* he exhorted:

Creep not upon the earth, my brother, like an animal. Put on those wings which Plato says are caused to grow on the soul by the ardour of love. Rise above the body to the spirit, from the visible to the invisible, from the letter to the mystical meaning, from the sensible to the intelligible, from the involved to the simple. Rise as by rungs until you scale the ladder of Jacob.

The next years, seeking support and repose for his scholarship, he traversed Europe. In England he secured the patronage of William Wareham, archbishop of Canterbury (to whom he dedicated his translations of Euripides). And he developed an intimacy with Thomas More, then a prominent young London barrister. Their shared enthusiasm for the satirical dialogues of Lucian (c. 115–c. 200) would soon bear fruit in More's *Utopia* and Erasmus' *Praise of Folly* (1508). Touring Italy as tutor to young English aristocrats, he visited Rome, where he was horrified by the corruption of the Church. In the countryside he saw poor peasants mulcted by papal tax collectors.

Pioneers of the new technology of printing became Erasmus' intimates. In Venice he was welcomed into the household of Aldus Manutius (1450–1515), whose Aldine press had published elegant editions of Greek and Latin classics, and who published a much-enlarged edition of Erasmus' *Adages* (1508). In Basel he became the friend and collaborator of Johann Froben (1460?–1527), settled in Froben's household and became his general editor and literary adviser. Froben published Erasmus' edited version of the Greek New Testament and his *Colloquies*. Done in haste, Erasmus' New Testament, Erasmus himself said, was "precipitated rather than edited" and failed to use some of the best surviving sources. But it was still the first published version of the printed text. Erasmus' reputation, and the book's low price and convenience, made it the stimulus to New Testament scholarship. It became a dominant influence on Luther's translation into German (1522) and William Tyndale's translation into English (1525–26). And it gave Erasmus his claim to be the father of New Testament scholarship. From all sides came attacks on his text, on his translation, his orthodoxy, and his omissions.

But, Erasmus asked, why be satisfied with the vulgar text of Saint Jerome? "You cry out that it is a crime to correct the gospels. This is a speech worthier of a coachman than of a theologian." An English critic, accusing him of the Arian heresy for having omitted the words supporting the Trinity, predicted that "the world would again be racked by heresy, schism, faction, tumults, brawls, and tempests." Erasmus retorted, "My New Testament has been out now for three years. Where are the heresies, schisms, tempests, tumults, brawls, hurricanes, devastation, shipwrecks, floods, general disasters, and anything worse you can think of?" The printing press had now become the collaborator and vehicle of the Protestant spirit. And so it opened the path to a popular scriptural theology—and the Reformation. Or, as it was later said, Erasmus laid the egg that Luther hatched.

The Champion of Simple Faith: Luther

It would be hard to imagine two more different responses to the challenge of Catholic Christianity at the end of the Middle Ages than Erasmus and Martin Luther. In the battle between Faith and Learning, Erasmus remained the champion of wit and learning, while Luther became the inspired champion of simple faith. While Erasmus had been raised as an orphan, Luther was the son of a domineering father. He was sent to a cathedral school in Magdeburg, then had some contact with the Brethren of the Common Life and entered the University of Erfurt to study the seven liberal arts. While Erasmus had entered the Collegia Pauperum in Paris for want of funds, Luther was denied financial aid because of his father's prosperity. Then, pursuing his father's wishes, he began the study of law, which came to an abrupt end in 1505. After only two months, and without asking his parents, Luther entered the Augustinian order of Hermits in Erfurt. "Not freely or desirously did I become a monk," he later wrote in *Monastic Vows* (1521), "but walled around with the terror and agony of sudden death, I vowed a constrained and necessary vow." The story in his *Table Talk* was that, fearing for his life when suddenly overtaken by a horrifying thunderstorm, Luther exclaimed, "Help, St. Anne, and I'll become a monk." On entering the monastery, he had kept only his Plautus and his Virgil, and sold all the rest of his books. He was ordained as a priest in 1507.

Erasmus never reported such a mystic experience, but found his own Christian faith confirmed by the sober wisdom of antiquity. He had wandered Europe seeking support for his retreat into scholarship. Erasmus' Greek New Testament was a search for sources. In contrast, Luther's translation of the Bible into German reached out to the wide audience and helped establish German as a national literary language. Erasmus wrote with humor, wit, and irony. His favorite literary form was the colloquy or dialogue of venerable classical lineage. But with no patience for dialogue, Luther asserted his Theses. How Luther came to his reformist enthusiasm is not clear. On his trip to Rome he, like Erasmus, was dismayed at the corrupt and worldly Church. Luther himself recalled his mystic experience of evangelical discovery of the "righteousness of God."

By 1517 Luther's ire was roused by the abuse of the Catholic practice of granting indulgences. These documents issued by authority of the pope claimed to be part of the sacrament of penance. As certificates commuting part of the temporal penalty of the sinner, they were sold through papal agents. Though theoretically they were not supposed to be effective unless the sinner was penitent, this requirement did not destroy their market. Indulgences, a welcome source of funds for the costly activities of the papacy, were managed by the Fuggers of Augsburg, one of the leading financial agents of the time. Pope Sixtus IV in 1476 had included the souls in purgatory in the saving effect of the indulgences. Luther's patron, the elector Frederick, had banned from his territory the sale of the Jubilee Indulgences, which were said to be sold to help the pope rebuild St. Peter's in Rome. What especially troubled Luther was the extravagant sales tactics of the German Dominican monk Johann Tetzel (1465?–1519), who had been authorized by the ambitious Archbishop Albert of Mainz.

Luther was so provoked by Tetzel's vulgar salesmanship that he put together his Ninety-five Theses arraigning the abuses of the Catholic Church on October 31, 1517. The appealing tradition of the outraged Luther "nailing his theses to the door of the Wittenberg castle church" gives a legendary vividness to his outrage and his anger. Whether or not he actually "nailed" his theses to a church door, Luther surely affixed his concerns deep into the hearts of believing Christians. And his declaration of defiance, even in that age of slow communication, soon made him notorious.

The legend of the "nailing" has not taken account of the ambiguities surrounding indulgences in Luther's time. The precise theological meaning had not yet been dogmatically defined by the Church. What actually was remitted by an indulgence? How serviceable was an indulgence to relieve a sinful soul from suffering in purgatory? These ambiguities had opened the opportunity for the extravagant salesmanship by Tetzel and his like, and for the extravagant indictments by Luther and others. The uses of the indulgences were so ill defined in the theology of the time that some Church historians have considered Luther's The-

ses to be little more than "probing inquiries." Luther himself said he issued them "for the purpose of eliciting truth." He did not deny the
pope's power to grant indulgences, but he did attack the abuse of the
power. And he insisted on the inwardness of the Christian religion.

Repentance, according to Luther, could not be attained by ecclesiastical fiat, but required a transformation within the believer. The true
power and glory of the Church were not in the papacy but in the Gospel.
Luther, lecturing at the new University of Wittenberg, had abandoned
the Aristotelian scholastic theology for the study of the Bible in the
original Hebrew and Greek. But his efforts to carry his message to other
universities did not succeed. He now believed that salvation came not
through works but through the divine gift of grace from God and
through Christ. He would express this dogma in his German translation
of the Bible, where he added the word "alone" in the crucial passage
"For we hold that a man is justified by faith alone, apart from the works
of man."

So Luther short-circuited the power of the Church, the priesthood, and
the sacraments. His combative theses, broadcast by the new art of printing, against the abuses of indulgence have attracted historians more
than his more fundamental affirmations of religious faith, autonomy,
and the priesthood of all believers. Without the printing press, Luther's
challenge might have made only a local flurry in Wittenberg. Luther
himself sent copies of his theses to the ambitious archbishop of Mainz
and to his own bishop. The printing press made it possible to circulate
them more widely and more speedily than ever before.

Luther would make the printing press the vehicle also for his reforming ideas. His address "To the Christian Nobility of the German
Nation concerning the reformation of the Christian Commonwealth,"
published in Wittenberg, offered his argument that the spiritual power
of Christianity came from the whole body of true believers, all of whom
had the power to read and interpret the Scriptures for themselves. He attacked the supremacy of the pope over the state, the theories of two estates (temporal and spiritual) and of two swords (pope and emperor).
He called for a national German Church, abolition of the celibacy of the
clergy, and reforms of schools and universities. This was his answer to
the papal bull excommunicating Luther, published in Rome in June

1520, and did more than Luther ever imagined or intended. He ignited the national spirit (not only in Germany) and sparked an overwhelming movement for reform of the Church. Published in mid-August 1520, by the eighteenth of the month his address had sold four thousand copies. In the sixteenth century it reappeared in seventeen further editions.

And Luther provided more than doctrine. He provided the treasure-house of Christian faith in a new form, which came to be called the Re-formation Bible. Simply by translating the Bible into German he had committed an act of reform that translated doctrine into deed. He de-mocratized the sources of Christian faith by putting them into the lan-guage of the marketplace. By 1522, after some two years of work, using the second edition of Erasmus' Greek text, he had translated the whole New Testament, now illustrated by Lucas Cranach (1472–1553), whose vivid full-page woodcuts depicted dragons and the Woman of Babylon wearing papal triple crowns. From there Luther went on to the Old Tes-tament, and the whole was published by 1534. So he made the Bible a popular cathedral. By this time some eighty editions of his New Testa-ment had appeared and became the basis of translations into Dutch, Swedish, Danish, and Icelandic. William Tyndale (c. 1494–1536) used it along with Erasmus' Greek New Testament for his translation, the first New Testament to be printed in English. So Luther had opened wide the gate to Scripture for all Christian Seekers, and helped destroy priestly monopoly on the sources of faith. Incidentally, he helped create a national language, for it was the eloquence of Luther's High German that overcame the many other dialects to become eventually the lan-guage of Heine and Goethe. The democratizing of the Bible was not the only consequence of Luther's work that far exceeded his intentions and expectations.

Calvin's Bridge to a Democratic World

Of the great trinity of the Protestant Reformation in Europe—Erasmus, Luther, and Calvin—it was Calvin who provided a way of organizing churches that opened paths to the modern Western world of democracy, federalism, and representative government. For the Christian Seeker, Erasmus had focused the humanist tradition; Luther had transformed theology into a doctrine of personal faith, with the independence and priesthood of all believers. Calvin, with a remarkable talent both for dogma and for organization—for the theory and the practice of Protestantism—made the newly Reformed Church in his Geneva into a model for Protestant Christianity across Europe and into the New World.

Born into a bourgeois family in Noyon in Picardy, France, in 1509, John Calvin (originally Jean Chauvin or Caulvin) seemed a most unlikely candidate to become intellectual leader of the Protestant Reformation. His father was secretary to the bishop and attorney for the cathedral. Calvin was raised and educated in an aristocratic family of the de Hangists who were relatives of the bishop. Intended for the Church, Calvin was sent to Paris with the de Hangist boys to study at the rigorous Collège de Montaigu. That was where Erasmus and Rabelais, too, had studied theology. After a falling-out with the bishop, Calvin's father directed him to give up theology for the law. And just as Luther's father had required Luther to turn to the law, the young Calvin dutifully obliged by going to the University of Orléans. When his father died excommunicate in 1531, Calvin's struggle to obtain a Christian burial for his father embittered his relation to the Church. At twenty-two he returned to Paris and to humanist studies. The fruit of these studies was his first book, a commentary on Seneca's *De clementia.* When Calvin helped his friend Nicholas Cop, rector of the University of Paris, compose an address that included ideas of the Lutheran Reformation, he and Cop were forced to flee for their lives. It was probably soon after this crisis that Calvin experienced the "sudden conversion" to Protestantism that he would later describe. He became, and remained, an exile from his native France.

And Calvin would spend his life expounding the theory and developing the practice of the Protestant Reformation. Few figures in history have shown such a talent to combine theory and practice in building institutions. Few have been so adept at combining opposites. Calvin's concept of the Church was both the most dogmatic, and the most practical; the most local, and the most universal. He preached the dogma of predestination, yet insisted that the participation of all believers was what God expected of his Church. Before he was thirty he had written *Christianae religionis Institutio* (translated as *Institutes of the Christian Religion*), the most important and comprehensive systematic statement of the Protestant cause (1536; definitive Latin edition 1559). It was in 1536, too, that he happened on his travels to pass through Geneva, where he encountered the fire-eating Guillaume Farel (1489–1565), whom he had known in Paris. Farel was now arousing the Geneva populace into an anti-Catholic fervor that resulted in image-breaking riots. And it was there, Calvin later said, that God "thrust him into the fray." Under Farel's influence, Geneva had revolted against its bishop, forbade the Catholic sacraments, and expelled all priests and members of religious orders who were not willing to conform to the Protestant faith. Since the Protestant rituals and system of education had not yet been established, Farel challenged Calvin to stay and help organize Geneva as a city in the biblical model. He threatened Calvin with the wrath of God if he refused.

Though Calvin had never intended to settle in Geneva, he was persuaded. Eventually his remarkable energy and courage would make Geneva famous as "the Protestant Rome." City and Church were to be a single community, both enforcing the model of a biblical commonwealth. Many of the rules of morality declared by Farel and Calvin had been in the city's code since the Middle Ages, but now the community feared they would be enforced. In 1538 a newly elected city council expelled both Farel and Calvin from the city. Calvin went to Strassburg, where he ministered to French refugees. Three years of chaos in Geneva, without the leadership of Farel or Calvin, led the citizens then in 1541 to recall Calvin, whom they provided with a comfortable house (including a wine cellar) and a good salary.

Calvin could now build the Reformed Church of Geneva in enduring form. He drafted ecclesiastical ordinances that would remain substantially the constitution of the Church of Geneva and be a model for Reformed Churches in Europe and the New World. He established four orders of the ministry: (1) teaching doctors (at first Calvin was the only one); (2) preaching pastors; (3) disciplining elders; and (4) deacons, charged with the works of charity. Morality would be strictly enforced, while Protestant doctrine would be expounded at the new University of Geneva, which he established. The program also included responsibility for a missionary effort to spread Calvinism abroad, which made it the only Protestant sect with universalist aspirations. While Calvin delivered regular biblical commentaries as public lectures, religious instruction was under a Company of Pastors, whose members were screened under Calvin's direction. The elders acted as "policemen" of the Reformation morality, and met with the pastors in a Consistory where, too, Calvin's voice was heard. They had the power to excommunicate, and were responsible for Geneva's reputed "reign of terror," which might have been called the reign of biblical morality. It was this regime that came to be called "Puritan." The deacons in a "Hospital-general" administered the orphanage, the distribution of free bread, and works for the poor, where also Calvin was active.

Calvin's energetic oversight of this ecclesiastical system did not go unchallenged. The melodramatic climax came when a Spanish doctor, Michael Servetus (c. 1511–1553), who had written a book attacking the doctrine of the Trinity, came to Geneva. Calvin had Servetus arrested and convicted of heresy, for which crime he had Servetus burned at the stake. And so Calvin obliged later Catholic partisans (including Lord Acton) with a spectacle of Protestant intolerance. After 1555, when Calvin was in full control in Geneva, he devoted his fierce energies to spreading Reformed Protestantism. He trained French refugees to serve as Reformed pastors and smuggled them back to France. Congregations on the Geneva model would be founded in Scotland and America, in England and the Netherlands.

While Calvin wielded dogmatic and dictatorial powers in Geneva and in some of the successor communities, the enduring influence of Calvinism on Christian religious and political institutions was quite otherwise. The presbyterian form of church government, of which Calvin was a founder, was very much in the spirit of modern Western representative political institutions. Calvin's theory of church government declared that only Christ was the head of the community, with all members being equal under him. The ministry then belonged to the entire church, though responsibilities might be distributed among several officers. All who held church offices would be elected by the members of the congregation, whom they represented. The church, then, was to be governed not by clergy but by persons (including officeholders, pastors, and elders) who represented the whole church. This, too, provided a federal relation among the local churches drawn together in an elected presbytery, or national or general assembly.

Calvinist doctrine centered on the local church. The power that resided in the membership as a whole created a decentralized form of organization that gave the Calvinist churches great strength and power to resist and defy persecution. If Calvinism was to be defeated, every one of the congregations had to be eradicated in turn. To arrest the minister would not silence the church, for the community itself was what survived, and could always elect new ministers. Based on the principle of representation, not of authority or dictation, Calvinism satisfied the modern need for participation—in church as well as state. And the transplantation of Calvinism to New England in a New World would nourish and encourage the dignity and participation of separate congregations and the independent faithful, out of which a new society would arise in North America.

BOOK TWO

COMMUNAL SEARCH

As you set out for Ithaka
hope the voyage is a long one,
full of adventure, full of discovery.
—C. P. CAVAFY (1910)

The great shift in the direction of seeking, which marked the opening of the modern mind, was the turn to experience. This was the turn from the upward reach of the Hebrew Prophets and the inward search of the Greek philosophers to the thrust outward and all around. This new way of seeking would bring Seekers back to community—not for orthodox dogma, but as a way of making the search continual, renewed in each generation. Modern liberal society would be a way of organizing for unending search. When the dyspeptic Thomas Carlyle (1795–1881) noted "the three great elements of modern civilization, gunpowder, printing and the Protestant religion," he was not far off the mark. Gunpowder expanded warfare—between nations and would-be nations. Printing endlessly widened the community of current and past experiences. The Protestant Reformation made personal experience the authentic avenue to religious faith. Discoverers in science—Galileo, Vesalius, Harvey, Newton, Malpighi, and others—were revealing how boundless were the still-uncharted areas of nature, while Columbus, Magellan, and Balboa awakened Europeans to how limited had been their experience of the earth and the seas. As science went public, societies pooled experience in parliaments of scientists. The growth of cities and the rising commerce of great colonial empires in America, Africa, and Asia widened European experience of exotic peoples and products. At every turn, enlarged experience revealed unimagined possibilities, there for the finding. And kept alive the Seekers' quest for meaning and purpose.

PART FOUR

WAYS OF DISCOVERY: IN SEARCH OF EXPERIENCE

*If the Past has been an obstacle and a burden,
knowledge of the Past is the safest and surest emancipation.*
—LORD ACTON

16

The Legacy of Homer:
Myth and the Heroic Past

In the past—the first universal source of experience—Seekers hoped to find clues to life's meaning and purpose. And in the Old Testament the ancient Hebrews left the most influential interpretation of the past ever to come to the West. Though it was the book of human destiny, the story belonged to God, His works of creation, His mercy, or His wrath. The story of God's covenant with His chosen people told how He rewarded or punished their response to His commands. And so affirmed Jewish national identity, confronting the powerful empire of Assyria, suffering exile and captivity in Babylon, and returning to the Promised Land. Though a work of many authors, it told a single theme—God's purposes.

The ancient Greek view of the past—the next great tradition for interpreting history—offered a stark contrast. Their heroic epics were tales of human deeds, despite the whims of gods and goddesses. In this, as in everything else, the Greeks found their own way, and marked new paths that we still follow. For the ancient Hebrews there was no doubt of how or by whom future events would be governed. The ancient Greeks explored the uncertainty of man's moral purposes. We think of the future as what lies before us, and the past as behind us. But the ancient Greeks, as Bernard Knox observes, took an opposite view. For them "behind" or "back" (*opiso* in Greek) referred not to the past but to the future. They saw their past (and their present) so plainly and vividly in front of them that it is no wonder they thought of the unknown and invisible future as behind them. In the *Odyssey,* Homer describes a wise old man as "the only one who sees what is in front and what is behind." Naturally, then, they saw themselves "backing into the future."

Long before they began writing what we call history, they had found their own vivid and persuasive way of organizing and interpreting the past. Their heroic myths, no mere tales of long-past happenings, became sacred texts of morality and religion. And long before they invented the writing of history, they had a confident and traditional view of the past that they could see plainly before them.

For the ancient Greeks it was myth—the heroic epic—that gave their past real and memorable form and filled it with meaning. In the reach for experience the first universal source is tradition: what grandparents told parents and what parents tell children. But for their tradition the Greeks did not rely on the casual spoken word heard at the mother's knee. In heroic myths, perpetuated in deathless poetry, they gave their past an enduring charm and what would seem an endless resource of meaning. While we see their myths as the realm of fantasy, for classic Greeks these were the treasured record of their past. Myth gave tradition its memorable drama. In myths all people learn of ancient times beyond everyday experience, of superhuman creatures and miraculous events. Unlike historical events, these need no proof. Their survival in the sacred word makes myths the first authentic story of purpose, of first causes and origins.

While our own modern Western society has not been fertile of myth, fortunately we have inherited the myths of ancient Greece. Familiar in our education, they brighten our lives. In them we can see how myths, serving our own need to know origins and purpose, sometimes frustrate our search for the true past. Their authority comes from being traditional and having no known author. They survive in the tradition of the spoken—or sung—word. So they dramatize our need to know why and our willingness to take poetry for truth.

The English word "myth" derives from the Greek *mythos,* which meant "word" in the sense of a final pronouncement. Its special meaning appears by contrast with the Greek *logos,* which meant "word" in the sense of a truth that can be argued and demonstrated. So myths are traditional statements of truths. Their anonymous source somehow added to their authenticity.

Greek myths, then, were an ancient "vulgate," a popular way of making the past known, as widespread a way of creating belief as journalism is today. And their "vulgate" was validated by the consensus of the ages. Just as the journalist nowadays expects the reader to take his word for the truth of the story, so did the ancient bards. Like modern journalists, they, too, were commonly silent on their "sources." Time itself gave authority to their utterances. "History is born as tradition," Paul Veyne observes, "not built up from source materials." Like the bard, the historian, when he begins to appear, also treats himself as a source. But he will have other purposes and find new paths in his search for the true past.

The *Iliad* and the *Odyssey*, at the end of the oral period of Greek culture, are a legacy of generations of bards. What we have learned about the ways of bards today in the Balkan mountains, where the Homeric bards once sang, suggests that there was a stability and continuity in the tales they told. For, unlike modern poets, Homeric bards were not concerned with "originality."

The Homeric epic had originated in long centuries before Homer and the eighth century B.C., in the creative period when bards were improvising, learning from older men, and even adding to the familiar heroic themes. While creative talent was still at work on the *Iliad* and the *Odyssey*, bards assimilated their individual contributions into these monumental poems. The Homeric word for poet is *aiodos,* or singer. And like all successful singers, bards were not reluctant to build their repertoires from the works of others.

When bards, enriched by the creative talents among them, found an attractive version, they could reproduce it for generations. The Homeric bards had probably reached this stage in the mid–seventh century B.C. But the rise of literacy and reliance on fixed texts brought the decline of the spontaneity of the bard, the *aiodos* singing to the accompaniment of his lyrelike *kitharis.* He was displaced by the *rhapsode,* or trained reciter. The rhapsode (the word means "song-stitcher" in Greek), who appeared in the fifth century B.C., was well trained, and probably had texts of Homer, though he still recited from memory. Rhapsodes then competed for prizes at public festivals. But while the bards were relied on for the authentic traditional myth, the very name "rhapsode" became a byword for unreliability as they continued to perform and compete for prizes into the third century A.D. The last stage in the degeneration of the tradition of the oral myth, rhapsodes were despised by educated people. Scholars can still detect their awkward additions to the works of earlier Homeric bards.

The Homeric epics were finally written down at the end of the true oral period—the "Dark Ages" of ancient Greece (c. 1100–900 B.C.). That Dark Age proved well suited for the thriving and transmission of oral poetry, which, unlike architecture, required no prosperity or any particular materials. The rudeness of daily life in an illiterate community that made literary culture impossible was no barrier to the seeking for heroes. Like the Norse sagas, the Homeric epics themselves suggest that ages of hardship and adversity, which reward courage, pride, and sheer survival, are fertile for heroic poetry.

Perhaps eras when other grand outlets for man's seeking, hopes, and ambitions are lacking naturally find expression in the only kind of monument that needs no material resource—the monumental epic. Such great monuments—to paraphrase Whitman—require great audiences. The Homeric epics found their audiences (and patrons) in the feasts of noblemen and in the religious festivals of the community. In other ways, too, the Homeric epics played the role of monuments. For a monument, as the origin of the word (in Latin, *monere,* to remind, admonish, or warn) suggests, aims not to surprise and astonish, but to remind.

Many of the special qualities of the Homeric epics are then easier to understand. The modern reader may feel disappointed that the *Iliad* and the *Odyssey* do not hold him in suspense but always have a familiar outcome—the more familiar and predictable because the gods are always ready to intervene to produce the predictable result. So in a Homeric epic there is no uncertainty about the outcome, toward which the gods have led events. Our interest is in the uncertain motives and reactions of the people. The focus is not on the unraveling of a usually predictable plot but on the tantalizing uncertainties of the reactions of Achilles or Hector. The *Iliad* and the *Odyssey,* recited entire at the annual Panathenaea festival, made myth and memory the handmaid of ritual. And an affirmation of the communal sense of purpose.

Still, fantasy has continued to give myth an undying universal appeal not found in later prosaic versions of the past. And no literature has been more fertile than myth in fostering Western humanism in young and old, awakening interest in other people's culture, other people's ways of seeking. Homer's apotheosis in antiquity as The Poet somehow survived in the Middle Ages even though his works were unknown in the Latin West. The Renaissance revival of Greek made the Homeric epics newly available and awakened enthusiasm, expressed in translation. George Chapman, who claimed to be directly inspired by the spirit of Homer (*Iliad,* 1611; *Odyssey,* 1614–15), was followed by passages of translation by Thomas Hobbes in quatrains (1674–75) and by John Dryden later in the seventeenth century.

Interest in Homer remained so alive that when the young Alexander Pope (1688–1744) published his first volume of his translation (containing the first four Books) of the *Iliad* in 1715, the excitement was said to be the greatest ever aroused by a book of verse. The King and the Prince of Wales subscribed substantial sums and the translation actually established Pope's financial independence. It was said that no poet before (not excepting Shakespeare) had been so highly paid. Nor perhaps has any since. When the six volumes of Pope's *Iliad* were completed, Pope had received from the publisher the unprecedented sum of £5,320.4*s*. The publisher, Bernard Lintot (1675–1736), played a heroic role. Even after Pope's work was pirated in Holland, Lintot went ahead and printed seventy-five hundred copies of a new edition of his own. And his faith in Pope's Homer was fully justified by the fortune he made from the enterprise—enough to secure for him and his son the posts of high sheriffs of Sussex.

It was Keats who united the English translator and the Greek epic past in immortality in his sonnet "On First Looking into Chapman's Homer."

> Then felt I like some watcher of the skies
> When a new planet swims into his ken;
> Or like stout Cortez when with eagle eyes
> He stared at the Pacific—and all his men
> Looked at each other with a wild surmise—
> Silent, upon a peak in Darien.

17

Herodotus and the Birth of History

Enjoying the heroic past with Homeric bards, why would anyone turn to the prosaic past that came to be known as history? The appearance of historiography—the writing of history—in classical Greece was one of their most remarkable and surprising achievements. For the cast of Greek thought in the age of Socrates and Plato was conspicuously anti-historical. According to Plato, the only subject of genuine knowledge was what was permanent and unchanging. So the ancient Greeks had the greatest respect for mathematical knowledge, and Pythagoras elevated numbers into the key to the universe. They dwelt on the distinction between true "knowledge" (*episteme*) and mere "opinion" (*doxa*). Then, why pursue the uncertain accounts of changing human actions, of societies born and decayed? At the same time, as we have seen, in the face-to-face community of the polis, the idealization of the evanescent spoken (over the enduring written) word, expressed in the way of dialogue, removed some temptations to make written records of their thoughts. "Poetry is something more philosophic and of graver import than history," observed Aristotle, "since its statements are of the nature of universals, whereas those of history are singulars."

The birth of history in ancient Greece was the legacy of two originals—Herodotus and Thucydides. Both were exiles, and so the readier to pursue a kind of knowledge not valued in their home-polis. Unlike the anonymous mythmakers, they signed their names at the outset of their work, and their twin legacy would suggest the questions of historians for millennia to come. What had really happened and why? What were the lessons of the past for the future?

The word "history" (*historie*) in Greek, of Ionian origin, meant inquiry. It had first connoted "research" into the nature of the physical world. Miletus, on the Ionian coast of the eastern Mediterranean, had been the home of Thales (born c. 624 B.C.), founder of the first Greek school of philosophy. From there, too, Hecataeus (c. 550–489 B.C.) appears to have been the first to apply this method of "investigation" from nature to the inhabited earth. He traveled widely and was one of the first logographers, recording local traditions and genealogies of mythical families. They were mostly interested in the legendary foundations of cities, and in the variety of local customs. Hecataeus' statement of purpose is a rudimentary credo of the historian: "What I write here is the account of what I considered to be true. For the stories of the Greeks are numerous and, in my opinion, ridiculous." His "Genealogies" tended to make the mythical past more credible. These logographers expressed the characteristic Greek interest—not surprising for a seafaring people—in the dominating power of the physical environment. His interests were more in geography—the variety of present phenomena on the earth—than in the shaping power of past events. The works of logographers survive only in fragments, and they left nothing that could be called a work of history. But the first such work did somehow grow out of their tradition, and when it appeared it opened paths into the past.

The exuberant Ionian intellectual adventure was not to be frustrated by a mere dogma of philosophy. Just as the French Enlightenment of the eighteenth century would dissolve Christian orthodoxies, defrock clergy, and guillotine kings, so the Ionian Enlightenment of the sixth century B.C. shook revered icons of Greek culture as it opened endless paths of inquiry. Thales had asked general questions about nature, and sought rational answers. As Bertrand Russell observed, Thales set philosophers on their paths to understand the world. Called "physicists" (from the Greek *physis* for nature), they tried to find the single substance—air or water—from which the world was made.

When the Ionians turned their inquiry on man himself, they took another look at their past, asking whether their myths were an adequate account. And what Socrates, at the cost of his life, did for Greek philosophy, awakening fellow Athenians to the discovery of their ignorance, Herodotus did for their quest for the past. This Ionian Enlightenment questioned the mythic view embodied in the Homeric epics and Hesiod. "Homer and Hesiod have attributed to the gods," Xenophanes (sixth century B.C.), the wandering Ionian poet from Colophon, observed, "everything that is disgraceful and blameworthy among men: theft, adultery, and deceit." So they "demythicized the past," in search of the qualities of man, and their past would not remain a vacuum. It would soon be filled by something quite new, of which Herodotus was to be the creator and the patron saint.

Myth, from the Greek for "word," was a name for the comforting authentic tale of origins. As we have seen, the Homeric bards sang a reassuring tradition, of the virtues and exploits of heroes. Their tales did not shock or surprise but solaced by the familiar themes—of Achilles or of Odysseus, Agamemnon, or Menelaus. The poetic epithets and embellishments, too, were in recognized formulas. But history was quite another world. The word *historie* in Ionian Greek meant "inquiry" or investigation focused on the seeking rather than on the finding. We have seen how myth, authenticated by generations of chanting bards, responded to the expectations of living audiences. So the bard's tales were being modified, not by newly discovered shapes of the past but by the novel expectations of each living listening generation.

History from this beginning would also become the name for a never-ending effort. Recollection of the past was an endless reaching. The past would no longer be a brilliant panoply of familiar verse but a dark continent of memory. Perhaps it could be newly illuminated in every generation. While myth was an anonymous product of community, history would be the work of the inquiring individual. We may speak of Homeric epics though there may never have been a Homer. But history begins with historians.

Herodotus, by consensus of scholars, is our first historian, the father of what we think of as history. And, unlike the anonymous Homer, from his first words Herodotus leaves no doubt of his authorship or of the nature of his enterprise:

> These are the researches of Herodotus of Halicarnassus, which he publishes, in the hope of thereby preserving from decay the remembrance of what men have done, and of preventing the great and wonderful actions of the Greeks and the Barbarians from losing their due meed of glory; and withal to put on record what were their grounds of feud.

So, with his word "researches" Herodotus announced one of the great shifts in human consciousness not often enough recognized. Here was the shift from mere recording and repetition of tradition to the scrutiny of experience. And so the historian opened the gateway to the infinite past, a new eternity. Before Herodotus, besides the Homeric epics in the oral tradition of the bards, there had been logographers. But they were not investigators asking whether or why.

The Father of History, the title given to Herodotus by Cicero, has been confirmed by centuries of scholarship. Before Herodotus, describers of the past, not inquiring, were simply recording or reporting. They were not writing history but (in R. G. Collingwood's phrase) "writing religion." They were recording "known facts for the information of persons to whom they were not known, but who, as worshippers of the god in question, ought to know the deeds whereby he has made himself manifest."

This new spirit of inquiry was conspicuously expressed in their language, in the shift from poetry to prose. The traditional epic themes of Homeric bards were perpetuated in verse, which was the common aid to memory for an illiterate society. History, the language of inquiry, would be written in prose. And Herodotus' *History* is the first masterpiece in Greek prose. The writing of history, a new branch of literature, as the Roman rhetorician Quintilian observed, brought Greek prose to a new height.

Some admirers of Herodotus have credited him as the creator of "scientific history." But this emphasis overlooks the uniqueness of the historian's task. The ancient Greeks were pioneers in many fields of science, other realms of "inquiry." But history was a literary art, because in history the subject and its audience were one. The effective historian is always telling us about ourselves, revealed in our human past. He cannot be a great historian unless he actually speaks to us. If he is a great historian, he never becomes obsolete, though he can be supplemented. With pleasure we still read Herodotus and Thucydides. It is no accident that the Father of History was in the vanguard of ancient Greek literature. So, our greatest historians, like Gibbon, hold as high a rank in literature as in history. Regardless of his place in the history of history, critics place Herodotus nearer to Shakespeare than to Thucydides and next to Homer. For Wordsworth, Herodotus' *History* was "the most interesting and instructive book, next to the Bible, which had ever been written."

How did it happen that our gateway to the infinite past was opened by this Herodotus (c. 484–c. 429 B.C.) of Halicarnassus? We know very little of his life beyond what he reveals in his *History*. Born of a prominent family in Halicarnassus on the west coast of Asia Minor, Herodotus was exiled by the tyrant of the city and traveled widely around the eastern Mediterranean. Herodotus visited Athens, he probably knew Pericles, and was reputed to have received ten talents for a public reading of his work there. His work, applauded as a celebration of the Athenian virtues, was actually parodied by Aristophanes. As an Athenian citizen he joined in founding Thurii, a Greek colony in southern Italy. He settled there and was buried in the marketplace. An Asiatic Greek by birth, he was a force of the Ionian Enlightenment in which Greek philosophy and literature first developed.

Out of Herodotus' own experience as exile and traveler came his grand theme—the struggle between Asia and Greece—between "East" and "West," between "Barbarian" and Greek. Herodotus would apply to human experience the method of rational inquiry, which the Ionian philosophers Thales of Miletus and Hippocrates of the island of Cos (born c. 460 B.C.) applied to physics and medicine. He had been raised on the myths of Greece in Homer and Hesiod. Then his providential exile set him out on travels across his known world. For the peoples he met, unlike the Greeks, had few myths. Only by inquiry—by asking people, noting their ways, and examining their monuments—could he learn of their past. And so it is not surprising that the Greeks' first reaching beyond myth into history was not about themselves.

Herodotus' great resource was boundless curiosity. He went not simply as an explorer nor to confirm what he already knew, but "to inquire." The travels that took him all over Asia Minor, to Egypt, and even to the mouth of the Dnieper River alerted him to all peoples' strange ways, customs, and legends. He took special pleasure in conversing with priests everywhere about their rites and doctrines. When he finally decided to write an account of the Persian Wars, he already had a rich miscellany about the peoples and places in the story. He was actually able to collect information from some who had fought the wars, and so he became the source of all later Greek accounts of the Persian Wars.

The inquiring spirit of Herodotus stands out in stark contrast to the bardic celebration of familiar themes. He rejects some stories because they seem too improbable. But he recounts others (like that of the circumnavigation of Africa by the Phoenicians) even if he has doubts. He is also willing to speculate more boldly than Christian doctrine would later allow. For example, he refused to fix a firm date for the Creation. Drawing on the experience of other alluvial deposits from rivers in the Aegean, he speculated on the time it must have taken to accumulate the alluvial deposits of the Nile Delta, perhaps some twenty thousand years. He concluded then that "nothing is impossible in the long lapse of ages." He doubts the Thracian account that lands beyond the Ister (the Danube) were impenetrable because of bees, for the simple reason that "it is certain that those creatures are very impatient of cold. I rather believe it is on account of the cold that the regions which lie under the Bear are without inhabitants."

Yet Herodotus does not deny all supernatural forces. The Homeric spirit survives in his combination of human causes with some deference to the prevailing religious beliefs. He respects oracles, and especially the oracle of Delphi. He seems to believe in the predicted fate of Croesus and in the loss of the acropolis of Sardis from the failure to follow carefully the Oracle's curious prescription to make the city impregnable by carrying a lion cub around its whole perimeter. The supernatural appears again and again in Herodotus' accounts of the divine jealousy (*phthonos*) that Aeschylus called "A venerable doctrine uttered long ago." This was the notion (which we might call *nemesis*) that the gods begrudge unlimited success to human beings. Therefore, too much success (especially if the lucky person brags about it) is apt to invite calamity. Herodotus also repeatedly reports the prophetic power of dreams, though he leaves the reader to judge.

Perhaps Herodotus first intended to improve on the work of Hecataeus by writing a kind of critical travel guide, focusing on geography and monuments. His chapter on Egypt shows how rich that book might have been. Fragments of his *Lydiaca, Aegyptiaca,* and *Scythica* survived as digressions in his *History.* Herodotus gave himself a more novel assignment, which put him in the vanguard of Seekers for the past. He would not merely collect interesting facts about the known world in his time. He would reach into the dark continent of memory, hoping by his "researches" to "preserve from decay the remembrance of what men have done, and of preventing the great and wonderful actions of the Greeks and the barbarians from losing their due meed of glory; and withal to put on record what were their grounds of feud." This enterprise in his new spirit of inquiry (history) was a venture without precedent and without end. For he set Western thinkers on a quest for the true past.

Today we delight in the fruits of Herodotus' omnivorous curiosity. In his one volume he opened for us a panorama of the ancient Mediterranean world—its beliefs, manners, customs, and institutions. While we enjoy his charming miscellany of fact and legend, we must not overlook his spirit—discriminating between what he is told by different informants and what he himself sees. He makes his own guesses and inferences. Extravagant beliefs seemed to him as much worth reporting as the commonplace facts of everyday life. Because of his sympathetic interest in the ways of all peoples, he is now sometimes recognized as the father of anthropology. Alongside his admiration of Athenian institutions he is not afraid to praise the great deeds of the Persians, and his reputation as an authentic reporter has risen as we have learned more about the people he described.

The enduring human issues, which before had been explored by the imagination of poets and the speculations of philosophers, Herodotus would now examine in the prosaic facts of experience. The Persian Wars—the conflict between Asia and Greece from the time of Cyrus the Great (c. 585–529 B.C.) and his conquest of Croesus, king of Lydia (reigned c. 560–546 B.C.), was a grand theme covering the whole eastern Mediterranean, the whole world known to Herodotus. It was the world war of his age. Extensive travels had acquainted him with the lands and peoples of the conflict. His achievement was to produce a vivid and coherent account when there were virtually no written records and nearly a generation had passed since the end of the war. Herodotus had interviewed survivors of the war, and he asked men of the next generation to recount the tales they had heard. So he has not inappropriately been described as "a journalist in search of a story that had been cold for thirty years." This was an amazing triumph of what has recently come to be called "oral history." Still, his rescue of the past from oral tradition had to be accomplished with the spoken word. With all its limitations, his account has remained the basis of all later histories of the war.

Herodotus had a mixed reception in his time. While Athenians applauded his celebration of their virtues, other Greeks who felt slighted called him "Father of Lies." Plutarch (c. A.D. 46–120) actually documented this slander in his essay "On the Malice of Herodotus."

Herodotus' unsavory reputation has not entirely disappeared; it survives in the praise of those who call him a fanciful storyteller. The classic Greek doubt of the value of transient human events was long in dying.

The example of Homer may have stirred Herodotus, for the Trojan War, too, was a war between West and East. The Persian War, longer in duration and on a vastly wider stage, also showed the great deeds of men.

The *History* by Herodotus that we read was divided into nine "books" by Alexandrian editors who named each after one of the Muses. The first two books, in the manner of the logographers, give the history of Croesus and the early history of Lydia and the exploits and empire of Cyrus, followed by the geography, manners, customs, and monuments of Egypt. In his detailed account of the building of the pyramids, Herodotus reports:

> The wickedness of Cheops reached to such a pitch that, lacking funds, he placed his own daughter in a brothel, with orders to procure him a certain sum—how much I cannot say, for I was not told; she procured it, however, and at the same time, bent on leaving a monument which should perpetuate her own memory, she required each man to make her a present of a stone. With these stones she built the pyramid which stands midmost of the three that are in front of the great pyramid, measuring along each side a hundred and fifty feet.

The following seven books recount the expeditions of Darius against the Scythians and Libyans, the Ionian revolt, the burning of Sardis, the subdual of the Ionians, the battle of Marathon, and the wreck of the Persian fleet at Mount Athos, the exploits and death of Darius, the battles of Thermopylae, Artemisium, and Salamis, the battle of Plataea, and the retreat of the Persians. The work appears to have been unfinished. The other books he may have written have not survived. Herodotus' *History* remains a miracle of lively narrative, vivid in the details of life and legend he had gathered in his years of travel.

The birth of history—inquiry into the human past—came with the shift of focus away from the will of God or the deeds of gods. The story moved from remote primordial time, the time of myths, to recent events in human time. While myths explained origins—how things began—history would explain consequences. Historical thinking is teleological.

"For history," J. H. Huizinga suggests, "the question is always 'Whither'?" This momentous shift is vivid in Herodotus.

But this change had not come all at once. The logographers had begun to gather current facts. Nor did the rise of history spell the disappearance of myth. Homer lived on in Western literature. And later the Romans, too, feeling their need for myth, found their Virgil, who followed the paths of Homer. We continue to follow and enjoy all paths to the vanished past. Newton would displace Aristotle's physics; Harvey, Galen's physiology. Though Herodotus survived in countless modern varieties of "scientific" history, he did not displace Homer, and he himself was never displaced.

Heroes led the way out of primordial to human time. In literature, myths survive as heroic epics—sagas of Gilgamesh, Achilles, and Odysseus, Beowulf and Roland. Heroes appear to be the first human beings in world literature. They reveal the shift in focus from immortal gods to mortal men—the wrath of Achilles, or "of that ingenious hero who travelled far and wide after he had sacked the famous town of Troy." Myths of the heroic age would live on in written literature as epic and tragedy.

Herodotus, though he wrote to recapture memory, opened our minds to the eternity that is the past. To view the historian's effort as "inquiry" transformed the past from an object into an ever-receding focus of activity, reaching through memory and monuments into a vanished eternity. So, too, he transformed the recounting of the past from an annual ritual into a perpetual adventure.

18

Thucydides Creates a Political Science

But Herodotus did not found a "school." The prevailing mood of Greek thought still favored the search for the unchanging. Plato, prophet of the search for the unchanging, wrote as if Herodotus had never lived. Greek philosophy and Greek science continued to flourish in the Academy.

Herodotus did have one great Greek successor. Thucydides (c. 460–c. 400 B.C.) read his work and carried on the pursuit of history, with his own style of inquiry. After the late fifth century B.C. Greek art declined, and so did the pursuit of history. The philosophers' and scientists' pursuits of changeless ideas went on. But in Greek historical writing the successors to Herodotus and Thucydides were not their equals.

While the epic spirit survives in Herodotus, his successor Thucydides writes in quite another spirit. Although we know few details of Thucydides' life we do know that he was a citizen of Periclean Athens who was active in its politics and was elected one of its ten generals. It was in 424 B.C., when he failed in his assignment to relieve Amphipolis in Thrace against the Spartan general Brasidas, that he was exiled from Athens. Thucydides' twenty years of travel gave him the opportunity to observe the rest of Greece and to write the work that he describes in his opening words:

> Thucydides, an Athenian, wrote the history of the war between the Peloponnesians and the Athenians, beginning at the moment that it broke out, and believing that it would be a great war, and more worthy of relation than any that had preceded it. This belief was not without its grounds. The preparations of both the combatants were in every department in the last state of perfection; and he could see the rest of the Hellenic race taking sides in the quarrel; those who delayed doing so at once having it in contemplation. Indeed this was the greatest movement yet known in history.

Though he read and seems to have admired Herodotus, he had his own way with the past. Herodotus had not entirely abandoned the Homeric heroic tradition. For, as we have seen, he aimed by his "researches" at "preserving the remembrance of what men have done, and of preventing the great and wonderful actions of the Greeks and the Barbarians from losing their due meed of glory; and withal to put on record what were their grounds of feud." He, too, hoped to rescue glorious deeds from the dark continent of memory, giving the historian the role that had been long filled by Homeric bards.

Thucydides added a new dimension to the historian's role. While he feared that "the absence of romance from my history will . . . detract somewhat from its interest," he would be content "if it be judged useful by those inquirers who desire an exact knowledge of the past as an aid to the interpretation of the future, which in the course of human things must resemble if it does not reflect it." As a leading Athenian citizen, he gave a high priority to the interests of the *polis*. And, naturally enough, when he came to recount the decisive events of his time, what he wrote was political history. In the famous passage where he says he has written his work "not as an essay which is to win the applause of the moment, but as a possession for all time," he is not merely hoping for literary immortality. He expects his book to provide *political* lessons for the future. In his Athens, knowledge was valued because it led to right action. And in "the greatest movement yet known in history," he sought lessons for everyday politics and the building and keeping of empire.

Thucydides could draw these lessons—the principles of political science—from the war in which he took part, and which was still going on as he wrote. The events of his own time illustrated the unchanging human nature for all future times. Perhaps, as R. G. Collingwood suggests, Thucydides was trying to justify himself for writing history at all, by turning it into something else—a new kind of political and psychological *science*. For him the present was a mirror of past and future in the careers of politics and empire. His concern for the meaning of events sometimes dominates his view of events. He is generally scrupulous in getting the facts. "And with reference to the narrative of events, far from permitting myself to derive it from the first source that came to hand, I did not even trust my own impressions." He tested the accuracy of reports "by the most severe and detailed tests possible." This demanded "some labor from the want of coincidence between accounts of different eye-witnesses."

But when it comes to general ideas and stating the principles behind each course of action, Thucydides himself remains in control. The speeches he includes by conflicting leaders at critical moments, he explains, are not "word for word" what they said. "My habit has been to make the speakers say what was in my opinion demanded of them by the various occasions, of course, adhering as closely as possible to the general sense of what they really said." So all the speeches are in Thucydides' own style. As he pairs them to speak the words he put in their mouths, they offer a symposium in political philosophy on the problem of that moment.

So, when Athens faces the question of whether to put to death the whole male population of Mytilene, a former ally who has turned against them, we hear the debate with the demagogue Cleon demanding the condign punishment because of his fear "that a democracy is incapable of empire." He urges his listeners to be wary of "the three failings most fatal to empire—pity, sentiment, and indulgence." Against Cleon, the large-spirited Diodotus says that "we are deliberating for the future more than for the present . . . we are not in a court of justice, but in a political assembly; and the question is not justice, but how to make the Mytilenians useful to Athens." Diodotus carried the day. And Thucydides has taken this opportunity to survey the arguments between firmness and compassion in a democracy's management of an empire. So, too, he uses the occasion of Pericles' funeral oration for his unexcelled eloquence in stating the patriotic ideals of Athens.

Thucydides' search for the large lesson, the general idea, explains, too, his economy of style. For a study of civil disturbance (*stasis*), since the detailed experience of Corcyra will suffice, he need not recount the numerous other such civil disorders during the war. And in Athens after Pericles he elides many others to put the spotlight on Cleon, in whom we can see clearly enough the character of the demagogue. He gives similar leading roles to Pericles (his model statesman), Themistocles, and Brasidas. This selectivity troubles the modern historian who relentlessly chronicles the whole succession of characters and events; for Thucydides it makes an economy of style focusing on lessons of politics and empire.

Some, denying the title to Herodotus, have called Thucydides the first "scientific" historian for abandoning all supernatural causes and finding a human cause for every event. His history of the Peloponnesian War, Maurice Bowra observes, is written in a "clinical" spirit—showing how an Athens in good health suffers the corruptions that bring its downfall. Perhaps his approach to political events owed something to the medical science of Hippocrates. Himself a victim of the plague of 430–429, he was lucky enough to survive and to describe the symptoms and course of the disease with a medical precision that still impresses clinicians. Still, Thucydides' momentous influence was as the creator of political history—a by-product of the Athenian polis. He interpreted his whole known world with a view to those political interests. That emphasis was not entirely wholesome, but has never ceased to dominate the writing of history in the West. And that same political obsession helps explain why, compared with other classic Greek forms of inquiry, Thucydides' kind of history in Greece was not fertile of successors.

But he did earn a high place among modern political theorists. Of all the Greek historians, Thomas Hobbes (1588–1679) "loved Thucydides best." In fact, he loved Thucydides so much that he gave his leisure hours to translating the *History of the Peloponnesian War* (1628) "in order that the follies of the Athenian Democrats should be revealed to his compatriots." "He made me realize," Hobbes notes in his autobiography, "how silly is democracy, and how much wiser a single man is than a multitude; I translated this author who would tell Englishmen to beware of trusting orators." Thucydides himself was wary of such simplicities. Athens under Pericles, he noted, was "nominally a democracy, but actually a monarchy under the foremost man." Yet there was never a more eloquent or more idealized picture of Athenian democracy than that Thucydides paints in his version of the funeral oration of Pericles. The constitution of Athens, he insists, is an original, a pattern for others to imitate. "Its administration favors the many instead of the few; this is why it is called a democracy." While all are equal before the law, in politics Athens is an aristocracy of merit. "As a city," he boasts, "we are the school of Hellas." So Thucydides fueled a debate that has never ceased.

19

From Myth to Literature: Virgil

While the Ionian spirit of inquiry added new ways of thinking about the past, it did not destroy the perennial appeal of ancient myth. In later centuries across the West, schoolchildren would be charmed by the Homeric epics, and especially by the adventures of Ulysses, though they had scant interest in Herodotus and Thucydides. While Homer survived in ancient Greece, the new spirit of history brought ways of giving myth and religion the plausibility of history. What was the relation between the gods, the traditional heroes of the epic bards, and the real events of history?

One of the most influential of those who asked this interesting question was Euhemerus of Messene (flourished c. 300 B.C.) on the southwest Peloponnese in the century after Thucydides' death. He must have been a bold imaginer, for he devised his own myth to give a historical basis for the traditional myths. He recorded his imaginary voyage to the mysterious island of Panchaea in the Indian Ocean. This fantasy was called "Sacred Scripture" from the inscriptions on a golden column at the center of the island. Inscriptions recorded the great deeds of Uranus, Cronus, and Zeus, who had once been benevolent kings of the island. The grateful people then worshipped them as gods.

This was a welcome precedent for Hellenistic rulers claiming worship from their subjects. Euhemerus' ingenious work had wide implications for Greek heroic traditions. It suggested that the Greek gods were originally heroic kings—later deified for their service to their people—and seemed to justify the ruler cults of Euhemerus' own time. The original work now surviving only in fragments was summarized by Eusebius, then translated and adapted by Ennius (born 239 B.C.). His Latin work *Euhemerus* had wide influence. Some saw it as rationalizing atheism, but Christian apologists like Lactantius (c. 240–c. 320) argued that Euhemerus had exposed the real foundation of Greek gods. The theory called Euhemerism argued that all gods may have originally been only human rulers elevated to divinity by later generations for their benefits to mankind. But Christian thinkers like Saint Augustine and Lactantius turned it to their purpose. The divinity assigned to human rulers, they said, came not from their virtues but from their demonic vices, which inspired fear in humankind. Then popular worship of them was not from adoration but for propitiation. The Roman author Statius (A.D. c. 40–96) had similarly observed, "The first reason in the world for the existence of the gods was fear."

Still the reach for the past was passionate and relentless. Myth, born in community tradition preserved and embellished by bards singing heroic epics, survived as a fertile form of literature. It produced its own classics tying past to future. The Romans had known writing since the seventh or sixth century B.C., and their pontiffs, guardians of the sacred books, had begun keeping archives. And this helps explain the poverty of Roman national myths, just as the rise of literacy in Greece had brought there the decline of the spontaneity of the heroic bards. In Rome the arts of oratory had developed and been celebrated by Cicero, under the republic. By the second century B.C. the new career of man of letters had been born. The full-time writers now depended on the patronage of the great families. When Octavian defeated Antony and Cleopatra at Actium in 31 B.C., power was concentrated in him as *princeps,* though republican forms survived. This did not call him a monarch, yet set him above all other citizens. The name Augustus was conferred on him in 27 B.C. The Augustan Age would be fertile of the great Latin writers—Horace, Ovid, and others. This new Roman Empire called for a new national literature, which soon would appear.

The hero of this re-creation was Virgil (70–19 B.C.). Like most of the great Roman writers, he was not born in Rome. He came from a respectable but not prominent family in what was still called Cisalpine Gaul near Mantua, not far from Venice. Educated at Cremona and Milan, Virgil then studied in Rome before returning to his Mantuan farm. There he began composing his *Eclogues* in 43 B.C. After his farm was confiscated during the civil wars, he lived for a while in Rome, where the powerful Maecenas (born between 74 and 64 B.C.) introduced him to the emperor Augustus. Maecenas himself had literary ambitions and was the patron of a literary circle that gathered in his mansion on the Esquiline hill. Virgil's *Eclogues,* a Latin adaptation of Theocritus' Greek pastorals, attracted the attention of Maecenas, who was close to Augustus. Maecenas may have suggested the subject of Virgil's next work, the *Georgics* (from Greek *georgos,* "farmer"), a didactic poem of two thousand lines on the model of Hesiod's *Works and Days* on agriculture, which Virgil dedicated to him.

Maecenas tried to persuade the poets in his stable to write epics in praise of his friend Augustus. Virgil took up his suggestion and spent eleven years composing the *Aeneid,* his epic of the wanderings of Aeneas. When Virgil had nearly finished his epic, he traveled to the East to verify his descriptions of sites in the poem. He fell ill en route, died, and was buried in Naples. Virgil's project had aroused Augustus' interest. The emperor had asked to see parts of it as it was written, and Virgil read portions to Augustus and his family in 23 B.C. Augustus appeared to see it as the epic of his vision of Roman grandeur. The work was never revised to Virgil's satisfaction. It was said that as he was dying Virgil ordered the manuscript destroyed, but this was countermanded by Augustus himself.

Virgil had led the life of a devoted man of letters, seeking perfection in his writing. He spent his life in poetry, he never married, never held a military or political position. The first half of his life he was a retiring scholar. After his poetry had made him famous, he won the friendship of leading Romans. But he never lost the awe of Rome that he felt from his youth as a provincial, an outsider. In the first Eclogue, one of his earliest poems, the visiting shepherd Tityrus reports:

> The city, Meliboeus, they call Rome,
> I simpleton, deemed like this town of ours. . . .
> Comparing small with great; but this as far
> Above all other cities rears her head
> As cypress above pliant osier towers. (trans. James Rhoades)

Although the *Aeneid* shows signs of not having been finally revised, it still survived as a model of Latin style. Just as Homer was the educator of Greece, Quintilian recommended that Virgil's works should be the basis of the Roman education. For all the centuries since, students of the classics have been enchanted by Virgil's epic of the adventures of Aeneas. In the Middle Ages, Virgil was Dante's guide through Hell and Purgatory toward Paradise. And the *Aeneid* would provide Milton his model for *Paradise Lost.* Translation of Virgil has invited the talents of English poets from John Dryden to William Morris, C. Day Lewis, and Robert Fitzgerald.

Myth, which had been the spontaneous accumulation of oral tradition over centuries, in Virgil's hands now became literature—the vehicle of nations and empires. He turned the kudos of myth to the needs of the new emperor Augustus and the grandeur of expanding Rome. It would have been difficult to write an epic with Augustus himself as the hero. Nor was the Battle of Actium, in which Octavian defeated Antony and Cleopatra in a naval battle, somehow an appealing theme. There had been very little fighting. It might have seemed absurd to feature the gods in such recent events. And perhaps there were too many suicides for a heroic epic. Antony had committed suicide on the false report of Cleopatra's suicide. Then Cleopatra, failing to seduce Octavian, and fearing being forced to adorn his triumph in Rome, did the same, while Egypt was added to the Roman Empire.

Octavian celebrated three triumphs and closed the temple of Janus to signal the restoration of peace throughout the Roman world. The Homeric bards, who sang of ancient times, had little fear of contradiction. But Virgil had taken on an epic foreshadowing the present and the future. Virgil once confessed in a letter that he must have been mad to attempt it. How to create a credible myth—in literature that would celebrate Roman virtues, encompass all Italy, and prophesy the glory of Augustan Rome? To do that while satisfying the envy and amour propre of his own age was an achievement. And at the same time to create an epic of pathos and tragedy that would long outlast the Roman Empire and delight generations who knew no Actium and cared nothing for Antony, Cleopatra, or Octavian. This was the *Aeneid,* Virgil's way of seeking meaning in the empire—encompassing past, present, and future.

Virgil succeeded in this first national epic by drawing on the Homeric epics, proven over centuries. It would have been folly not to build on themes so long tested. So he found ways to adapt the themes of a preliterate heroic age to the aspirations of a world-reaching empire. But how tie the imperial future to a mythic past? A secondary figure in the *Iliad,* Aeneas, son of Anchises and Aphrodite (Venus) and a member of the younger branch of the royal family of Troy in disfavor with Priam, gave him his clue. In the *Iliad*, "The shaker of the earth Poseidon" predicted that "the might of Aeneas (Aineias) shall be lord over the Trojans and his sons' sons, and those who are born of their seed hereafter." Aeneas was thus the one legendary Trojan who had a promising future. While Romans naturally looked to Greek legends for their founding epic, in a time when they were conquering Greece they preferred a hero from among the enemies of Greece. The image of the Trojan Aeneas, refugee from Greek brutality, with his father Anchises on his back and leading his son Ascanius by the hand, filled the prescription. In the *Iliad,* Aeneas is said to have been respected equally with Hector and to have been honored like a god. While his recorded deeds are not heroic, Aeneas is noted for his piety, a conspicuous Roman virtue. Roman *pietas* meant not mere religious piety, but devotion to father and mother and the gods and to the grand destiny of Rome. By Virgil's time there was already a legend of Aeneas' flight from Troy with his ancestral gods (Penates), of his wanderings and his founding of cities. Towns with names resembling Aeneas or with temples of Venus claimed him as their founder. The Sicilian Greek historian Timaeus in the fourth century B.C. had mentioned Aeneas as the founder of Lavinium on the coastal plains of the Tiber, from which settlers were said to have come to found Alba Longa, birthplace of Romulus and Remus, about twenty miles from the future site of Rome. Drawing on these and other legends, Virgil composed the *Aeneid.*

While inspired by Homer, Virgil was wonderfully free in adapting his models. He reversed the order of the Homeric story. He made the *Odyssey* his model for his first half, starting with six books on the wanderings of his hero Aeneas, after his flight from Troy (his *Odyssey*). The next six books (his *Iliad*) was a saga of battle scenes of Aeneas enlisting allies and founding Rome. And he reenacts Homeric themes in an exhilarating Roman manner. When Ulysses visited the Underworld, the world of the dead, he saw the shades of his mother and his fellow Greeks killed at Troy or on their way home, along with heroes of the mythic past. Similarly, Virgil's Aeneas in the Underworld, guided by his father, sees the heroes of the Roman future. While the canny Ulysses personifies the bold Greek seafaring adventurer, Aeneas personifies *pietas,* the Roman morality of discipline and duty that built a world-encompassing empire.

At the same time Virgil depicts the tragic choices that were the price of Roman destiny—personal sacrifices like Aeneas' abandonment of

Dido. The Roman destiny was also a costly choice—to turn away from the gentler Greek tasks of art and philosophy to the hard tasks of government and empire. As Anchises prophesies to Aeneas in the Underworld:

> Others will cast more tenderly in bronze
> Their breathing figures, I can well believe,
> And bring more lifelike portraits out of marble;
> Argue more eloquently, use the pointer
> To trace the paths of heaven accurately
> And accurately foretell the rising stars.
> Roman, remember by your strength to rule
> Earth's peoples—for your arts are to be these
> To pacify, to impose the rule of law,
> To spare the conquered, battle down the proud. (*Aeneid,* Fitzgerald trans.)

So Virgil's national epic takes the form of myth and prophecy. "To these I set no bounds in space or time," declares Jupiter, "I have given them rule without end." Which is fulfilled in Virgil's time, as Anchises foresaw in the Underworld:

> Turn your two eyes
> This way and see this people, your own Romans.
> Here is Caesar, and all the line of Iulus,
> All who shall one day pass under the dome
> Of the great sky: this is the man, this one,
> Of whom so often you have heard the promise,
> Caesar Augustus, son of the deified,
> Who shall bring once again an Age of Gold
> To Latium, to the land where Saturn reigned
> In early times. (*Aeneid,* Fitzgerald trans.)

In the Middle Ages Virgil would have a new mythic appeal. In his fourth Eclogue (written 40 B.C.) he had recalled the Sibyl's prophecy:

> The ages' mighty march begins anew.
> Now comes the virgin, Saturn reigns again:
> Now from high heaven descends a wondrous race.
> Thou . . . look with favor on the newborn babe—who first shall end
> That age of Iron, bid a golden dawn
> Upon the broad world . . .
> Shalt free the nations from perpetual fear.

This came to be called the Messianic Eclogue and was said to contain imagery reminiscent of the Bible. It is likely that Virgil was referring to the expected child of Antony and Octavia. But this and other supposedly prophetic passages earned Virgil his medieval reputation as seer and magician, and his role as Dante's guide through Hell and Purgatory.

20

Thomas More's New Paths to Utopia

The Age of Discovery of continents and oceans was also an age of European self-discovery. The science of society was no longer channeled into Aristotelian paths. New ways of thinking about society would leave their permanent mark on ways of seeking. The wide spectrum of novelty was revealed in the lives and works of two antithetic brilliant Renaissance contemporaries, Seekers from opposite sides of Europe. The saintly Englishman Sir Thomas More (1478–1535) in his fantasy of *Utopia* (1516) gave a name and a new form to the poetry of politics, to the search for the ideal community. At the same time the Italian Niccolò Machiavelli (1469–1527) in *The Prince* (written in 1512) gave birth to a modern science of politics and nations.

More spoke from the limbo between the medieval Christian and the modern ways of seeking. Son of a prominent lawyer and judge, he was sent to Oxford and then trained in law at Lincoln's Inn. Tempted toward the priesthood, he decided instead to pursue the law as a profession. But he remained pious, prayed regularly, fasted on the holidays. He even wore a hair shirt, and seemed to be preparing himself for martyrdom. He became a good friend of Erasmus, who while he was More's houseguest wrote his *Praise of Folly* (*Encomium moriae*), and dedicated it to More with a title which was a pun on the name of More.

More's *Utopia,* in Latin, which was still the international language of the learned in Europe, was printed in Louvain in 1516, under Erasmus' supervision. The word "Utopia" (from Greek, "nowhere") was invented by More for his classic political fantasy, which would become a model for many others in succeeding centuries. Cast as a traveler's tale, it bore the unmistakable mark of the Age of Discovery. The mythical narrator, Raphael Hythloday, had gone to America with Vespucci, whose travels had been published in 1507. When Vespucci sailed back to Europe, Hythloday preferred to stay on the ideal island, discovered by one of Vespucci's crew. More uses the dialogue, the dramatic structure of Plato's *Republic,* for the first half of his tale. In search of the ideal society, More gives over the first part of his book to a survey of the evils of European society in his time. The second part describes life on the island of Utopia off the coast of America.

More's Utopia is an idealized version of the medieval monastic life. Its main feature is the communal ownership of property (also found in Plato's *Republic*). "In other places men talk very literally of the common wealth, but what they mean is simply their own wealth; in Utopia, where there is no private business, every man zealously pursues the public business." "Though no man owns anything, everyone is rich." They hold "precious metals" up to scorn in every conceivable way, and make their chamber pots of gold. A national system of education gives women the same education as men.

The invading king, Utopus, had found the island easy to conquer "because the different sects were too busy fighting one another to oppose him, . . . he decreed that every man might cultivate the religion of his choice, and might proselytize for it, provided he did so quietly, modestly, and rationally and without bitterness toward others. If persuasions failed, no man was allowed to resort to abuse or violence, under penalty of exile or enslavement." The king Utopus, "because he suspected that God perhaps likes various forms of worship and has therefore deliberately inspired different people with different views," allowed the widest toleration. "The only exception he made was a positive and strict law against any person who should sink so far below the dignity of human nature as to think that the soul perishes with the body, or that the universe is ruled by mere chance, rather than divine providence."

The "justice of the Utopians," unlike that of Europe, did not reward noblemen or goldsmiths or moneylenders who made their living "by doing either nothing at all or something completely useless to the public" while laborers who did the necessary work were treated like beasts of burden. The book appealed at once to the community of impecunious humanists, and was soon translated into French (1550) and English (1551).

More's fanciful imagination somehow did not prevent his success at the bar. He entered the service of the king, and championed Erasmus' program of the Christian humanists, the study of the Greek classics, the Bible, and the Church Fathers. Henry VIII appointed him Lord Chancellor in 1529 in place of Cardinal Thomas Wolsey when Wolsey failed to secure the king's divorce from Catherine. But this was as far as More would go in indulging the whims of Henry VIII. When More refused to attend the coronation of Anne Boleyn after the divorce from Catherine, he was a marked man. He was included in a bill of attainder, and continued to refuse to swear to the whole Act of Succession, which would have denied the supremacy of the pope and have made Henry VIII the head of the Church.

More never lost his orthodox Catholic faith, and despite his wife's pleas, he refused the conciliation with Henry VIII that would have saved his life. Found guilty of treason, he was sentenced to be "drawn, hanged, and quartered," but instead he was beheaded in 1535. His courage and good humor at his execution became proverbial. "See me safe up," he said to the lieutenant, "and for my coming down let me shift for myself." More blindfolded himself. As he put his head on the block he moved his beard aside, since, he said, it had done no offense to the king.

More declared that he was not dying for treason but "in the faith and for the faith of the Catholic Church, the king's good servant and God's first." Erasmus praised him as a man "whose soul was more pure than any snow." He was canonized by Pope Pius XI in 1935 as Saint Thomas More. And he was immortalized in Erasmus's phrase as *omnium horarum homo,* translated as "A Man for All Seasons" in a popular play and film (in 1966) by Robert Bolt. Other English Catholics have shared G. K. Chesterton's adoration of him as "the greatest Englishman, or at least the greatest historical character in English history."

While the waning Catholic faith around him led Saint Thomas More to seek his ideal community not in the monastery but in a mythical island of the New World, in Italy the worldly ambitions of the Church would provide the laboratory for a new political science.

21

Francis Bacon's Vision of Old Idols
and New Dominions

If we are awed by the powers of man, the learned animal, we must also be appalled that he has been such a slow learner. And there has been no greater obstacle to his learning than the stock of accumulated learning that he has made for himself with his illusions of knowledge. How else to explain that two thousand years passed after Socrates' martyrdom for his discovery of ignorance before Western thinkers looked around them and turned to experience for their avenues to the purpose of their lives?

The appearance of Francis Bacon (1561–1626) on the English scene signaled a dramatic transformation in the role of "philosophers" and the expectations of philosophy—from crusades to convert the pagan to voyages of discovery into the unknown. The vastly enlarged world of the Renaissance overwhelmed literate Europeans. Now aware of being part of the whole continental experience of "Europe," they glimpsed other continental experiences—Asia, Africa, and America. The travels of Marco Polo and the voyages of Columbus (newly interpreted by Vespucci and Magellan) had broadened the dimensions of earthly experience as never before. López de Gomera in his *History of the Indies* (1552) saw the discovery of the "new" continent as "the greatest event since the creation of the world, excepting the incarnation and death of Him who created it."

Before Bacon, great philosophers had been teachers who could claim the dignity of their profession for what they taught. But Bacon was a man of affairs, active in politics, member of Parliament, counselor of sovereigns. He set a new style in philosophers, who would put their ideas to the public tests of their times. Yet they were seldom saints. Saint Thomas More was an exception.

Bacon's life story was a relentless push for position. Born in London, he was the youngest son of Sir Nicholas Bacon, Lord Keeper of the Seal and Chancellor, the highest legal post in the realm. On his father's death in 1579, receiving only the "narrow portion" of a younger son, he had to make his way in the world. Naturally choosing to go to the bar, he studied at Gray's Inn and then was admitted to practice in 1582.

From then ambition drove him to seek the highest legal positions. When James I succeeded to the throne in 1603, Bacon's skill at letter-writing and at sycophancy and his adeptness at intrigue soon brought him appointments as solicitor general (1607), attorney general (1613), and finally Lord Chancellor (1618). Advancing by a barrage of self-serving letters and shameless flattery, he incidentally became the uncompromising champion of the powers of his royal master.

Soon after his appointment as Lord Chancellor, Bacon was surprised by charges of bribery. Gifts to judges by parties appearing were common at the time. And judges were expected to show character by not being influenced by the gifts. Bacon admitted twenty-eight charges and was pronounced guilty by the High Court of Parliament. King James could not interfere; Bacon was disabled from holding future public office and forbidden to come "within the verge of the court." Finally, Bacon secured relief from the worst penalties of his conviction for bribery by bribing a court favorite with a gift of York House, his mansion by the Thames.

None of these events would diminish the appeal to future generations of his *Essays,* which were cogent exhortations to honesty and prudence. And the generations would further profit from his being forced to abandon public life, for Bacon would spend his remaining five years writing important books.

After following Bacon's breathless public career, we must wonder how he found time for reflection, for experiment, or to write the books that changed the course of thinking about science. While Bacon's great works—*The Great Instauration, The Advancement of Learning,* the *Novum organum, The New Atlantis*—would be forward-looking, positive, and constructive, he appears to have been led to his vision by reaction against the "learning" into which he had been inducted.

What he had seen of conventional knowledge during his precocious years at Cambridge had a cathartic effect on his own view of the world. Sent to Trinity College, Cambridge, at thirteen, he had completed the undergraduate program in less than three years with a reputation for diligence. The Cambridge curriculum was still not substantially different from that of the great medieval universities. The way of disputation ruled. Dialectica—grammar, rhetoric, and logic based on the texts of Aristotle—was the heart of the undergraduate education. A series of public disputations, beginning with "sophisms" and culminating in "demonstrations of truth" (the propositions of Aristotle) by syllogism, marked the student's career. Mathematics, though traditional in the quadrivium, was not offered, as there were no tutors who knew the subject. At the age of sixteen, Bacon told his early biographer, "he fell into the dislike of the philosophy of Aristotle; not for the worthlessness of the author, to whom he would ever ascribe all high attributes, but for the unfruitfulness of the way; being a philosophy . . . only strong for disputation and contentions, but barren of the production of works for the benefit of the life of man; in which mind he continued to his dying day."

"Being convinced that the human intellect makes its own difficulties," Bacon offered his vivid catalog of the illusions of knowledge—"idols which beset men's minds." And even now it is hard to find a better catalog of menaces to thought than his short list of four "Idols" in his *Novum organum* in 1620. "The *Idols of the Tribe* [italics added] have their foundation in human nature itself, and in the tribe or race of men. For it is a false assertion that the sense of man is the measure of things. . . . And the human understanding is like a false mirror, which receiving rays irregularly, distorts and discolors the nature of things by mingling its own nature with it." "The *Idols of the Cave* are the idols of the individual man. For everyone . . . has a cave or den of his own, which refracts and discolors the light of nature; owing either to his own proper and peculiar nature or to his education and conversation with others. . . . Whence it was well observed by Heraclitus that men look for sciences in their own lesser worlds, and not in the greater or common world."

"There are also idols formed by the association of men with each other, which I call *Idols of the Market-place.* . . . For it is by discourse that men associate; and words are imposed according to the apprehension of the vulgar. And therefore the ill and unfit choice of words wonderfully obstructs the understanding. . . . Lastly there are idols which have immigrated into men's minds from the various dogmas of philosophies, and also from wrong laws of demonstration. These I call *Idols of the Theater;* because in my judgment all the received systems are but so many stage-plays, representing worlds of their own creation after an unreal and scenic fashion." All these betray the same universal weakness. "The human understanding is of its own nature prone to suppose the existence of more order and regularity in the world than it finds."

How is man to dissolve these illusions and advance to a grasp on the real world? Bacon declared this his lifelong object—"The Great Instauration" ("Great Renovation")—"a total reconstruction of sciences, arts, and all human knowledge, raised upon the proper foundations." When he called the first part of his project "The Advancement of Learning," he signaled his object to be not the capture of empyrean truth but the processes of increasing knowledge. So he deplores those who pursued knowledge "as if there were sought in knowledge a couch whereupon to rest a searching and restless spirit; or a terrace for a wandering and variable mind to walk up and down with a fair prospect; or a tower of state for a proud mind to raise itself up upon; or a fort or commanding storehouse for the glory of the Creator and the relief of man's estate." His aim is not once and for all to find salvation. Rather he hopes to renew that "dominion over creatures" once forfeit at the Fall of Man, and forfeit a second time by "admiring and applauding the false powers of the mind." "Dwelling purely and constantly among the facts of nature," Bacon sees that knowledge is power.

When in the next century Bacon came to write his own Utopia, he saw a different, strikingly modern path to the ideal society. His *New Atlantis* (published posthumously in 1627) was, like More's *Utopia,* an island off the coast of Peru in the New World. But his fable was not focused on the classical problems of justice and distribution of property. His whole story was a frame for "Salomon's House; the noblest foundation . . . that ever was upon the earth." Here was a prototype of the modern research and development laboratory, but without limits of geography or subject matter. The members of this college were dedicated to the "interpreting of Nature and the producing of great and marvelous works" for the benefit of mankind. There was a mathematical house with astronomical instruments, botanical and zoological gardens for research, an aquarium, a theater for anatomical dissections, and numerous other laboratories, together with instruments to measure sounds and earthquakes, and for making optical instruments, and for boats to travel underwater or in the air, along with every imaginable facility for the fabrication of textiles and the concoction of chemicals.

Fellows of Salomon's House sailed out to collect knowledge and materials everywhere. "But thus you see we maintain a trade, not for gold, silver, or jewels, nor for silks, nor for spices, nor any other commodity of matter; but only for God's first creature, which was light: to have light, I say, of the growth of all parts of the world . . . The end of our foundation [of Salomon's House] is the knowledge of causes, and secret motions of things; and the enlarging of the bounds of human empire, to the effecting of all things possible." This fantastic research college included "Merchants of Light," who collected information; "Mystery-men," who collected experiments of the mechanical arts; "Pioneers or Miners," who try their own new experiments; "Compilers," who collect data for drawings and tables; "Benefactors," who seek ways to apply knowledge for human benefit; "Lamps," for suggesting new experiments; "Inoculators," who pursue these new experiments; and, finally, "Interpreters of Nature," who find ways to generalize from the works of all these others. Two long galleries offered "patterns and samples of all manner of the more rare and excellent inventions; in the other we place the statues of all principal inventors. There we have the statue of your Columbus, that discovered the West Indies: also the inventor of ships . . . the inventor of printing . . . and many others."

Salomon's House was no romantic figment. It became real in England when royal charters were issued (1662–63) for the Royal Society of London for the Improving of Natural Knowledge (better known as the Royal Society). Its founding and early members were a galaxy that included Robert Boyle, Robert Hooke, and Sir Christopher Wren. When theology and metaphysics were excluded from their transactions, the Society became a shining symbol of the new turn to experience. It also became an attractive target for know-nothings and theological diehards, who even attacked its language, which defenders celebrated as a "close, naked, natural way."

The New Atlantis was not published till after Bacon's death. During his lifetime he offered his guide for future generations of Seekers into the paths of fruitful experience. The ambitious Bacon, seeing that "the sovereignty of man lieth hid in knowledge" and that "the monuments of wit survive the monuments of power," proposed a grand scheme of works to come. *The Great Instauration* was "to commence a total reconstruction of sciences, arts, and all human knowledge." And his "monuments of wit" would outlive and overshadow his fall from positions of power. He was not troubled by excessive modesty. "I have as vast contemplative ends," he boasted at the age of thirty-one, "as I have moderate civil ends, for I have taken all knowledge for my province." In the Proemium to his projected great work, he soberly listed his qualifications:

> For myself, I found that I was fitted for nothing so well as for the study of truth; as having a mind nimble and versatile enough to catch the resemblances of things (which is the chief point) and at the same time steady enough to fix and distinguish their subtler differences; as being gifted by nature with desire to seek, patience to doubt, fondness to meditate, slowness to assert, readiness to reconsider, carefulness to dispose and set in order; and as being a man that neither affects what is new nor admires what is old, and that hates any kind of imposture.

Bacon was not hasty in offering his epochal renewal. He was in his sixtieth year before he borrowed the title of Aristotle's treatise on logic for his *New Organon, or True Directions Concerning the Interpretation of Nature.* He had been thinking about the project ever since his dissatisfaction as a boy of sixteen at Cambridge with the "unfruitfulness of the way" of Aristotle and had been surveying the realms of "sciences, arts, and all human knowledge" ever since. With his *Advancement of Learning* (1605), dedicated to King James I, he offered the first part of his Great Instauration—a defense of the Dignity of Learning followed by his Survey of Learning. "The parts of human learning have reference to the three parts of man's understanding, which is the seat of learning: history to his memory, poesy to his imagination, and philosophy to his reason." For Bacon, the realm of reason (*scientia*) included all the sciences. And for their *Encyclopédie,* Diderot and d'Alembert would adopt Bacon's scheme. When Thomas Jefferson arranged his large personal library (which became the core of the Library of Congress) he, too, chose Bacon's threefold division.

When Bacon was ready to publish his *New Organon,* in 1620, he published his Plan for the whole of his Great Instauration. The foundation of the whole would be "laid in natural history." The first part, a survey of the state of knowledge, described the sciences still unknown and to be cultivated. The second part, or *New Organon,* would describe Bacon's new inductive method—not seeking agreement with principles and definitions already assumed, but discovering axioms drawn from actual observations of nature. Then a collection of natural history prepared by the methods of the second part. Followed by striking examples of results of the new inductive method, and a fifth part (for temporary use) offering tentative conclusions from still-incomplete observation—resting places on the way to fuller experiments. And finally the New Philosophy based on the inductive interpretation of natural history.

Significantly, the *New Organon* begins not with a dogmatic statement of "first principles" but with discrete "Aphorisms concerning the Interpretation of Nature and the Kingdom of Man." His first Aphorism declares, "Man, being the servant and interpreter of nature, can do and understand so much and so much only as he has observed in fact or in thought of the course of nature: beyond this he neither knows anything nor can do anything." Bacon's four "Idols" were offered here as a list of Aphorisms. In the second part of the *New Organon* he illustrates his inductive method by a study of the forms of heat, of which he offers twenty-seven instances, with more to be added, dramatizing his departure from the Aristotelian Peripatetic philosophers. Bacon's search for the "forms" of nature is quite different from a search for elements. "To inquire the form of a lion, or of an oak, of gold, nay, even of water or air, is a vain pursuit; but to inquire the form of dense, rare, hot, cold, heavy, light, tangible, pneumatic, volatile, fixed, and the like . . . which (like the letters of the alphabet) are not many and yet make up and sustain the essences and forms of all substances:—this, I say, it is which I am attempting. . . . And inquiries into nature have the best result when they begin with physics and end in mathematics."

Although Bacon would be widely recognized as the pioneer of the modern scientific method, he was not in the vanguard of the sciences in his age. Despite his occasional good words for mathematics he underestimated the importance of mathematics for the future of science. Himself an inveterate Seeker, he still failed to recognize the epochal advances made by others of his time. He did not note the invention of logarithms by the Scottish mathematician John Napier (1550–1616). He seems not to have known Vesalius' anatomy, or Gilbert's works on magnetism. The great Sir William Harvey attended him as a physician, but Bacon had no knowledge of Harvey's discovery of the circulation of the blood (published after Bacon's death).

Still, Bacon showed a remarkable clairvoyance. He approved rejection of the tradition that the planets moved in perfect circles and he applauded Galileo's improvements and uses of the telescope for astronomy. He also anticipated Newton by suggesting that the earth and the heavens consisted of common matter with "common passions and desires." And so he foresaw a new alliance between astronomy and physics. He favored an empirical approach to medicine and belief in the kinship of man with all nature.

Before the end of the seventeenth century, Bacon's campaign against the syllogism was overwhelming Aristotle in English universities, and so helped bring to an end what has been called "the longest tyranny ever exercised." But Aristotelian texts continued to be used as exercises in definition. Only gradually did Bacon's ideas for the curriculum overcome the stigma of "mechanics." Descartes's teachings would lack that stigma. But Bacon had turned Seekers from the way to salvation toward ways to increase man's sovereignty over nature. And within a century, John Evelyn (1620–1706), the polymath diarist who became secretary of the Royal Society, when surveying the society's work, was gratified to observe that "Salomon's House . . . however lofty, and to appearance Romantic, hath yet in it nothing impossible to be effected."

22

From the Soul to the Self: Descartes's Island Within

The travail of the Seeker is nowhere better revealed than in the life of the father of modern philosophy. A versatile scientist, obsessed by the wonders of the world out there, René Descartes (1596–1650) was also creator of the modern idea of the self. At home and well drilled in the dogmas of Aristotle and the scholastics, he made a career of dissolving them. It was in a mysterious dream that he had his call to produce a universal science built by reason. Making doubt the fertile beginning of his philosophy, he made certainty the first principle of his method. His life showed the power, the temptations, and the tribulations of a seeking spirit. And he marked a new era of the sovereign self, when philosophers now were scientists—not retailers of conventional doctrine but explorers on the frontier. His background gave no clue to his revolutionary role.

Descartes was qualified to move on from Aristotle and the medieval scholastics, for, like Bacon, he was trained in them from his earliest years. He was born into the *noblesse de robe* in Touraine, where his father was a lawyer and a judge. His mother died when he was only one, and he was raised by a nurse to whom he remained devoted all his life. At eight he was sent to the newly opened Jesuit college at La Flèche, which soon became noted for its intellectual distinction. There he received the best Jesuit education based on Aristotle and Aquinas and polished with the gentleman's social graces of riding and fencing. Ten years as an industrious student prepared him to assess the extent and the limits of the conventional Catholic learning, and he acquired a Catholic faith that he never lost. He was sent to the University of Poitiers to fulfill his family's hope that he would become a lawyer.

When he had already decided "to abandon the study of letters," a lucky inheritance left him free for a vagrant, restless way of life. And he determined to give up scholarly books for what he called "the book of the world." His first adventure was in the military life, not hard to find in seventeenth-century Europe. In Holland he joined the army of Maurice of Nassau, Prince of Orange, against the Spanish forces seeking to recover

Holland for Spain. Though a Catholic, he saw no incongruity in joining the Protestant forces of a Protestant prince. But he received no pay and probably never saw action. The idle, debauched life of the barracks did not please him, but did provide leisure for his scientific pursuits.

In Holland "the book of the world" opened for Descartes in surprising ways. He was awakened by a casual encounter with a Flemish doctor, Isaac Beeckman, who shared his mathematical interests and would remain a lifelong intellectual companion and catalyst. In March 1619 Descartes went to Middelburg to visit Beeckman, then returned to Breda, where he spent six days with his compass working out mathematical problems. Beeckman had stirred his creative urge. "And so as not to hide anything from you about the nature of my work," Descartes wrote, "I would like to give to the public not an *Ars brevis* but a completely new science which would resolve generally all questions of quantity, continuous or discontinuous." But before he could fulfill his promise, he had another inspiration.

"Where will destiny lead me? Where shall I come to rest?" he asked himself. His unlikely answer was to seek "repose" in another military assignment in the armed forces of Duke Maximilian of Bavaria. So, too, he was plunged into the religious maelstrom of the Thirty Years War. When he found that Maximilian was fighting against the Protestant cause, he took another military assignment that brought not action but enforced leisure, which he spent at Neuberg on the Danube.

There he lodged not in barracks but in a rented room that would become famous as the site of his life's crisis. He called this room his "*poêle*" (stove). At the age of twenty-three, according to his own account, locked in this heated solitude, he reflected on his knowledge and on his mission to create a single universal science. With melodramatic irony, his mission as founder of modern rationalist philosophy came to him on the night of November 10, 1619, in a mystic experience. His three dreams on that Saint Martin's Eve have aroused much scholarly speculation. Some uncharitably attribute them to heavy drinking or indigestion. Descartes himself took the trouble to note that he had had no wine for three months. For Jacques Maritain the experience had "a divine origin . . . a holy intoxication . . . like a Pentecost of Reason." Descartes claimed now to possess "everything at once" as the "foundations of a marvelous science" were revealed in his three successive dreams.

First was a nightmare in which he was lame and bent over, driven by a whirlwind against a church. A strange person told him to go in search of a Monsieur N. who would give him something, which proved to be a melon from a foreign country. Turning from his left to sleep on his right side, he prayed for protection from the ill omens of the dream. His second dream frightened him with loud noises like thunder, and he was awakened by sparks all around the room. Falling asleep once more, he had a less frightening and more explicit third dream. In it he saw a book on his table entitled *Corpus poetarum,* which he opened to the line "*Quod vitae sectabor iter?*" (What path of life shall I follow?) A stranger handed him some verses beginning with "Est et non" (Yes and No). Descartes identified the verses in the *Idylls* of Ausonius, a fourth-century Latin poet and Roman official of Bordeaux. When this book mysteriously disappeared it was replaced by a dictionary. In his dream Descartes was beginning to wonder whether what he saw was only imagined, when he awoke.

In those pre-Freudian days, Descartes sought meanings elsewhere than in his childhood experience. Instead he found revelations for his future path: Perhaps the first two dreams were parables of punishment for his sins, and his need for remorse. Perhaps the book of poets signified the incorporation of wisdom in the works of poets. Then the *Est et Non* (from Pythagoras) could be the divisions between truth and error in human knowledge. And the melon stood for the charms of solitude. But the third dream carried omens of his future. The dictionary that replaced the poems of Ausonius augured the unifying of all the sciences.

Descartes himself appeared to have thought his dreams were the divine inspiration for what would be his "marvelous invention." To show his gratitude, and his hope for more guidance from the Holy Virgin, he vowed to make a pilgrimage to the church of Notre Dame of Loretto in central Italy. He promised—if he had the strength—to travel there on foot from Venice. Some years later he did fulfill his vow.

Descartes declared that this revelation of reason was "the foundations of a marvelous science" (*mirabilis scientiae fundamenta*). But not until eighteen years later did he sketch the outlines of that science. This sense of a higher authority behind the operations of his human reason never left him. During the next years he kept up his vagrant life, having his last taste of military experience with the imperial army in Hungary, before traveling in Germany and France. At a meeting of Catholic theologians in Paris exploring alternatives to Aristotle, Descartes gave hints of his own method and the wider use of mathematical reasoning. Cardinal de Bérulle (1575–1629), leader of a Catholic renaissance, was there and was much impressed. He invited Descartes to visit him privately and he urged Descartes that it was his divine duty to benefit the human race by applying his (still undefined) techniques to medicine and mechanics.

In 1628 Descartes settled in Holland, where he would stay for the next twenty years. Though he changed his residence almost every year, he used the opportunity for solitary reflection and writing. While his frequent moves rescued him from trivial social activities, he kept up a wide correspondence, much of which has survived. And he studied at the universities of Franeker and Leiden. His insatiable curiosity about "the book of the world" led him after 1630 to wide-ranging self-assigned research in the physical and natural sciences—on the nature of light, in optics, meteorology, physics, and biology.

By 1633 Descartes finally had his *Le Monde* (The World), his work of marvelous unified science, ready for publication. But just as he was about to send off the finished manuscript to his friend Marin Mersenne, he had a piece of shocking news. For his own research he had sought a copy of Galileo's *Dialogue of the Two Chief Systems.* He shared Galileo's view that the earth did move and that the earth was not the center of the universe. Now he learned that though Galileo's work had been published in 1632, all copies had been burned and the author had been sentenced by the Inquisition to an indefinite term of imprisonment. To Mersenne, Descartes explained:

> I was so astounded that I quasi resolved to burn all my papers or at least not to show them to anyone. I cannot imagine that an Italian, and especially one well thought of by the Pope from what I have heard, could have been labeled a criminal for nothing other than wanting to establish the movement of the earth. I know that this had been censured formerly by a few cardinals, but I thought that since that time one was allowed to teach it publicly even in Rome. I confess that if this is false, then, all the principles of my philosophy are false also. . . . And because I would not want for anything in the world to

be the author of a work where there was the slightest word of which the Church might disapprove, I would rather suppress it altogether than have it appear incomplete—"crippled," as it were.

Leading Dutch and French scholars in Holland had taught Galileo's view of the solar system, but that did not satisfy Descartes. "I have decided to suppress my treatise entirely and thus lose almost all of my labor during the past four years in order to render entire obedience to the Church. . . . I am seeking only rest and tranquility of spirit which are gifts which cannot be had by those who harbor either animosity or ambition." *Le Monde* and Descartes's other earlier philosophical works were not published till after his death.

Although Descartes had been experimenting, writing, and researching all his life, not till he was forty did he publish. Then his *Discourse on Method* (1637), a slim volume, gave him his claim to be the first modern philosopher and one of the first modern scientists.

Everything about this work expressed a modern emphasis. The focus on "Method" itself revealed the Seeker rather than concern for the Sought. Descartes begins with autobiography, and the aura of personal experience overcasts it all. He aims to free the reader from the burden of ancient erudition (Aristotle and the scholastics), to allow exercise of the individual intelligence. "Thus my design here is not to teach the Method which everyone should follow in order to promote the good conduct of his Reason, but only to show in what manner I have indeavoured to conduct my own." He opens with a reminder that "Good sense is of all things in the world the most equally distributed." "And if I write in French which is the language of my country, rather than in Latin which is that of my teachers, that is because I hope that those who avail themselves only of their natural reason in its purity may be better judges of my opinions than those who believe only in the writings of the ancients." And "Truths are more likely to have been discovered by one man than by a nation." Every self must make its own discoveries "because no one can so well understand a thing and make it his own when learnt from another as when it is discovered for himself."

Having recounted his personal experience and how he came to distrust the traditional resources of philosophy—"Seeing that it has been cultivated for many centuries by the best minds that have ever lived, and that nevertheless no single thing is to be found in it which is not the sub-ject of dispute"—and seeing so many conflicting opinions all supported by learned people, he "esteemed as well-nigh false all that only went as far as being probable." So he ended by "resolving to seek no other sci-ence than that which could be found in myself, or at least in the great book of the world." A restless Seeker, he was committed to years of re-flection, travel, and personal experiment.

This explained why, as he told Mersenne, what he wrote was not a "Treatise" but a *Discourse,* with a plainly practical purpose explicit in his title "On the method of rightly conducting the reason and seeking for truth in the sciences." His emphasis on *Method* told all, for it be-trayed his greater interest in the process than in the product of seeking. That the rules of his method (in Part II) seem so obvious nowadays sim-ply confirms the extent to which his self-centered search has come to dominate the modern consciousness. Ever since Descartes, Western philosophers have been preoccupied with theories of knowledge, and modern philosophers have been challenged by his questions but not im-pressed by his answers. Instead of the many precepts of the Aristotelian logic, he proposes his simple rules that have the charm of common sense and the familiarity of the commonplace. First, "to accept nothing as true which I did not clearly recognize to be so." Second, "to divide up each of the difficulties which I examined into as many parts as possi-ble." Third, "to carry on my reflections in due order, commencing with objects that were the most simple and easy to understand." And finally, "to make enumerations so complete and reviews so general that I should be certain of having omitted nothing."

Descartes further shows his practical concern by providing us with his "code of morals for the time being"—not daring to tear down what was there until he could provide better. This meant obeying the laws and customs of his country, and staying with the "truths" of its religion. His morality, too, sets him on the path of "Cartesian doubt." For he resolves "to try always to conquer myself rather than fortune, and to alter my de-sires rather than change the order of the world, and generally to accus-tom myself to believe that there is nothing entirely within our power but our own thoughts." His ruthless quest for certainty leads him "to reject as absolutely false everything as to which I could imagine the least ground of doubt."

So by starting with doubt as the catalyst of his philosophy he makes the doubter the center of his universe. More basic even than the maxim that became so famous, *Cogito, ergo sum* ("I think, therefore I am"), would have been the axiom "I doubt, therefore I am" (*Dubito, ergo sum*). For his way of seeking aimed not at reaching for transcendent empyrean truths, but at allaying personal doubt and satisfying the ego. It is no wonder that his way of seeking led him toward a private world that never intersected with the world of universals out there.

"If I had only ceased from thinking . . . I should have no reason for thinking that I existed. From that I knew that I was a substance the whole essence or nature of which is to think, and that for its existence there is no need of any place, nor does it depend on any material thing; so that this 'me'; that is to say, the soul by which I am what I am, is entirely distinct from the body." Lest it appear that this focus on self should leave out God, Descartes ingeniously makes the imperfection of the doubter a basis for his belief in God. "Reflecting on the fact that I doubted, and that consequently my existence was not quite perfect (for I saw clearly that it was a greater perfection to know than to doubt), I resolved to inquire whence I had learnt to know of anything more perfect than I myself was . . . it could but follow that it had been placed in me by a Nature which was really more perfect than mine could be . . . — that is to say, to put it in a word, which was God." Thus Descartes founded his belief in God not in the wondrous order of nature, but in the superiority of God to the imperfect doubting self.

The rest of his *Discourse* applies his Method to questions of physics and medicine (especially the movement of the heart), and the difference between the soul of man and that of the brutes, and finally offers a prospectus for the future of the sciences. Having "never remarked that by means of the disputations employed by the Schools any truth has been discovered of which we were formerly ignorant," he hopes "to attain knowledge which is very useful in life, and that instead of that speculative philosophy which is taught in the Schools, we may find a practical philosophy by means of which, knowing the force and the action of fire, water, air, the stars, heavens and all other bodies that environ us, as distinctly as we know the different crafts of any artisans, we can in the same way employ them in all those uses to which they are adapted, and thus render ourselves the masters and possessors of nature."

The exhilarating conclusion is "that all that men know is almost nothing compared with what remains to be known." And as a token of his hope for those vistas of the unknown, he ends his *Discourse* by declaring his resolve not to spend his remaining life "in any other matter than in endeavouring to acquire some knowledge of nature, which shall be of such a kind that it will enable us to arrive at rules for Medicine more assured than those which have as yet been attained." Descartes was plainly not frightened by paradox. His declaration of the independence of the self by no means prevented him from seeking the forces that shaped the outer world.

Descartes hoped to share discoveries to improve the condition of the human race, and yet not disturb the state or dissent from established religion. Appending *Essays in This Method* "to show that this method is applicable to all sorts of investigations," he included a section called *Dioptric* on the eye, vision, and optics, *Meteors* on the winds, weather, and colors of the rainbow, and *Geometry* on his method for solving unsolved problems. No mere speculations, each added substantially to man's mastery of nature.

Here he formulated the law of refraction, related the weather to changes in barometric pressure, and offered the momentous new techniques of analytic geometry, applying algebra to the problems of geometry. Descartes's faith in mathematics as a means to certainty in the solution of problems was reinforced by his own system of mathematics, of which his analytic geometry was the most widely known. Incidentally, he invented much of the basic vocabulary of algebra and mathematics. This included the form of the equation, the use of a and b for knowns, of x and y for unknowns, of numerals (instead of words) to express powers, and the form of the square-root sign. He had simplified algebraic notation by substituting letters for numbers to designate quantities, and numbers for arbitrary symbols to indicate powers. He made it possible to represent a point by a pair of numbers and to represent lines and curves by equations. So his Cartesian coordinates had made possible his analytic geometry, which reduced all geometric problems to the formulas of his new algebra, and opened unimagined new opportunities for the sciences. It is hard to enlist modern physical sciences without the use of this vocabulary. And it is not so surprising that Descartes himself harbored extravagant hopes for applying mathematical techniques to all problems.

While Descartes believed that "there is nothing entirely within our power but our own thoughts," he gave his thought a wonderful centrifugal character. Perhaps no other great philosopher except Aristotle spent so much time or was so versatile in experiments. Among these were studies of anatomy, dissection of embryos of birds and cattle, observations on the weight of air, the vibrations of strings, optical phenomena, and the reproductive generation of animals and men.

Another sign of his modernity, besides his focus on the self, was his close connection of physiology with the axioms of his philosophy. From his earliest writings on philosophy he suggests that all animal and subrational human movements are controlled by unconscious physical mechanisms. He imagined a two-step process by which external physical stimuli entered the human body to a "pineal" gland (at the base of the brain), which then directed the human response. A kind of mechanism or automatism underlay it all. Except only for phenomena caused directly by the human will, then, everything in the world could be explained by mathematics, measurable forces, shape, and motion.

It was appropriate, too, that he did not lead the life of the monastery or the university, nor did he surround himself with disciples. Instead he sought repose for his reflection and experiment, even suppressing publication where it was necessary to secure that repose, and he did not seek public position or responsibility. Lucky in having inherited property that gave him independence, he spent his life as he wished—in travel, study, and experiment. He formed warm, continuing, and fruitful intellectual companionships. His chance encounter at the age of twenty-two with Isaac Beeckman had encouraged his mathematical interests and ambitions for twenty years. His schoolmate Marin Mersenne (1588–1648) became a scientist of note, remained his lively correspondent, and defended Descartes against clerical critics.

Descartes had a remarkable capacity for lively friendships with young women intellectuals. In 1640, when he was forty-seven, he met the charming twenty-four-year-old Elizabeth of Bohemia, Princess Palatine. She had a talent for languages, had read some of his work, and was receiving instruction from university professors in philosophy and the sciences. She brought friends to visit Descartes, then living in a remote village in the marshes. Thus began a correspondence of which there remain twenty-six letters from Elizabeth and thirty-three from

Descartes, on all sorts of philosophic and scientific subjects. Although he was a confirmed Catholic and she had been raised a Protestant, in an age of religious wars they still shared theological concerns. She needed his solace, especially on receiving news of the beheading of her uncle Charles I in England on February 9, 1649. Up to a point she shared Cartesian doubt, but oddly wrote that "you . . . alone have kept me from being skeptical." They also shared mathematical puzzles like the ancient problem of the three circles, which she delighted him by solving.

The young intellectual Queen Christina of Sweden (1626–1689), who had been receiving Descartes's writings from his friend and admirer who was the French minister in Sweden, wished to add him to the circle of brilliant celebrities at her court. He was reluctant to leave his village retreat at Egmond, but she pressed him with an offer of a naval vessel to take him to Stockholm. When he finally gave in and arrived in October 1649, he was impressed by the twenty-three-year-old queen's lively mind. In that "land of bears between rock and ice" he observed that "men's thoughts freeze during the winter months." She set the bitter-cold hour of five o'clock in the morning for their tutorial sessions, which gave him chills, brought on pneumonia, and led to his death in February 1650. He received the last rites and died as a Catholic. During the French Revolution his remains were removed to the Pantheon.

PART FIVE

THE LIBERAL WAY

Liberty is not a means to a higher political end.
It is itself the highest political end.
—LORD ACTON, *HISTORY OF FREEDOM* (1907)

23

Machiavelli's Reach for a Nation

The Renaissance in Europe, a great age of poetry, the arts, and architecture, and epochal adventures of discovery, never produced a great work of theoretical philosophy, nor a work of history to live alongside Herodotus and Thucydides. The widening vistas of experience diverted man's seeking spirit from the ways of the Creator to new areas of man's own dominion. So the age did produce the pioneer work of modern political science. It grew out of the experience of a perceptive and eloquent Florentine Seeker, active in the life of the Italian city-state and its battles with the papacy. The name of this first modern political scientist would become an eponym for the evil and devious ways of politicians. The reputation of Niccolò Machiavelli (1469–1527) has suffered in history. He has been treated as a shallow polemicist for political immorality when he was a subtle interpreter, a Seeker of the grand truths of European political experience. His thought, judged solely by his hundred-page essay, *The Prince,* has been as little appreciated as Karl Marx's ideas would have been if judged solely by *The Communist Manifesto* without referring to *Das Kapital.* To rediscover Machiavelli is to see the foundations of modern political science.

Born in Florence to an impoverished father of a noble family, who had been denied public office as an insolvent debtor, Niccolò did not receive the education customary for his prominent family. As a youth he was mostly self-educated by the books he read and by an occasional private tutor. He learned Latin, but not Greek. So, luckily for his later work, he was never overwhelmed by pedantry or erudition and retained the alertness and curiosity of the amateur. In the turnover in the government of Florence after Savonarola had been tortured, hanged, and burned, the young Machiavelli in 1498 was employed in the new government in the "second chancery," which dealt with foreign affairs and defense.

Minor diplomatic missions to France opened his eyes to the working of strong government. Returning to Florence, he saw how the ruthless Cesare Borgia had created a new state for himself in central Italy. Determined to strengthen his home city of Florence, Machiavelli promoted his idea of displacing the usual foreign mercenaries by a militia drawn from the people themselves. Missions to Pope Julius II, and across the Alps to Germany, produced his perceptive reports on the strength of the enemies of Florence and the invaders of Italy. He commanded his militia successfully in the capture of Pisa and in defense of Florence against the invaders. In the volatile wars of the city-states his patron the gonfalonier (chief magistrate) Soderini was removed, and in 1512, when the Medici returned to power in Florence, Machiavelli lost his place in the government. The Medici imprisoned and tortured him on suspicion of conspiracy, but he gave no false confession.

Having tried unsuccessfully to win the favor of the Medici, Machiavelli retreated to his family property near Florence where he wrote his influential books. He had been well baptized in the currents of political power. To his friend Francesco Vettori at the papal court in Rome in a familiar letter, he recounted the new delights of his life with books in his study.

> On the threshold I slip off my day's clothes with their mud and dirt, put on my royal and curial robes, and enter, decently accoutred, the ancient courts of men of old, where I am welcomed kindly and fed on that fare which is mine alone, and for which I was born: where I am not ashamed to address them and ask them the reasons for their action, and they reply considerately; and for two hours I forget all my cares, I know no more trouble, death loses its terrors: I am utterly translated in their company.

We owe Machiavelli's passionate and illuminating primers of political science to his retreat from active politics during his fourteen-year exile on that farm outside Florence. If he had been a more successful politician, the literature of modern Seekers in political science would be much poorer.

He wrote his short book, *Il Principe* (The Prince), in a few months in 1513. It was dedicated to Lorenzo de' Medici (the Magnificent), presented to him, and circulated in manuscript. His long work, his *Discourses* on the first ten books of Livy, was written over those many years of retreat. He was well aware that he was on a new track, as he explains in his introduction:

Although the envious nature of men, so prompt to blame and so slow to praise, makes the discovery and introduction of any new principles and systems as dangerous almost as the exploration of unknown seas and continents, yet, animated by that desire which impels me to do what may prove for the common benefit of all, I have resolved to open a new route, which has not yet been followed by any one, and may prove difficult and troublesome.

In the last chapter of *The Prince,* "Exhortation to Liberate Italy from the Barbarians," Machiavelli gives us a clue to the new purpose he sees taking shape in modern history. The strategy of power that he describes will not be for its own sake but to fulfill a nation. It was said that "it was necessary in order that the power of Moses should be displayed that the people of Israel should be slaves in Egypt." Similarly, Machiavelli ventures, "in order that the might of an Italian genius might be recognized, it was necessary that Italy should be reduced to her present condition, and that she should be more enslaved than the Hebrews, more oppressed than the Persians, and more scattered than the Athenians; without a head, without order, beaten, despoiled, lacerated, and overrun, and that she should have suffered ruin of every kind." He calls on Lorenzo de' Medici and his "illustrious house" "to follow those great men who redeemed their countries" so "in order to be able with Italian prowess to defend the country from foreigners." He saw the nation as a way of organized liberation from alien dominion. The modern state in Italy that Machiavelli glimpsed was not to become real until the nineteenth century. Three centuries earlier he had prescribed ways to create and preserve such a nation-state.

The Italian peninsula in his day, split into numerous small states whose lives were complicated by the papal reach for power, was again and again overrun by French, German, Spanish, and Swiss armies. The tiny states, trying to defend themselves with mercenaries, lacked the power to repel the invaders. It is no wonder, then, that Machiavelli saw the primary "aim or thought" of the Prince to be "war and its organization and discipline." And that he should foresee the "redeeming" of Italy in a strong, centralized state, defended by militias of its own people. So Machiavelli's classic guide to national power came out of the desperate confusion of the numerous warring states of Renaissance

Italy. The Italians needed his insights. But even with them, his Italy would be among the last of the great modern nations of Europe. "This barbarous domination stinks in the nostrils of everyone." What Machiavelli provided, and what his country wanted, was not a political theory but political science and technology. He offered not a theory of the state but a manual for creating and preserving a state. No other part of Europe more desperately needed his prescriptions for political community.

A passionate pursuer of experience, he greatly admired the ancient Roman republic. And in his sprawling *Discourses* on Livy's Roman history he reveals the special strengths of the government of the Roman republic—the balance of forces of the tribunes, the consuls, the Senate, and the people. In his rambling, suggestive exploration of the strengths and weaknesses of ancient society, he always has an eye on the recent experience of Florence and of Italy. So he cannot underestimate the power of religion, "the most necessary and assured support of any civil society." And he sees ancient Roman society held together by religion. "The people of Florence are far from considering themselves ignorant and benighted, and yet Brother Girolamo Savonarola succeeded in persuading them that he held converse with God. I will not pretend to judge whether it was true or not, for we must speak with all respect of so great a man; but I may well say that an immense number believed it, without having seen any extraordinary manifestations that should have made them believe it."

So Machiavelli offers us an incisive chapter on "the importance of giving religion a prominent influence in a state, and how Italy was ruined because she failed in this respect through conduct of the Church of Rome. . . . We Italians then owe to the Church of Rome and to her priests our having become irreligious and bad; but we owe her a still greater debt, and one that will be the cause of our ruin, namely that the Church has kept and still keeps our country divided. And certainly a country can never be united and happy, except when it obeys wholly one government, whether a republic or a monarchy, as is the case in France and in Spain; and the sole cause why Italy is not in the same condition and is not governed by either one republic or one sovereign is the Church; for having acquired and holding a temporal dominion, yet she has never had sufficient power or courage to enable her to seize the rest of the country, and make herself sole sovereign of all Italy."

Machiavelli laments that while jurists and physicians in his time drew on the experience of the ancients, "yet to found a republic, maintain states, to govern a kingdom, organize an army, conduct a war, dispense justice, and extend empires, you will find neither prince, nor republic, nor captain, nor citizen, who has recourse to the examples of antiquity!" The main reason for this, he said, was less the weakness of education than "the evils caused by the proud indolence which prevails in most of the Christian states, and to the lack of real knowledge of history. . . . Thus the majority of those who read it take pleasure only in the variety of the events which history relates, without ever thinking of imitating the noble actions, deeming that not only difficult, but impossible; as though heaven, the sun, the elements, and men had changed the order of their motions and power, and were different from what they were in ancient times." So in exploring ancient Rome he draws from "the variety of events" lessons for those who would transform the chaos of Italy in his day into a unified expression of "the might of an Italian genius." His *Discourses* offer simple prescriptions for princes, republics, captains, and citizens toward that grand end, but not until three centuries had passed, in the age of Mazzini (1805–1872), had his hopes for a unified republican Italy, liberated from foreign dominion, begun to be realized.

24

John Locke Defines the Limits of Knowledge and of Government

The creators of dogma and champions of absolutes have a clear advantage before the bar of history. They offer attractive banners and clear targets. It is not as easy to give historic stature to the apostle of experience and of the modern liberal spirit John Locke. His life, buffeted by the winds of everyday politics, is lacking in drama or romance. His ideas were not strikingly original or subtle. His style was prosaic. So his career and his writings would illustrate the paradox of liberal thought. Openness to grand new ideas, the tradition of tolerant institutions, would be a by-product of the compromises of society's daily problems, rather than of the sharp-edged visions of systems of philosophy. This man who provided a modern epistemology and leading ideas for democratic revolutions is one of the least systematic of the great social thinkers of modern times. Paradoxically, this prophet of revolutions would be a philosopher of limits. Yet if any modern thinker merits the title of a latter-day Aristotle, it is probably John Locke. He, too, offered ways of thinking equally applicable to science and society, ever ready to be arbitrated by common sense.

Born in 1632, son of a country attorney who had fought in the English Civil War on the side of Parliament, John Locke received the most conventional formal education. After Westminster School he took his B.A. at Christ Church College, Oxford (1656), which was still dominated by scholastic methods. Though his college offered advantages to those in orders, after reflection he decided not to become a clergyman.

His informal education awakened him to the new experiences of his age and encouraged him to seek a this-worldly solace. His growing interest in science was casually sparked by his providential contact with two of the most lively scientists of the day—the physicist Robert Boyle (1627–1691) and the physician Thomas Sydenham (1624–1689). Both provided antidotes to the scholastic methods still dominating the university. Not attached to any college, Boyle made his house on High Street in Oxford a laboratory and meeting place for experimental scientists whom he stimulated and encouraged. His air pumps (devised with the aid of Robert Hooke) made possible Boyle's Law, and he showed how to make the barometer into a weather indicator. Passionately empirical and independent, Boyle had "purposely refrained" until he was thirty from reading Descartes's works or Bacon's *Novum organum* "that I might not be prepossessed with any theory or principles till I had spent some time in trying what things themselves would incline me to think." Locke's warm friendship with Boyle lasted till Boyle's death.

After a brief tour as secretary to the British diplomatic mission in Brandenburg, Locke returned to Oxford to his experimental interests, and the influence of the eminent physician Thomas Sydenham, "the English Hippocrates," a pioneer in clinical medicine and the treatment of smallpox and malaria. He became Sydenham's intimate, and the doctor praised Locke's intelligence as having "few equals and no superiors" in his time. Sydenham so bitterly opposed the professional dogmas that he was excluded from the College of Physicians. He believed the function of a physician to be "industrious investigation of the history of diseases, and of the effect of remedies, as shown by the only true teacher, experience." Sharing this view, Locke—still without a medical degree—became a practicing physician.

It was as a physician that Locke began his momentous association with Anthony Ashley Cooper, first earl of Shaftesbury (1621–1683). A leading Parliamentary figure in the Civil War, Cooper was one of the commissioners sent by the House of Commons to invite Charles II to resume the throne. And he sponsored legislation to grant toleration to Protestant Dissenters. Cooper brought Locke into his large household as staff physician, but Locke soon became counselor in politics as well. The affinity of their thinking strengthened Locke in his liberal attitudes. Both favored a constitutional monarchy, the Protestant succession, civil liberty, and religious toleration. Locke also enjoyed the spectacle of rising commerce and flourishing trade with the colonies, which he identified with toleration and a more open society. The example of Holland showed how toleration could nourish commerce, and how both could nourish culture. Locke was made secretary of Cooper's group to promote trade with America, and he served as secretary of the newly founded Council of Trade and Plantations. Just as Boyle and Sydenham put Locke in the vanguard of new experience in the world of nature, so

Anthony Ashley Cooper kept him in close touch with new currents in government and commerce.

Remarkably, none of these practical concerns distracted Locke from wider speculations that would place him in the vanguard of Seekers. Somehow these experiences stimulated him to pursue the large questions of philosophy and political theory, which made him a prophet of the English empirical spirit. Locke's checkered active life as he shared the volatile political career of Anthony Ashley Cooper delayed the leisure needed for his works of philosophy and political theory, but enriched his understanding. In his early years at Oxford, Locke had been stimulated to do his most important work when he explored problems of philosophy and science in regular meetings in his chamber with five or six friends. These meetings, he explained in the Introductory Epistle to his *Essay Concerning Human Understanding,* while "discoursing on a subject very remote from this, found themselves at a stand by the difficulties that arose on every side." Locke decisively led them "to examine our own abilities and see what objects our understandings were or were not fitted to deal with." The group agreed that Locke had hit on the basic question—the limits of human knowledge.

Out of this casual beginning arose the work that would give Locke his repute as the philosopher of modern revolutions. By 1671 Locke had begun making drafts of his *Essay.* Four years in France would have as decisive an effect on his thinking as Locke himself would have on the French Voltaire a half century later. There he became acquainted through lectures with the ideas of the French philosopher Pierre Gassendi (1592–1655), who had been a friend of Galileo and Kepler, and had attacked the ideas of both Aristotle and Descartes, urging a return to the Epicurean emphasis on sense experience. Locke had lost his powerful English patron when Shaftesbury, who had been tried for treason, after acquittal fled to Holland. In 1683 Locke, too, fled to Holland, where he found the tolerant commercial atmosphere congenial and made new friends. His five years in Holland gave him the leisure to draw together his thoughts and prepare for publication. In 1688 when Princess Mary crossed to England to be crowned queen beside William of Orange as king, Locke was in her party. He retired to the house in Essex of his friends Sir Francis and Lady Masham. There as guru of the Whigs he continued to counsel the leaders of Parliament, and saw the fulfillment of the bloodless Glorious Revolution that would be a basis of Western liberal societies in the next centuries. For England it meant a constitutional monarchy with Parliament supreme, the rule of law and an independent judiciary, and freedom of speech and the press.

Displacing theology by philosophy, Locke sought not a system of truths but something more modest—a definition of the limits of human knowledge. His political ideas, too, were a by-product of his refutation of divine absolutes. And his thoughts on education were simply letters of advice to a good friend on how to raise his son. Locke's notions of toleration were based on his view of government as the protector of all persons and material interests. With some reason, detractors alleged that Locke favored toleration (as he saw it in Holland) because it "tended to the advancement of trade and commerce."

Over all hovered Locke's cautionary spirit and hostility to absolute government along with all other absolutes. "We should do well to commiserate our mutual ignorance," he warned in his *Essay Concerning Human Understanding,* "and endeavor to remove it in all the gentle and fair ways of information; and not instantly treat others ill, as obstinate and perverse, because they will not renounce their own, and receive our opinions." So "our assent ought to be regulated"—not by the dictates of some imagined Truth, but only "by the grounds of probability."

Locke's efforts as Seeker for the proper ends of thought and of government were thus not the product of sudden insight or inspiration but developed over decades, in the bright light of the scientific and political experience of his day.

In an age replete with pioneer scientists, Locke was alert to the advances of science yet not unaware of the quibbles of theologians and the visions of mystics. While he was a patient and loyal friend of "the incomparable Mr. Newton" (as Locke called him), it is not certain that Locke had a firm grasp of Newton's *Principia.* But the broad interests of both Locke and Newton in religion and science brought them together. Newton shared with Locke his critical thoughts on the New Testament texts of John and Timothy and looked forward to Locke's further "judgment upon some of my mystical fancies."

When "the commonwealth of learning" boasted such "master-builders" as Boyle, Sydenham, Huygens, and Newton, Locke explained in his Epistle to the Reader of his *Essay,* "it is ambition enough to be employed as an under-labourer in clearing the ground a little, and removing some of the rubbish that lies in the way to knowledge." With that modest profession, Locke sounded the leitmotif of the modern Seeker.

Locke's *Essay Concerning Human Understanding* (1690–1700), the constantly revised product of his last thirty years, thus set out to define the limits of human knowledge, so man could economize his efforts by ventures into the possible. "If we can find out how far the understanding can extend its view, how far it has faculties to attain certainty, and in what cases it can only judge and guess, we may learn to content ourselves with what is attainable by us in this state." The modesty and the limits of his project were displayed even in his title. This was no "treatise" but a mere "essay" or trial. Montaigne (1533–1592) had given the word French literary form and meaning, and in this sense the word had only lately come into the English language. The tentative spirit of the "essay" and the hope to reach beyond the learned was already expressed in Francis Bacon's *Essays* (1597–1625). "Essays" would have increasing vogue in English literature—for Addison, Pope, Macaulay, Arnold, Lamb, and countless others. Locke's focus, too, was not on Truth but only on "human understanding." His day did not know our distinction between the philosopher and the scientist. Both shared Locke's objective—"Nothing but the true knowledge of things."

Incidentally, Locke expressed another modern obsession—not with the empyrean Truth to be known, but with the idiosyncrasies and vagaries of the knowing self. Here was a new, more ruthless, and more punishing application of the ancient Greek motto "Know thyself." Locke revealed anew how modern man felt imprisoned in the self. The first "rubbish" that Locke set out to clear away from our paths to knowledge was the notion of "innate" knowledge—or ideas supposed to be inborn and universal. So he opens his *Essay* with an attack. If there were "some primary notions . . . as it were stamped upon the mind of men, which the soul receives in its very first being, and brings into the world with it," all men would have these same ideas. But, he argued, there are no ideas that are universally assented to—not even the idea of God. Innate ideas naturally had a special appeal to preachers and teachers. Such notions "eased the lazy from the pains of search and stopped the inquiry of the doubtful concerning all that was once styled innate." A pioneer in the sociology of knowledge, Locke showed how liberation from the notion of innate ideas freed each man to do his own thinking. The path from the empirical mind to a liberal society was laid open.

Then Locke offers his own deceptively simple answer to the mind's source of knowledge. "Whence comes it by that vast store, which the busy and boundless fancy of man has painted on it with an almost endless variety? Whence has it all the materials of reason and knowledge? To this I answer in one word, from EXPERIENCE; in that all our knowledge is founded, and from that it ultimately derives itself." This antidote to absolutes offered everyone a personal arena of independence.

Though experience was the source of knowledge, according to Locke, the *objects* of thought were always ideas. And so, paradoxically, Locke's way of seeking was both the Way of Experience and the Way of Ideas. Locke saw no contradiction here because his two sources of ideas were both forms of experience. One was *sensation,* or external experience, those "sensible qualities" that external objects convey into the mind. And the other was *reflection,* or internal experience—"the perception of the operations of our own minds within us, as it is employed about the ideas it has got, which operations, when the soul comes to reflect on and consider, do furnish the understanding with another set of ideas which could not be had from things without."

Locke significantly concludes his *Essay*—Book IV: Of Knowledge and Opinion—with miscellaneous observations on the degrees of knowledge and on a resounding cautionary note. Rounding out his Way of Ideas, he describes Knowledge as the perception of the agreement or disagreement of two ideas. The perception of this agreement or disagreement he calls *intuitive knowledge.* "We can have knowledge no farther than we have ideas," so he warns against unfounded universal propositions, the facile wisdom of maxims, and the extravagant uses of "self-evidences." Not surprisingly, in one of his least original and least persuasive chapters he piously asserts, "We are capable of knowing certainly that there is a God." But beware of "*enthusiasm,* which laying by reason, would set up revelation without it. Whereby in effect it takes away both reason and revelation, and substitutes in the room of it the ungrounded fancies of a man's own brain."

It was as an amateur—not as a professional philosopher—that Locke had come to philosophy. While Locke called his work on philosophy a mere "Essay," on government he wrote "two Treatises." Both are concerned with limits—the *Essay* on the limits of human knowledge, the *Treatises* on the proper limits of government. The *Two Treatises*, as Peter Laslett has shown, were not written after the fact to "justify" the Revolution of 1688. They originated as early as 1679, and were, in fact, a demand for a revolution still to happen, not a rationalization of revolution that had already happened.

The *Treatises*, like the *Essay*, begin with a negative. Just as "innate ideas" provide a foil against which to outline the true sources and limits of our understanding, so now in the first *Treatise*, "The False Principles and Foundation," the Divine Right of Kings (in the writings of Sir Robert Filmer and his followers), provides Locke's point of departure. The Second *Treatise* then is "An Essay concerning the True Original, Extent and End of Civil-Government." It is surprising that a work so ill proportioned and labored, in a style so awkward, flat, and uninspired could itself have become an inspiration and justification of great Western political revolutions in succeeding centuries. It is the persuasive simplicity of the ideas that explains the enduring power of the work.

The power and originality of the Second *Treatise*—a gospel for Jefferson and the makers of the American Revolution of 1776—was its novel emphasis on *limits*. Just as the *Essay* was an antidote to absolutes in thought—against "enthusiasts" and champions of innate ideas—so the *Treatises* were an antidote to absolutes in government. Earlier political philosophers had enchanted with their visions of political perfection—Plato's *Republic*, More's *Utopia*, and Hobbes's *Leviathan*. They all had the appeal of a constructive poetic imagination. Locke's *Treatise* on *limits*—the proper and necessary limits of civil government—lacked the poetry of the grand vision. But it offered a commonsense prosaic frame for the Seeker, a plan for community where all could make their personal sallies.

Locke's argument, though not beautifully logical or systematic, was appealing. Few of Locke's ideas were original, but the form that he gave to mostly familiar ideas was simple and intelligible enough to encourage revolutions, to justify revolutions, and to help reshape institutions after revolutions. These cataclysmic possibilities may not have been entirely unimagined by Locke. He not only refused publicly to avow his authorship when the *Two Treatises* was published. He actually acted irritated when good friends "accused" him of authorship and demanded his confirmation.

In his *Two Treatises* Locke did not appeal especially to the facts of English history. But he did appeal to all human history, what he called the universal experience of mankind. He based his theory of government on a parable describing how government first came into being. He argued that it was not fair to object to his account of the origins of government just because there were no examples in recorded history of its happening in the way he suggested.

> And if we may not suppose Men ever to have been in a State of Nature, because we hear not much of them in such a State, we may as well suppose the Armies of Salmanasser or Xerxes were never Children, because we hear little of them, till they were Men, and imbodied in Armies. Government is everywhere antecedent to Records, and Letters seldom come in amongst a People, till a long continuation of Civil Society has, by other more necessary Arts provided for their Safety, Ease, and Plenty. And then they begin to look after the History of their Founders, and search into their original, when they have out-lived the memory of it.

In that early preliterate era before government, men everywhere lived in a State of Nature. And, as Josoph Acosta's history of the Indies had recently shown, the people of Peru had once actually lived with "no Government at all." Men were then free to live as they pleased, "but by consent were all equal, till by the same consent they set Rulers over themselves. So that their Politick Societies all began from a voluntary Union, and the mutual agreement of Men freely acting in the choice of their Governours, and forms of Government." All depended on the original "State of Nature."

If Locke's history (or prehistory!) was speculative, it nevertheless purported to be history. And his explanation was a momentous departure from earlier ways of justifying government. Like Filmer's Divine Right, those accounts generally had traced the origins of political power to God's delegation of authority to sacred persons. Such authority could be revoked only by its donor, who was God. But Locke's civil government was wholly a matter of this world, founded in human convenience, in the people's need and desire to preserve their lives, liberty, and property. These agents of the people, creatures of the people's consent, then held their authority within the strict limits under which it had been given. So, if a government ceased to satisfy its earthly creators, its authority was dissolved. Experience, the foundation of Locke's knowledge, was equally the basis of his civil government. To that earliest experience he traced majority rule.

25

Voltaire's Summons to Civilization

When we talk of the history of "civilization," we are speaking in a thoroughly modern vocabulary. For "Civilization" is our legacy from the French Enlightenment—the Age of Voltaire. It is our inheritance from the way Voltaire (1694–1778) and other French *philosophes* saw human achievements (and weaknesses) in their time.

At 9:30 A.M. on November 1, 1755, an earthquake shook Lisbon, a commercial center of the continent, killing some fifteen thousand people and leaving the city in ruins. In that catastrophe the wise men of Portugal and Europe saw the wrath of God—His Providence in punishing a profligate people's sins. They even saw meaning in the few sacred images that had been spared. And they saw strangely confirmed the devout dogma of Alexander Pope's recent (1732–34) *Essay on Man:*

> All Nature is but art, unknown to thee;
> All chance, direction, which thou canst not see;
> All discord, harmony not understood;
> All partial evil, universal good:
> And, spite of pride, in erring reason's spite,
> One truth is clear: Whatever IS, is RIGHT.

Voltaire the Seeker promptly refuted that pious optimism in his long poem *The Lisbon Earthquake: An Inquiry into the Maxim, "Whatever is, is right."* A few years later, Voltaire's classic tale depicted his mock-hero Candide with his companion Pangloss, the world's greatest philosopher, in Lisbon on that disastrous morning.

Pangloss seized the opportunity to console the dying inhabitants "by assuring them that things could not be otherwise. 'For,' said he, 'all this is for the best; for, if there is a volcano at Lisbon, it cannot be anywhere else; for it is impossible that things should not be where they are; for all is well.' " Then, as Voltaire reports in *Candide,* the wise men of Lisbon, in an earnest effort to prevent another earthquake, "could discover no more efficacious way . . . than by giving the people a splendid *auto da fé.* It was decided by the University of Coimbra that the sight of several persons being slowly burned in great ceremony is an infallible secret for preventing earthquakes." As part of this entertaining ceremony the irrepressible Pangloss was hanged and Candide was flogged to the rhythm of lovely plainsong music. In his Preface to his poem on the earthquake, Voltaire maintained "that ancient and sad truth that there is evil upon earth." "If the various evils by which man is overwhelmed end in general good, all civilized nations have been wrong in endeavoring to trace out the origin of moral and physical evil."

Voltaire is most widely quoted for a tragic view of history—"that history in general is a collection of crimes, follies, and misfortunes, among which we now and then meet with a few virtues, and some happy times; as we sometimes see a few scattered huts in a barren desert." But in retrospect, this pessimism is not what Voltaire the Seeker has added to our mosaic of belief. Though a passionate skeptic and enemy of religious dogma and fanaticism, Voltaire should be remembered as a long-term optimist. A hallmark of this optimism is Voltaire's notion of "civilization." Surprisingly, civilization in its modern sense does not enter our historical thought until Voltaire's day, and is in large part due to what he and his fellow *philosophes* saw and wrote about in their time.

On March 23, 1772, James Boswell reports, he tried to persuade Dr. Johnson to admit the noun "civilization" in our modern sense into his landmark *Dictionary of the English Language*. Still Dr. Johnson would admit the word only in the technical legal sense of "A law, act of justice, or judgment, which renders a criminal process civil."

> He would not admit *civilization,* but only *civility.* With great deference to him, I thought *civilization,* from *to civilize,* better in the sense opposed to barbarity, than civility.

In the lexicon of Voltaire's French Enlightenment, civilization was coming to be a name for the enlightened state of which all mankind was capable. In his own lifetime, Voltaire was witnessing in France a climax of civilization and in Russia he was seeing the process by which civilization came to other countries.

The ancient Greeks, too, had distinguished themselves from the Barbarians. But for them the Barbarians (*Barbaroi*) were people who spoke any language other than Greek. Only after the Persian wars did "Barbarism" denote the condition of all vulgar and uncultivated people. This was the Greek way of expressing the superiority of Greeks to all other nations. Originally they included the Romans, with other non-Hellenic people, among the Barbarians. But after the Roman conquest of Greece, the Romans eventually took a leaf from Greek chauvinism and used "barbarian" to describe nations outside the orbit of Greco-Roman language and culture. Cicero (106–43 B.C.) used "barbarians" to describe all savage, rude, or uncultivated peoples.

For Voltaire, then, barbarism was no chauvinistic term of contempt. Instead it simply described the failure of any people to fulfill the possibilities of all humankind—"that reason and human industry will continue to make further progress." He was a bold young man of twenty-one at Louis XIV's death. Voltaire's brilliant *Age of Louis XIV,* on which he spent some twenty years and which he called his lifework, was seen by some as a work of sheer French patriotism. But for Voltaire it described a climax of the human spirit (*l'esprit humain*). The Age of Louis XIV was the latest and greatest of the "four happy ages when the arts were brought to perfection and which, marking an era of the greatness of the human mind, are an example to posterity."

Civilization, then, according to Voltaire, was no monopoly of France, nor of any one people or language. The first of the three earlier happy ages was classical Greece in the time of "Philip and Alexander, or rather of Pericles, Demosthenes, Aristotle, Plato, Apelles, Phidias, Praxiteles . . . the rest of the known world being in a barbarous state." The second was the era of Caesar and Augustus, "distinguished by the names of Lucretius, Cicero, Livy, Virgil, Horace, Ovid, Varro and Vitruvius." The third was the Renaissance, "the hour of Italy's glory." "The arts, for ever transplanted from Greece to Italy, fell on favourable ground, where they flourished immediately. France, England, Germany, and Spain, in their turn, desired the possession of these fruits." "The fourth age is that which we call the age of Louis XIV; and it is perhaps of the four the one which most nearly approaches perfection." Enriched by the earlier discoveries, it accomplished more than the other three together. "All the arts, it is true, did not progress further than they had under the Medici, under Augustus or under Alexander; but human reason in general was brought to perfection." Finally "rational philosophy" came to light and spread its beneficent influence to England, Germany, Russia, and a revived Italy.

With his *Age of Louis XIV* (1751) Voltaire earned his title as "the first historian of civilization." He named his work after the Sun King of Versailles, for, he wrote, "no single person could epitomize the high level that European civilization had reached in the late seventeenth century better than Louis XIV." Voltaire's *Charles XII* (1730) had focused on a few leading figures, mostly military and political. In this later work, too, he gave ample accounts of Louis's diplomatic and military exploits, salted with anecdotes of the court and the condition of Europe. And he puzzled and piqued critics by abandoning the simple chronological for a topical treatment. A third of his pages, which sum up the work, are finally devoted to social and fiscal institutions, laws, science, literature, and the arts, religion, and ecclesiastical affairs. He includes a brisk polemic chapter illustrating his "terrible reproach" that the Christian Church had caused that "blood should have been shed for so many centuries by men who proclaimed the god of peace. Paganism knew no such fury. It covered the world in darkness, but shed hardly a drop of blood save that of beasts." "The spirit of dogma bred the madness of religious wars in the minds of men." In a surprising final chapter, Voltaire savors the irony of how Dominican opposition to Chinese ceremonies for reverencing ancestors led to the banning of Christianity in China.

Voltaire surveys the achievements of Molière, Corneille, Racine, Boileau, and La Fontaine, the painting of Poussin, Colbert's Academy of Painting, the Academy of Science, and the countless minor advances with "useful arts." Revealing his ecumenical view of Europe as a community of civilization, he offers a chapter on "the Useful Arts and Sciences *in Europe* during the Reign of Louis XIV." The *Age of Louis XIV* was planned and arranged (in Gustave Lanson's phrase) "as an apotheosis of the human spirit." With his customary elegance Voltaire summed up what his concept of civilization added to familiar ways of thinking about history:

> Of those who have commanded battalions and squadrons, only the names remain. The human race has nothing to show for a hundred battles that have been waged. But the great men I speak to you about have prepared pure and lasting *pleasures* for men yet to be born. A canal lock uniting two seas, a painting by Poussin, a beautiful tragedy, a newly discovered truth—these are things a thousand times more precious than all the annals of the court or all

the accounts of military campaigns. You know that, with me, great men come first and heroes last.

I call great men all those who have excelled in creating what is useful or agreeable. The plunderers of the provinces are merely heroes.

Voltaire's personal experience proved to him that the progress of the human spirit (*l'esprit humain*) carried promise for all enlightened mankind. "Voltairism," John Morley observes, "may be said to have begun from the flight of its founder from Paris to London." It was "the decisive hegira." Voltaire's two and a half years in England (May 1726–February 1729) inspired him with admiration for "that intellectual and fearless nation," which he soon expressed with his usual irony and eloquence in *Letters Concerning the English Nation* (1733). In these essays he succinctly celebrated some distinctive triumphs of civilized enlightenment in England: the Parliament; the Quakers; inoculation against smallpox; the physics and optics of the adorable Newton ("who was buried like a king who had benefited his subjects"); the spirit of toleration; and the persons of rank who cultivate learning. Voltaire's hegira showed how nations could enrich one another, and share their civilization. That experience, if no other, would have cured Voltaire of French chauvinism. It had no such effect in France. Under its title of *Lettres Philosophiques* his brief volume was condemned on June 10, 1734, by the Parlement of Paris to be lacerated and burned by the hangman as "likely to inspire a license of thought most dangerous to religion and civil order."

But how did barbarous peoples become civilized? Voltaire saw a melodramatic example in his own lifetime. Russia, he observed, occupied the whole of northern Asia and Europe from the frontiers of China to the borders of Poland and Sweden. "Yet the existence of this immense country was not even realized by Europe before the time of the Czar Peter. The Russians were less civilized than the Mexicans at the time of their discovery by Cortez; born the slaves of masters as barbarous as themselves, they were sunk deep in ignorance, and unacquainted with the arts and sciences, and so insensible of their use that they had no industry."

Yet Voltaire would actually see Russia become "civilized." The process and the hero, Peter the Great, fascinated him. In his *History of Charles XII,* he had given almost as much attention to Peter as to the announced subject of the book. "If I were younger, I would make myself Russian," he was reported to have told Catherine the Great, who herself had actually gone through that process. To participate in analyzing a great barbarous nation was a tempting prospect for Voltaire. And he dramatized the encounter of cultures in his poem "The Russian in Paris" (1760). In 1744, when he had proposed to write a biography of the civilizer of Russia, Peter the Great, the reigning empress of Russia, Elizabeth, offered to provide him with all the documents. Then, as he proceeded, in order to avoid emphasizing Peter's personal weaknesses, he refocused his work under the title *History of the Empire of Russia under Peter the Great* (1759). In this work his praise of the civilizer of Russia was so extravagant that it irritated his correspondent Frederick the Great of Prussia. After Frederick saw the book, he stopped writing to Voltaire. Only when Voltaire learned that Frederick had been ill did he succeed in resuming the correspondence.

Voltaire reports in detail how Peter "civilized" Russia. How, for example, "in a desolate district," Peter built Petersburg in 1703 to be his "window into Europe," which he made his national capital in 1712, and which he made a lively center of culture. "The sciences, which in other parts have been the slow product of centuries, were, by his care, introduced into his empire in full perfection." The climax of Voltaire's *History of Charles XII* is Peter's victory at the decisive battle of Poltava (1709) "between the two most famous monarchs that were then in the world . . . the one [Charles XII] glorious for having given away dominions; the other for having civilized his own." Alert to the ironies of history, Voltaire reminds us, "He civilized his people, but remained savage himself. He carried out his sentences with his own hands, and at a debauch at table he displayed his skill in cutting off heads."

Civilization, in Voltaire's eyes, is an achievement of all mankind, not just of the Europeans. And in his longest work, his *Essay on the Customs and the Spirit of Nations* (1756), a pioneer effort at an Enlightenment universal history, he reaches all across the globe. He abandons the biblical chronology and Bossuet's eloquent espousal of divine Providence. Beginning with geography and the different races of men, through "the Usages and Sentiments Common to Almost All Ancient

Peoples," Voltaire gives way to the Chaldeans, Indians, and Chinese—"the first nations to become civilized." He sees the piecemeal progress of civilization. "Even in these uncivilized times [thirteenth and fourteenth centuries in Europe], certain useful inventions were made, the fruit of the mechanical inventiveness which nature has given to men and which is quite independent of their scientific or philosophical knowledge." Among these in the fifteenth century, his surprising examples are the invention of spectacles to aid eyesight, then windmills, faience, glass, and mirrors. But he notes that the compass, paper, and printing were still hidden in the future.

As Voltaire recounts it, the progress of civilization is seldom easy. The king of France, Charles V, who collected about nine hundred volumes a hundred years before the Vatican library was founded by Nicholas V, "tried in vain to encourage talents; the soil was not prepared for these exotic fruits. Some of the wretched compositions of these days have been collected, but this is like hoarding a heap of stones from some ancient hovel when one lives in a palace." Voltaire concludes his universal history by reminding us of the task of the historian—"to give posterity an account of all the misfortunes which man has suffered, to describe all the pillage, the crimes, the losses, the ineffective measures and the inadequate resources." All other civilizations serve Voltaire as sticks to beat the cruel fanaticism of religion in his age. He finally acknowledges those who accused him of "having painted crimes, above all those of religion, in too somber colors, and of having made fanaticism execrate and superstition ridiculous." Voltaire declares his fault is that he has not said enough. "It is clear that there are still unfortunates who are the victims of this spiritual disease and who are afraid to be cured." Still the undaunted Voltaire "cannot but believe that reason and human industry will continue to make further progress."

In the idea of civilization, Voltaire encourages us with hope for the common possibilities of the human spirit everywhere. He observes in his *Philosophical Dictionary*:

> The use of history consists above all in the comparison which a statesman or an ordinary citizen can make between the laws and customs of other countries and those of his own; this is what leads modern nations to emulate each other in the arts, in agriculture and in commerce.
>
> The great faults of the past are also very useful in many ways; the crimes

and misfortunes of history cannot be too frequently pondered on, for whatever people say, it is possible to prevent both.

While Voltaire was chronicling the triumph of civilization in the France of Louis XIV and witnessing the rise of civilization in Russia, his France saw the building of a magnificent literary monument to civilization, a witness to the powers of collaboration of an enlightened people. The *Encyclopédie ou Dictionnaire Raisonné des Sciences, des Arts et des Métiers,* edited by Voltaire's friend Denis Diderot, had begun as the ambitious commercial venture of the French bookseller-publisher Le Breton, who owned the largest printing house in Paris. He planned to publish a French translation of the Scottish Ephraim Chambers's *Cyclopaedia, or Universal Dictionary of the Arts and Sciences,* which had appeared in 1728. But when Le Breton put his project in the hands of d'Alembert and Diderot, it became a monument far overshadowing its model. The twenty-eight volumes (seventeen of text; eleven of illustrations; 1751–65), covering all knowledge and the arts, 71,818 articles and 2,885 plates, was the work of the leading French thinkers of the age. It included some of the best essays of Voltaire and articles by Rousseau, Turgot, d'Holbach, and Quesnay. It was both a compendium of the latest knowledge and a manifesto of the Enlightenment. Its comprehensive view of the world came to be called Encyclopedism.

There were some two thousand subscribers to the first volume, and the subscribers multiplied with each volume despite (or because of) the increasing opposition of the authorities. Without doubt this was a dangerous—even explosive—book, for it urged readers to consult only reason and their own senses in place of the dictates of church and state. What the *Encyclopédie* offered was not just a point of view but the whole of knowledge. Traditional learning was treated as prejudice or superstition. Here was the harvest of new science in an age of brilliant scientists and Seekers—from the physics of Bernoulli to the natural history of Buffon, and the sociology of Quesnay. Its articles challenged the ideas on which the tottering *ancien régime* relied. Diderot's article on "Political Authority" degraded the authority of the king to the mere consent of the people. D'Holbach urged a constitutional monarchy. Rousseau espoused his subversive ideas of the general will. And articles on many subjects dissolved the Bourbon and Catholic dogmas.

Diderot's work was an omen of the revolution to come, which only the blind could fail to see. The king revoked the privilege of publishing the book in 1759. In that same year, too, Pope Clement XII put the *Encyclopédie* on the Index of Forbidden Books and warned all Catholics who owned the book to have it burned by a priest or face excommunication. The great intellectual monument of the age stood overwhelmingly condemned by the age's highest authorities. But it attested the enduring powers of "civilization" toward which Voltaire and other *philosophes* were collaborating.

26

Rousseau Seeks Escape

If a skillful dramatist had sought a foil for Voltaire, he could hardly have done better than to invent Jean-Jacques Rousseau (1712–1778), a Seeker who idealized the savage and believed that "a thinking man is a depraved animal." Rousseau, like Voltaire, purported to base his view of "civilization" on history. But while Voltaire founded his opinions on his work as a pioneer historian of civilization and the achievements of enlightened mankind, Rousseau sought his views in introspection. The same epoch that produced Voltaire's unexcelled paeans to civilization and man's power to enlighten himself and his neighbors produced Rousseau's influential polemics against civilization.

Rousseau, always the self-obsessed Seeker, proved adept at transforming his personal grievances into a philosophy of history. He was born "feeble and ill" into the repressed society of Geneva in 1712. His mother, niece of a Calvinist minister, died a few days after his birth. And his father, a watchmaker, citizen of Geneva, commonly beat Jean-Jacques, whom he blamed for the death of the boy's mother. Jean-Jacques was self-educated, mostly by the books in his father's workshop.

When Jean-Jacques was only ten his father left Geneva, and he was sent to live with a minister, Jean-Jacques Lambercier, and his family outside the city. His boyhood experience with Madame Lambercier revealed the masochism that stayed with him. After reporting in his *Confessions* that he enjoyed being spanked by Madame Lambercier, he naively asked: "Who would believe that this punishment received at the age of eight from the hands of a girl of thirty determined my tastes, my desires, my passions for the rest of my life?" Using his talent for melodrama to make his point, he even misstated their ages—he being eleven and she forty. Back in Geneva he was apprenticed to an engraver. But, mistreated by his master, he left Geneva for Annecy and Turin, where he was converted to Roman Catholicism.

Rousseau would spend much of the rest of his life as an intellectual and emotional vagabond—always seeking a *maman.* He seemed to have an uncanny appeal for women—especially married women. When he met Madame de Warens, who had left her husband, she soon became Rousseau's mistress and his patron. He earned his living as a tutor to a prominent family before going to Paris to publish his new scheme of musical notation.

After a brief tour in Venice as secretary to the French ambassador, with whom he quarreled, he returned to Paris. There he became friendly with Denis Diderot, and wrote the articles on music for the *Encyclopédie*. There, too, he was enamored of Thérèse Le Vasseur, a chambermaid at his hotel. The children he had by her were all sent to a foundling home, a not unusual procedure in those days in Paris. When he returned briefly to Geneva in 1754, he returned also to Calvinism. Instead of settling in Paris, he went to Montmorency, where Madame d'Epinay had lent him her country house, and there he devoted himself to writing. When his books were condemned by the Parlement of Paris, he fled again to Switzerland, then to England where he enjoyed the friendship and patronage of the philosopher David Hume. But when Rousseau's paranoia led him to suspect Hume of a plot against his life, he returned to France in 1767. To protect himself against these imagined "conspirators," he took an assumed name, "Renon." He wrote a plan to reform the government of Poland, he married Thérèse Le Vasseur, and he wrote the *Confessions,* which would be his most durable and widely read work. He died in 1778. His remains were moved to the Pantheon in Paris during the Revolution.

Rousseau's intellectual life was a saga of conflict between a need for discipline and a demand for freedom. He curiously resolved this conflict in his political theory, *The Social Contract* (1762), which would become a sacred text of the French Revolution of 1789. This populist dogma made the "General Will" of the people inalienable, indivisible, and infallible (pedantically distinguished from "the will of all"). So he designed a populist totalitarianism that has appealed to revolutionaries ever since, often with disastrous consequences.

With little information about man in the state of nature, which he idealized, Rousseau focused his lifelong polemic on the evils of civilization, of which he thought he had enough personal knowledge. He first secured public notice by his winning essay in the competition of the Dijon Academy (1750) on the question "Has the Restoration of the Arts and Sci-

ences had a purifying effect upon morals?" And this essay was well designed to shock. The arts, literature, and the sciences, he argued, "fling
garlands of flowers over the chains which weigh them down. They stifle
in men's breasts that sense of original liberty, for which they seem to
have been born; cause them to love their own slavery, and so make of
them what is called a civilized people. . . . It is not through stupidity that
the people have preferred other activities to those of the mind . . . useless
thinkers were lavish in their own praises, and stigmatized other nations
contemptuously as barbarians. . . . The arts and sciences owe their birth
to our vices. . . . Astronomy was born of superstition, eloquence of ambition, hatred, falsehood and flattery; geometry of avarice; physics of an
idle curiosity and even moral philosophy of human pride."

Rousseau rounded off his indictment of civilization by a "Discourse
on the Origin of Inequality," which disposed of any evils he had not yet
attributed to enlightenment—surprisingly dedicated (with explicit
sycophancy) to the Republic of Geneva. He seemed not to regret
the destined power of women to govern men. But he is eloquent on the
countless other inequalities born of civil society—of property and the
power to govern. "Man," he concludes, is "subject to very few evils not
of his own creation." "Man is naturally good but in Society finds profit
in the misfortunes of his neighbor." Contrary to vulgar prejudice,
Rousseau explains, man was not miserable in a state of nature, but was
in better health than he would ever be in civilized society. He needed no
medicine, for he had not yet suffered the weakness that all animals
show when they are domesticated. He was free, healthy, honest, and
happy, for he had not yet multiplied his needs or begun to suffer the inequality of civil society.

Rousseau's nostalgia for the state of nature, the foundation of his political philosophy, also shaped his philosophy of education. He explained at the opening of his *Émile* (1762):

> God makes all things good; man meddles with them and they become evil.
> He forces one soil to yield the products of another, one tree to bear an-
> other's fruit. He confuses and confounds time, places, and natural condi-
> tions. He mutilates his dog, his horses, and his slaves. He destroys and
> defaces all things; he loves all that is deformed and monstrous; he will have
> nothing as nature made it, not even man himself, who must learn his paces

like a saddle-horse, and be shaped to his master's taste like the trees in his garden.

For Rousseau, then, education would have to be a way not of instilling the ideals of civilization but rather of liberating the young from civilization and its evils.

Much of the program he described in his didactic novel *Émile* is what he calls "negative education," an antidote and inoculation against the pervasive evils of civilization. It has come to be called "The Child's Charter"—a basis for modern child psychology. And it would be the prospectus and statement of principles for "progressive education" in the United States, led by John Dewey (1859–1952), who conceived it as a way of bringing democracy into the classroom (*The School and Society,* 1899; *Democracy and Education,* 1916). The movement attended to the child's physical and emotional as well as his intellectual development, favored "learning by doing," and encouraged experimental and independent thinking. The teacher, then, aimed not at instilling a body of knowledge but at developing the pupil's own skill at learning from experience.

In *Émile* the child was to be kept from books—except one, *Robinson Crusoe,* which Rousseau called "the happiest treatise of natural education." "Children begin by being helped, end by being served," he warned. They become masters, using their tears as prayers. The teacher must guide without seeming to, must never use corporal punishment, but must provide situations in which the child can learn for himself. The teacher, too, must know the stages of a child's development and introduce subjects only when the child is emotionally prepared. At the age of twelve the pupil must learn a useful trade. "Émile must work like a peasant and think like a philosopher in order not to be as lazy as a savage." Not until the age of eighteen should Émile turn to moral science and religion, and then he can choose his religion. For "at an age when all is mystery there can be no mysteries properly speaking." The child must have compassion, "love those who have it, but fly from the pious believers." But also shun the philosophers ("angry wolves"), who are "ardent missionaries of atheism and very imperious dogmatics who will not endure without fury that one might think differently from them."

Just as Voltaire sought a common vision for all mankind, to be fulfilled in "civilization," of which the France of Louis XIV had provided
a model, so Rousseau, having witnessed the varied spectacle of war and
civilization in the enlightened Europe of his day, envisioned a liberated
mankind. It was only civilization—the arts and sciences and institutions—that separated men from one another and set them at war in pursuit of the unnecessary. If men would only somehow return to their
natural bliss they would be free to fulfill their human possibilities. But
what were these possibilities? Was there any way of knowing?
Rousseau was made the paradoxical patron of the guillotine of Reason
of the French Revolution to come. But he was also godfather of the liberated romantic imagination about to create a rich and fantastic new
legacy of arts and literature.

Among the surprising consequences of Rousseau's vagabond life
and encyclopedic writing was the role assigned to him in the early
twentieth century as the archenemy of the New Humanism. This American movement in the 1920s, of which Irving Babbitt (1865–1933) was
the popular spokesman, made the human elements of experience, embodied in the ancient classical tradition, the source of meaning, and opposed the appeal to nature or the supernatural. In his *Rousseau and
Romanticism* (1919) Babbitt described Rousseau's role as apostle of the
wild, romantic spirit. The New Humanists urged instead a seeking spirit
of restraint and proportion. They saw freedom as the "liberation from
outer constraints and subjection to inner law."

27

Jefferson's American Quest

In a happy coincidence Voltaire's Age of Enlightenment in Europe, which celebrated and explored the still-unfulfilled possibilities of civilization, saw a vast and fertile continent sparsely settled and little explored in America. This New World challenged Western Seekers to find new meanings in nature and in society, and stirred spokesmen for New World ways of seeking. Perhaps the most eloquent and effective of these was Thomas Jefferson (1743–1826). A leader of the Virginia planter aristocracy, and not entirely exempt from its attitudes, he gave enduring voice to the American quest for new forms of self-government. The American War for Independence drew on the constitution and laws of the mother country to justify the colonies' independence.

Jefferson the lawyer had expounded the right of the colonies to seek their own form of government in his *Summary View of the Rights of British America* (1774). And when the Continental Congress voted independence, Jefferson led the committee drafting its declaration. The Declaration of Independence, adopted on July 4, 1776, became a manifesto in the next centuries for the communal seeking of people across the world. The document, with wide appeal despite its form as a legal indictment, declared that "the history of the present King of Great Britain is a history of repeated injuries and usurpations, all having in direct object the establishment of an absolute Tyranny over these States." The crucial phrases that made this a credo for revolutionaries in later generations first affirmed the "self-evident" truths of man's "unalienable Rights" to "Life, Liberty and the pursuit of Happiness." Then it declared the revolutionary communal right of Seekers: "That whenever any Form of Government becomes destructive of these ends it is the Right of the People to alter or to abolish it, and institute new Government, laying its foundation on such principles and organizing its powers in such form, as to them shall seem most likely to effect their Safety and Happiness."

The Declaration of Independence was thus dual—both a classic declaration of the ends of government and a declaration of the communal right to seek forms of a government better suited to those ends. It proclaimed the right of "the people" to carry on their search. To this political quest Jefferson committed himself and his political partisans in the new nation.

And an auspicious time it was, too, for exploring the experience of a New World. Benjamin Franklin, in his circular letter of 1743 gathering the American Philosophical Society, reminded Americans that the time was ripe for a communal seeking of all that could be learned from nature and from earlier settlers in the New World. "The first Drudgery of Settling new colonies, which confines the attention of People to mere Necessaries, is now pretty well over," Franklin observed, "and there are many in every Province in Circumstances that set them at Ease, and afford Leisure to cultivate the finer Arts, and improve the common Stock of Knowledge." Jefferson would become president and guiding spirit (1797–1815) of the Society during the most creative years.

The "American Philosophical Society, held at Philadelphia, for promoting useful Knowledge" had been consciously modeled on the Royal Society of London. But its scope, its publications, and its discussions were shaped by the novel openness of the New World and the host of unfamiliar phenomena in nature and among the native peoples. Never before in Western culture had people at a distance from the ancient centers so effectively organized to seek the meaning of their whole environment. The Society brought together a galaxy of asking minds, which included the astronomer and inventive genius David Rittenhouse (1732–1796); the pioneer psychologist and physician Dr. Benjamin Rush (1745–1813); the great American botanist of the age Benjamin Smith Barton (1766–1815); the chemist and philosopher of revolution Joseph Priestley (1733–1804); the artist, museum founder, and amateur archaeologist Charles Willson Peale (1741–1827); and a variety of other scientists and political philosophers. The transactions of the Society reveal a lively openness to a novel environment.

Just as the Declaration of Independence announced that Americans would find their own political way in the New World, Jefferson's *Notes on the State of Virginia* would reveal a similar spirit at work on nature and all society. This, Jefferson's only full-length book, was written in answer to the Secretary of the French Legation in Philadelphia, the Marquis de Barbé Marbois, who had posed twenty-three questions that

Jefferson answered in detail. Too little read nowadays, it is a remarkably compendious and readable survey of Jefferson's Virginia—from the geography, mines and minerals, the forests and agricultural products, to the institutions, peculiarities of the Indians, plantation life and slavery, the history and laws, manners and customs of the colony, the manufactures, taxation, standard of living, and commerce.

The book was an unexcelled prospectus of the promise of this New World. And it provided Jefferson the Seeker with the opportunity to reflect on the meanings of the American experience. In answering Query XIX about manufactures in the colony, after describing the self-sufficiency of plantation life and the relative insignificance of commerce compared with that in the urban life of Europe, he observes:

> In Europe the lands are either cultivated, or locked up against the cultivator. Manufacture must therefore be resorted to of necessity not of choice, to support the surplus of their people. But we have an immensity of land courting the industry of the husbandman. . . . Those who labor in the earth are the chosen people of God, if ever He had a chosen people, whose breasts He has made His peculiar deposit for substantial and genuine virtue. It is the focus in which he keeps alive that sacred fire, which otherwise might escape from the face of the earth. Corruption of morals in the mass of cultivators is a phenomenon of which no age nor nation has furnished an example. It is the mark set on those, who, not looking up to heaven, to their own soil and industry, as does the husbandman, for their subsistence, depend for it on the casualties and caprice of customers. Dependence begets subservience and venality, suffocates the germ of virtue, and prepares fit tools for the designs of ambition.

Jefferson's *Notes on the State of Virginia* would perhaps be the most influential scientific book written by an American. For it invited the Old World to the opportunities of the new. First published anonymously (at Jefferson's own expense) in Paris, in an edition of only two hundred copies in 1784, it was soon widely translated. French liberals were impressed by Jefferson's description of free republican institutions and inspired by his vision.

For Jefferson, America was not only a pristine continent to be discovered but a laboratory of new meanings and purposes for society. When thirty years later, as president, he sent his secretary, Meriwether Lewis, and William Clark on their exploring expedition (1804–1806) into the American West, the narrative of their travels would provide, in an adventure story, a similar inventory of the vast continental territory acquired in the Louisiana Purchase from France in 1803. Again, a priceless resource for seeking the meaning of civilization for a new nation on an unexplored continent. Jefferson, the president, would energetically explore these distinctly American possibilities. And he foresaw still more to come. "So we have gone on, and so we shall go on," he wrote to John Adams in 1812, "puzzled and prospering beyond example in the history of man."

This theme of the new American nation as a place for seeking the future possibilities of civilization would resound in the eloquence of political leaders. And would be declared again and again even before the great influx of adventuring immigrants and refugees from the Old World. The seeking spirit resounds in Lincoln's Gettysburg Address—affirming that the history of this "new nation, conceived in Liberty, and dedicated to the proposition that all men are created equal" was a "testing whether that nation, or any nation so conceived and so dedicated, can long endure."

28

Hegel's Turn to
"The Divine Idea on Earth"

There is no more surprising or ironic episode in Western thought than the story of how the threads of the Enlightenment and Western Europe's quest for freedom were brought together by G. W. F. Hegel (1770–1831) into dogmas that would be used to justify the totalitarian movements of the twentieth century. The seventeenth, eighteenth, and nineteenth centuries were an era of emerging modern nations when the communal search for meaning and purpose would find forms arising out of the peculiar history and experience of each nation. The vortex of Italian city-states had led to the quest for a nation that provided Machiavelli with the experience and precedents for his search for an Italian nation and his prescriptions for nation making. The English experience provided Locke and his followers with a theory of limits—limits of knowledge and of government. Voltaire and his companions of the French Enlightenment saw civilization—human renewal everywhere—foreshadowed in the culture of France and the promise of its Revolution. So, too, the trials and travails of numerous small contesting German states and principalities would include a quest for national unity. Perhaps this would have to be a kind of coherence not yet seen in history or on earth. This distinctively German quest was expressed in the miraculously abstract ideas of Hegel, which would have an uncanny appeal across the world in later centuries.

The appeal of idealism, which Hegel gave its most influential political expression, is understandable in a land of peoples speaking a common language but fragmented into many small communities. While the emerging new nations of Western Europe were unified into governments that could be restrained by constitutions and influenced by public opinion, in eighteenth-century Germany there was yet no central government that could be influenced by debate or revolution. Political power was diffused into warring small communities—sometimes loosely confederated, but not organized into a nation. Since there was not yet a central government to be influenced by public opinion, unlike the age of Voltaire and Rousseau in France and Pitt and Burke in England, it is not remarkable that no comparable shapers of public opinion appeared in a diffuse Germany.

Thinkers in these numerous small competing German communities took refuge in abstraction and introspection—idealizing their thought and the state. So it was that in the late eighteenth century Germans were coming to think of their land as the refuge of philosophy and poetry. For this idea there was ample evidence in the bright constellation of German writers in the eighteenth and early nineteenth centuries: Winckelmann (1717–1768), a leader in the rediscovery of Greek art; the critic and dramatist Lessing (1729–1781), librarian to the Duke of Brunswick; Schiller (1759–1805), poet and playwright, who led the *Sturm und Drang* movement, a revolt against convention inspired by Rousseau; and the lyric poet and critic Heine (1797–1856). The great figure of German literary awakening was, of course, Goethe (1749–1832), who spent most of his life under the patronage of the Duke of Weimar, and directed the ducal theater there.

It was Hegel who gave an appealing new form to the idealism of the period that would shape thinking about the communal quest. Hegel's ideas were built on those of Immanuel Kant (1724–1804), founder of German idealism. Kant, who spent all his life in and around Königsberg in Prussia, was the prototype of the obsessed and focused philosopher. His neighbors would set their watches by his daily walks. An early sympathizer with the French Revolution of 1789 (until the Reign of Terror), Kant admired Rousseau's works, and was so engrossed in *Émile* that he allowed reading it to disrupt his rigorous schedule.

Kant is commonly considered the greatest modern philosopher, but his works are difficult to grasp and their influence is most visible through his followers, among whom Hegel is conspicuous. His copious, involuted works do not bear concise summary and should be explored in the histories of modern philosophy. But the influence of Kant's leading ways of thought appears in the writings of Hegel. The axiom of Kant's ethical system—that every man must be treated as an end in himself and not as a means—has sometimes been considered a form of the French Revolutionary doctrine of the Rights of Man. His own concept of freedom was that every man must legislate for himself. Which led him to believe "that there can be nothing more dreadful than that the actions of a man should be subject to the will of another." For Kant, then, freedom did not mean mere personal whim, but was the highest realization of law in the universe. His "categorical imperative" is widely known even to those who have not read his philosophy: "Act only on that maxim through which you can at the same time will that it should become a universal law." Adapting the natural rights doctrine of the seventeenth and eighteenth centuries to his new critical idealist philosophy, Kant separated the natural laws of the physical world from the laws of society. So he created his own philosophic universe in which the "noumenal" world of the intellect was opposed to the "phenomenal" world of the senses. And this opened the way to his definition of freedom.

Hegel, building on Kant, produced his own system, which was an elusive marvel of abstraction and construction. His ideas had wide influence, not merely among philosophers. Academic philosophy, by the end of the nineteenth century, in England and America, would be dominated by Hegelian ideas.

His father was a civil servant when Hegel was born in Stuttgart, and his mother taught him Latin by the time he entered grammar school. Hegel himself led a focused academic life. His family had intended him for the ministry, but he early steered himself to the university. He was never active in politics, but wrote and pursued his interests in classics and philosophy, while making his living as a private tutor or on the faculty at Jena, Nuremberg, Heidelberg, and finally at Berlin. Hegel became a patriotic Prussian and loyal civil servant. He was early attracted by the teachings of Kant, and by Kant's defense of the rationality of the teachings of Jesus. And his faith in reason permeated all his works.

But Hegel soon became preoccupied with history—an interest that distinguished him from Kant, and was expressed in his approach to all subjects. Hegel, obsessed by the wholeness of experience, believed that the separateness of items in the world was illusory. This led him to doubt the reality of time and space—the modes of separation. Hegel expressed the wholeness, unity, and rationality of experience in his elusive idea of "the Absolute," which was spiritual. And so Hegel's philosophy, not easy to grasp, was based on his arcane idea that "The Absolute is Pure Being." In history he saw the Absolute being fulfilled. His great influence was through his simple but abstract triadic scheme of the "dialectic." This was the progression of "thesis," "antithesis," and "synthesis" later best known for its influence on Karl Marx, who inverted the scheme into his own "dialectical materialism." And interest in Hegel's "dialectic" was kept alive in socialist thought in the nineteenth and twentieth centuries. It was a universal illustration of his belief that the real is rational and the rational is real. "Reason," he observed, "is the conscious certainty of being all reality."

Into his triadic scheme Hegel forced the whole of world history, which he expounded in his lectures on "The Philosophy of History," the best popular exposition of his system. In these lectures, published posthumously, we can see Hegel's genius at oversimplification—at forcing the most disparate and ancient facts into his ideal scheme. Unsympathetic readers like Bertrand Russell, while admiring his cosmic interests, charge that he made his theory (like other historical theories) plausible only by "some distortion of facts and considerable ignorance." Still, there is no denying that if we can penetrate Hegel's viscous style (even when translated into readable English), we can sense soaring grandeur in his ideas and an admirable cosmopolitanism in his spirit.

Hegel's history, as he repeatedly notes, is meant to be "universal." No part of the human experience on this planet is omitted—however, little may be known (or Hegel may know!) of the facts.

His subject, he explains at the outset, is "the Philosophical History of the World . . . not a collection of general observations . . . but Universal History itself." The other approaches, which he will not pursue, he briefly explains as "Original History" (e.g., Herodotus and Thucydides) and "Reflective History," which includes much of historical writing in modern times. But Hegel's, he explains, is the third kind of history, "the Philosophical":

> The most general definition that can be given is that the Philosophy of History means nothing but the thoughtful consideration of it. Thought is, indeed, essential to humanity. It is this that distinguishes us from brutes. In sensation, cognition and intellection, in our instincts and volitions, as far as they are truly human. Thought is an invariable element.

Even this brief passage gives us a clue to the vast and vague generality of Hegel's doctrines of history, and their soaring suggestiveness. And he goes on with some hints of what he means by Thought, and how he makes it the theme of his Universal History.

The only Thought that Philosophy brings with it to the contemplation of History, is the simple concept of Reason; that Reason is the Sovereign of the World; that the history of the world, therefore, presents us with a rational process. . . . On the one hand, Reason is the substance of the Universe, viz., that by which and in which all of reality has its being and subsistence. On the other hand it is the Infinite Energy of the Universe; since Reason is not so powerless as to be incapable of producing anything but a mere ideal. . . . It is the infinite complex of things, their entire Essence and Truth.

Advancing further and more grandly into the world of abstraction, Hegel gives his own definition of his subject for Universal History. He christens this "the World-Spirit—that Spirit whose nature is always one and the same, but which unfolds this one nature in the phenomena of the World's existence . . . the ultimate result of History."

The vast generality of this "World-Spirit" does not prevent Hegel from dividing it into three phases: the Oriental; the Greek and Roman; and the Germanic. His world-history is divided into the states in which "the Spirit knows itself," always moving toward an ever-fuller self-consciousness. And with a bold unconcern for troublesome facts, Hegel confidently explains that "the Orientals have not attained the knowledge that Spirit—Man as such—is free; and because they do not know this they are not free."

"The consciousness of Freedom," he writes, "first arose among the Greeks, and therefore they were free; but they, and the Romans likewise, know only that some are free—not man as such." And as we might have expected, Hegel defines the climax of man's discovery of his freedom. "The German nations," Hegel insists, "under the influence of Christianity, were the first to attain the consciousness that man, as man, is free: that it is the freedom of Spirit which constitutes its essence." Which leads Hegel to one of his more cryptic and arithmetically simple summaries. "The history of the world is the discipline of the uncontrolled natural will, bringing it into obedience to a universal principle and conferring subjective freedom. The East knew, and to the present day knows, only that *One* is free; the Greek and Roman world, that *some* are free; the German world knows that *All* are free."

The more we read Hegel, the more we are impressed with the truth of Benjamin Franklin's aphorism: "So convenient a thing it is to be a rational creature, since it enables us to find or make a reason for every thing

one has a mind to do." This insight helps us understand the unlikely climax of Hegel's doctrine of Freedom in a Prussia struggling toward na-
tionhood, recently (1806) humbled by Napoleon's victory at the Battle
of Jena. For Hegel, a nation is a community in search of its meaning.
And Freedom—self-realization—Hegel sees being achieved through the
community organized as a state. So, in *The Philosophy of History* Hegel
plausibly concluded that "The State is the Divine Idea as it exists in
earth. . . . The State is the embodiment of rational freedom realizing and
recognizing itself in an objective form. The State is the Idea of Spirit in
the external manifestation of human Will and its Freedom." For the individual, then, Freedom means the right to obey the law.

More surprising than Hegel's idealization of the Prussian state is
how he fits the New World into his ideal universal scheme. "America
is . . . the land of the future, where, in the ages that lie before us, the
burden of the World's History shall reveal itself,—perhaps in a contest
between North and South America. It is a land of desire for all those
who are weary of the historical lumber-room of old Europe. Napoleon
is reported to have said '*Cette vieille Europe m'ennuie.*' "

This was only one (and not the least plausible) of the extravagant
speculations that Hegel drew from his view that the history of the world
was a repetition of his triadic dialectic—with its inevitable progression
from thesis to antithesis, to synthesis, and so on. As Time and Space
would fragment experience, Hegel had conveniently found them unreal.
For Hegel, only the whole—the World-Spirit—is real. Still Hegel offers
us no convincing reason to believe that the later processes of history
embody higher categories than the earlier. For this lacuna in Hegel's
scheme, Bertrand Russell offers a Hegelian explanation—"the blasphemous supposition that the Universe was gradually learning Hegel's philosophy." Other heirs of the Enlightenment, as we shall see, were not so
ready to believe that the world had to go through Hegel's laborious triadic stages. In the world of experience all about them, European
thinkers would find other, less abstract clues to the meaning of history.

BOOK THREE

PATHS TO THE FUTURE

Many discoveries are reserved for the ages still to be.... The world is a poor affair if it does not contain matter for investigation for the whole world in every age.

—SENECA, *NATURAL QUESTIONS*

Theories thus become instruments, not answers to enigmas in which we can rest.

—WILLIAM JAMES, *PRAGMATISM*

Just as Western Seekers discovered their power and duty to build civilization and so fulfill the common mission of humanity, they invented a new science of history. As the Age of Discoverers had found in America realms of experiment and self-government, so the Age of Science produced new views of historical forces that carried along men and societies. They invented historicism, a theory that events were determined by conditions beyond individual human control, and they snatched history away from God and from community, in a modern version of prophecy. Again, they sought solace in the future. Ideology, reinforced by the social sciences, gave people a new view of the extent and limits of their control. Dogmas of the way the world was destined to work overcame the liberal way of communal seeking. Religious faith retreated before the certitudes of science. And these stirred Seekers to find sanctuaries of doubt—on the way to make the seeking itself a source of meaning.

PART SIX

THE MOMENTUM OF HISTORY: WAYS OF SOCIAL SCIENCE

Seek, Seeker
The future is made of Seeking.
—ORTEGA Y GASSET

29

A Gospel and a Science of Progress:
Condorcet to Comte

The first modern ideology, the first "scientific" dogma of human history, was the idea of progress. It was heard in many voices in an era of dramatic changes in Western Europe, where the chorus of progress began to be sung in the late eighteenth and early nineteenth century. For this was an age of increasing wealth, growing cities, expanding empires, scientific advance, new technologies of communication and transportation, and political revolutions. "The confluence of French theory with American example," Lord Acton explained, "caused the Revolution to break out" in France and across Europe. "The American Revolution," as Condorcet would observe, ". . . was about to spread to Europe; and . . . there existed a country where the American cause had diffused more widely than elsewhere its writing and its principles, a country that was at once the most enlightened and the most enslaved of lands . . . that possessed at the same time the most enlightened philosophers and the most crassly and insolently ignorant government. . . . It was inevitable, then, that the revolution should begin in France." Change was in the air. With their Enlightenment enthusiasm, French *philosophes* preached the infinite powers and infinite increase of knowledge—the fruit of endless seeking. But would the idea of progress itself be only a way station in the search? Dogmas of social science would, in their turn, eventually be embodied in institutions whose mission it was to enforce a frozen ideology. Which would again stir rebellious spirits to continue the search.

Of the many spokesmen for a new science of history, there were two high priests, both French—the Marquis de Condorcet (1743–1794) and his follower, Auguste Comte (1798–1857). They impressed their scheme of progress on the compulsory currents of history. No longer mere "inquiry" nor only a narrative of past events, history now seemed a process that man dared not defy.

Ancient Greek mythology had begun with the Golden Age of Kronos, when men lived like gods, from which men and society had degenerated. The Hebrews, too, had begun with their own version of a Golden

Age in the Garden of Eden, until man's disobedience—the Fall, from which ever since he had been trying to recover. Christianity offered a Savior to redeem sinful man, which made history an effort to recover lost innocence. Ancient pessimism was sometimes tempered by a belief in cycles, a never-ending repetition of rise and fall. "The thing that hath been, it is that which shall be; and that which is done is that which shall be done: and there is no new thing under the sun." Classical writers had their own way of describing the cycles. Our rational mind, observed the philosophical Roman emperor Marcus Aurelius (A.D. 121–180), "stretches forth into the infinitude of Time, and comprehends the cyclical Regeneration of all things, and discerns that our children will see nothing fresh, just as our fathers too never saw anything more than we." The idea of novelty in history, that man's lot had improved from the beginning of time, had to await the experience of Europe in modern times.

The first classic statement of the modern idea of progress and the indefinite perfectibility of the human race was the work of the Marquis de Condorcet. Born to an old aristocratic family in the French provinces, after education in Jesuit schools he joined the community of *philosophes* in Paris. There he shared the lively salon of his beautiful and witty wife. He worked on the mathematical articles of the *Encyclopédie,* and on the Supplement, and came to be called "the last of the *encyclopédistes.*" During the turbulent days of the French Revolution he wrote a draft constitution that was never adopted, but his original scheme for universal state education did shape policy. He was one of the first to propose a republic, and he drafted the summoning of the National Convention in August 1792. But he opposed the execution of Louis XVI, and his moderation earned the enmity of Robespierre.

So Condorcet was outlawed, and under threat of the guillotine he went into hiding. There, within less than a year and without access to a library, he wrote his classic work on the progress of the human mind and the perfectibility of man. He called what he offered a mere *Sketch of a Historical Picture of the Progress of the Human Mind* (1795). A larger work was to follow. But this Sketch would have an influence on modern thought quite out of proportion to its modest brevity. It bears marks of haste. Parts were written on the backs of proclamations and other sheets of used paper. The manuscript in Paris shows numerous mistakes of spelling, punctuation, and grammar. Condorcet must have had an incorrigibly sanguine temperament—to write in the shadow of the guillotine so persuasive and passionate a paean to the progress of the human mind and to human perfectibility. Yet he did see the Revolution of which he was now a victim as a modern climax of human progress!

An admirer (and biographer) of Voltaire, Condorcet offers in his brief *Sketch* a cogent statement of the Enlightenment spirit that animated Voltaire's hundred volumes. He sees the increase of knowledge, of science, and the liberty that comes with them as collaborating forces for human progress throughout history. Condorcet discovers nine epochs, beginning with men united in tribes, coming through the rise of agriculture and the invention of the alphabet, the progress of the sciences in Greece, the invention of printing and "the time when philosophy and the sciences shook off the yoke of authority"; the ninth stage begins with Descartes and climaxes in the founding of the French republic. The tenth stage, the future, he prophesies, will be marked by "the abolition of inequality between nations, the progress of equality within each nation, and the true perfection of mankind." Following Locke's method and Locke's view of the limits of human knowledge, he saw philosophers finding, for the sciences of morals, politics, and economics, "a road almost as sure as that of the natural sciences."

Condorcet's antireligious passion prevents his valuing the achievements of the European Middle Ages.

> During this disastrous stage we shall witness the rapid decline of the human mind from the heights that it had attained, and we shall see ignorance following in its wake. . . . Nothing could penetrate that profound darkness save a few shafts of talent, a few rays of kindness and magnanimity. Man's only achievements were theological day-dreaming and superstitious imposture, his only morality religious intolerance. In blood and tears, crushed between priestly tyranny and military despotism, Europe awaited the moment when a new enlightenment would allow her to be reborn free, heiress to humanity and virtue.

He sees printing as the agent of knowledge, and knowledge as the agent of freedom. Progress, then, is a coherent, inevitable process. Religion, the enemy of progress, was a system of hypocrisy in which priests "frighten their dupes by means of mysteries."

> Has not printing freed the education of the people from all political and religious shackles? It would be vain for any despotism to invade all the schools. . . . The instruction that every man is free to receive from books in silence and solitude can never be completely corrupted. It is enough for there to exist one corner of free earth from which the press can scatter its leaves. How with the multitude of different books, with the innumerable copies of each book, of reprints that can be made available at a moment's notice, how could it be possible to bolt every door, to seal every crevice through which truth aspires to enter?

So printed books opened paths for political freedom.

And Condorcet foresaw the rise of a new power. "The public opinion that was formed in this way was powerful by virtue of its size, and effective because the forces that created it operated with equal strength on all men at the same time, no matter what distances separated them. In a word, we have now a tribunal, independent of all human coercion, which favours reason and justice, a tribunal whose scrutiny it is difficult to evade, and whose verdict it is impossible to evade."

Progress actually transformed, and enlarged, the very subject matter of history. "Up till now, the history of politics, like that of philosophy or of science, has been the history of only a few individuals: that which really constitutes the human race, the vast mass of families living for the most part on the fruits of their labour, has been forgotten. . . ." So the historian himself was now to be transformed from biographer into social scientist. Formerly he needed only to "collect facts; but the history of a group of men must be supported by observations." Only Enlightenment could guide the historian to the observation of groups.

Condorcet had thus sketched an enticing scheme of history past and future, with a momentum not apt to be deflected by individuals. This was an ideology. But he never made of it a religion, a dogma to be enforced by institutions. Whether he might have made his theory into an enforced orthodoxy we will never know. His arrest was ordered in July 1793, but he remained hidden in Paris in the house of a Madame Vernet until the end of March of the following year. During these few months he wrote his influential *Sketch*. Then when he left the house he was identified as an aristocrat, arrested for being without papers, and confined in the prison of Bourg la Reine. He was found dead in his cell the following day. Perhaps he had committed suicide by taking poison.

While Condorcet was fortunate in not having seen his theory become an enforced ideology, he did have some prophetic notions of the future of the social sciences. In his scheme of universal education he included a new science that he called Social Mathematics. His "*art social*" was the "application of mathematics to the moral sciences," believing as he did that "the truths of the moral and political sciences can be as certain as those that make up the system of the physical sciences." With a flair for mathematics, Condorcet proposed the statistical description of societies and applying the calculus of probability to human phenomena. He applied the technique himself to a theory of voting that sought ways of structuring voting to produce the maximum probability of collective choice of a "true" solution.

Condorcet's *Sketch,* brief and unpolished, has survived as a monument in the liberal tradition. His view of modern Western civilization, though overly optimistic, was uncannily prophetic. Except for his dogma of human equality, his view of society remained open-ended, aiming at human "perfection," whatever that might be.

While Condorcet did not live long enough to make a religion of his ideology, his more influential disciple, Auguste Comte, would do just that. In fact, Comte did everything with the idea that Condorcet had not done. What his predecessor had made into a suggestive *Sketch,* Comte would elaborate into a massive system. While Condorcet had casually touched on some sources and results of progress, Comte would document and define the "laws" of progress. Comte would play the role of a learned Aquinas to his predecessor's inspired Saint Paul.

A precocious, independent boy in a royal and passionately Catholic family in Montepellier, the young Comte early rebelled against the conventions of his community. His erratic and troubled personal life was in dramatic contrast to the rigor of his philosophic system. He offended his family by abjuring Catholicism at the age of fourteen. When his brief career at the École Polytechnique was cut short by his refusal to follow the school rules, he stayed in Paris occasionally teaching and writing for magazines, educating himself by wide reading and conversation with the lively intellectual community. The most influential of his young acquaintances was Henri de Saint-Simon, whose ideas he would adapt and develop. Comte's abnormally short legs made people call him ugly, and troubled his relations with women. One of his first amorous adventures was with a prostitute, Caroline Massin, whom he married in a civil ceremony—in order to have her removed from the police register.

By 1826, when Comte was only twenty-eight, he was presenting his "system of positive philosophy" in a series of lectures to a private audience of leading Paris intellectuals. But after only two lectures he could not continue, and was so disturbed that he was taken to an asylum. To satisfy his mother, his marriage to Caroline was solemnized in a Catholic ceremony, but he was unable to sign the register. In deep depression, he attempted suicide by jumping off the Pont des Arts into the Seine, but was rescued by a passing soldier. He gradually recovered his faculties and successfully resumed the lecture series in 1829. Over the next twelve years the lectures were published in six volumes—the *Cours de philosophie positive.*

Here Comte proposed his "law of human development," which became famous with its appealingly simple three stages. Human progress (and each branch of our knowledge), he observed, had passed through three stages—"the Theological, or fictitious; the Metaphysical, or abstract; and the Scientific, or positive." In the first stage, explanations depended on supernatural beings, gods or spirits; in the second stage explanations were by abstract forces, essences, and final causes. "In the final, the positive state, the mind has given over the vain search after absolute notions, the origin and destiny of the universe, and the causes of phenomena, and applies itself to the study of their laws. . . . Reasoning and observation, duly combined, are the means of this knowledge . . . the establishment of a connection between single phenomena and some general facts, the number of which continually diminishes with the progress of science." The second, or "abstract," stage was necessary because "The human understanding, slow in its advance, could not step at once from the theological into the positive philosophy. . . . an intermediated system of conceptions has been necessary to render the transition possible."

Each of the sciences in turn had also gone through these stages, and Comte arranged his "hierarchy" of the sciences—beginning with the simplest or most general, the inorganic, and proceeding to the most complex, the organic. Each science depended on the science below it in the hierarchy. "Thus we have before us Five fundamental Sciences in successive dependence—Astronomy, Physics, Chemistry, Physiology, and finally Social Physics." And this Social Physics—for which unifying science, the highest of the hierarchy of sciences, Comte invented the name Sociology—"is what men have now most need of; and this it is the principal aim of the present work to establish."

Comte's own life would dramatize the weaknesses of the rigid rationalism that he had preached. His wife, Caroline, left him and he taught erratically at the Polytechnique. He then fell in love with Clotilde de Vaux, the married sister of one of his pupils, who had been abandoned by her husband. But she died in 1846, after only a year of their passionate association, and he never recovered from his loss. He made a ritual of her memory, regularly visited her tomb, and wrote her a letter each year. His life became a ritual, in which he ended his evening dinner with a crust of dry bread, "meditating on the numerous poor who were unable to procure even that means of nourishment in return for their work."

By the time Comte finished the final volume of his *System of Positive Philosophy* in 1854 his works had been translated and exerted a strong influence in England. Positivist societies were growing around the world. When Harriet Martineau condensed Comte's *Cours de philosophie positive* into two volumes and translated it into English, the pious Martineau explained that "The supreme dread of every one who cares for the good of nation or race is that men should be adrift for want of an anchorage for their convictions. . . . a very large proportion of our people are now so adrift. . . . The work of M. Comte is unquestionably the greatest single effort that has been made to obviate this kind of danger." Comte, too, was well aware that the progress of science and industry had created a crisis of belief.

Comte did not see science as a cure-all for the loss of moral convictions in a science-obsessed society. "Monotheism in Western Europe," he observed in his *General View of Positivism* (1848), "is now as obsolete and as injurious as polytheism was fifteen centuries ago. The discipline in which its moral value principally consisted has long since decayed. . . . The noblest of all practical pursuits, that of social regeneration, is at the present time in direct opposition to it. For by its vague notion of Providence, it prevents men from forming a true conception of Law. . . . Sincere believers in Christianity will soon cease to interfere with the management of a world, where they profess themselves to be pilgrims and strangers."

Comte is ready with his answer to this need for meaning. "We tire of thinking and even of acting," he made his motto for *The General View of Positivism.* "We never tire of loving." "The new general doctrine aims at something more than satisfying the Intellect. . . . it is in reality quite as favourable to Feeling and even to Imagination." So Comte rounds out his system by elaborating "the Religion of Humanity." "Love . . . is our principle; Order our basis; and Progress our end." "Positivism becomes, in the true sense of the word, a Religion; the only religion which is real and complete; destined therefore to replace all imperfect and provisional systems resting on the primitive basis of theology." The successor to Christianity, his religion surpasses it.

And the Religion of Humanity will have its own festivals. "In every week of the year some new aspect of Order or Progress will be held up to public veneration; and in each the link connecting public and private worship will be found in the adoration of Woman. . . . All the points in which the morality of Positive Science excels the morality of revealed religion are summed up in the substitution of Love of Humanity for Love of God." A new kind of Worship of the Dead will be the services commemorating those eminent persons in the past who have served morality and progress. The most important object of the regenerated polity will be "the substitution of Duties for Rights; thus subordinating personal to social considerations. The word *Right* should be excluded from Political language, as the word *Cause* from the language of philosophy."

Since Catholicism, according to Comte, is now no more than "an imposing historical ruin," he offers us what T. H. Huxley called "Catholicism minus Christianity." Comte's world, governed by the iron laws of sociology, has no need for the liberty of mere opinions. Progress, for Comte, unlike Condorcet, is not indefinite, but continuous. And there is no room for surprise or the whims of personal liberty. It was no wonder, then, that the doctrines of Enlightenment and social science, touted to liberate man from the tyranny of the priesthood, would soon establish their own tyranny. Comte and his successors could not imagine that their gospel of progress might prove as ephemeral as the fictions of theologians or the abstractions of metaphysicians.

30

Karl Marx's Pursuit of Destiny

The most influential of the new "scientific" historians was also the prophet of worldwide revolution. "As Darwin discovered the law of evolution in organic nature," Friedrich Engels declared at the graveside of his hero, "so Marx discovered the law of evolution in human history." But while Darwin shook faith in the prevailing religion of Western Europe, Karl Marx (1818–1883) created a new religion of Revolution. His new historicism charted the destiny of Western civilization in an ideology that revealed the shaping forces of which men were part but which gave little freedom for mankind to deflect the material forces. Marx might have said, as Bertrand Russell has observed, that he did not advocate socialism but only prophesied it. The movement for which Marx supplied the sacred text would command a life-risking passion no less than the faith of the Christian saints and martyrs of the Middle Ages.

Marx's personal background was marked by conflicting loyalties. Trier, the town where he was born, had some of the most important Roman remains of northern Europe as well as an elegant Gothic cathedral, and prospered from factories making iron and leather goods. It had been a French department under Napoleon, but passed to Prussia after his fall. Marx's father was a lawyer, a devotee of Voltaire and the Enlightenment philosophers. Marx was one of seven children. His grandfather was a rabbi in Trier who was succeeded in the synagogue by his uncle. Marx's mother, who came from Holland, was also descended from a line of rabbis. She spoke only broken German. About a year before Karl was born, his father, Heinrich, was baptized in the Evangelical Established Church of Prussia, and Karl himself was baptized when he was six. The conversion was convenient, and probably necessary for Heinrich's position as a practicing lawyer. Karl happily married Jenny von Westphalen, a beautiful and spirited girl four years his senior, who came from a non-Jewish Prussian aristocratic family.

After the Trier high school, Marx attended the University of Bonn in 1835. The high school at Trier had been under police surveillance for suspected liberal teachers, and student life at Bonn was disrupted by the arrest of students for disturbing the Federal Diet at Frankfurt. Marx joined in the student life, fought a duel, and was once jailed for being drunk and disorderly. Then he went on to the University of Berlin to study law and philosophy. There he became one of the Young Hegelians. In 1841 he offered his doctoral dissertation for a degree at Jena, known to have lower academic standards. He used the Hegelian dialectic to expound the differences between the materialist philosophies of Democritus and Epicurus. He idolized Prometheus, and in his foreword he already revealed his aggressive spirit. "As long as one drop of blood still pulses through the world-conquering and untrammelled heart of philosophy it will always defy its enemies with the words of Epicurus: not he is Godless who scorns the Gods of the multitude, but he who accepts the opinions of the multitude concerning the Gods."

Another influence toward a materialist philosophy entered Marx's life with the publications of Ludwig Feuerbach (1804–1872), who argued (1839) that "Christianity has in fact long vanished not only from the reason but from the life of mankind." In his own philosophy Marx managed to combine Hegel's dialectic with Feuerbach's materialism in what became his materialist interpretation of history ("Dialectical Materialism"). When Marx left the university he became a journalist, reporting and editorializing on the miseries of the Berlin poor as well as on other issues. His liberal alarms were so effective that the paper he wrote for, the *Rheinische Zeitung,* was soon suspended by the Prussian authorities. After a jury in Cologne in 1849 acquitted him of press offenses and inciting to armed insurrection, he went to Paris to study communism. But within the year he was expelled from Paris, and emigrated to London, where he remained in exile till his death in 1883. After 1851 he was European correspondent for *The New York Tribune,* for whom he wrote some five hundred articles and editorials.

Marx lived in conflict between his two vocations—as the scholarly social scientist and as the passionate prophet of social justice. He was equally committed and equally vigorous in both. His restless exploring mind helped him assimilate and review the elusive abstractions of Hegel, Feuerbach, and others into explanations of the facts of life that he observed and reported around him. The everyday horrors of the newly flourishing industrial system that he observed in England and learned about through his close friend the Manchester industrialist

Friedrich Engels documented the findings of English Royal Commissions, fueled his moral indignation, and inspired his hopes for a better society. In both roles he had the advantage of a restless pen, equally fluent of wit and vitriol.

Karl Marx proved to be the perfect transitional figure between the Age of the Religious Why, which sought to explain the world by the end (To what purpose?), and the Age of the Science Why (From what cause?). From Salvation to Evolution. He somehow preserved a sense of meaning and purpose in history while revealing the laws of social change. So for his followers Marx was able to avoid the emptiness of a valueless world ruled by impersonal forces by assuring them of the triumph of justice in the long run. His moral prophecies were all encapsulated in the security of science. The Marxian history would offer salvation without Christianity.

How did he manage to provide so persuasive and powerful an ideology? In harmony with the modern empirical spirit Marx's ideology was not a theology, a metaphysic, or a moral philosophy, but purported to be a pure science of history. Before he was thirty he had laid out the outlines of his materialist theory—which came to be called "dialectical materialism." He had developed his ideas in journalistic articles and polemics, including *The Holy Family* (1845), *The German Ideology* (1845–46), *The Poverty of Philosophy* (1847), and *The Communist Manifesto* (1848). Marx himself would describe the "guiding thread" of these works and the essence of his theory in a famous summary passage:

> The mode of production in material life determines the general character of the social, political and spiritual processes of life. It is not the consciousness of men that determines their existence, but, on the contrary, their social existence determines their consciousness.

So far in history all methods of production ("the Asiatic, the ancient, the feudal, and the modern bourgeois") had depended on "antagonism"—between the producers and the beneficiaries of production. He forecasts that "the bourgeois relations of production are the last antagonistic form of the social process of production . . . at the same time the production forces developing in the womb of bourgeois society create the material conditions for the solution of that antagonism." This will be "the closing chapter of the prehistoric stage of human society." So Marx's "science" of history ends on an apocalyptic note.

According to Marx, Darwin's great achievement was to interest us in "the history of nature's technology." Engels, as we have seen, eulogized Marx for having similarly "discovered the law of evolution in human history." For Marxists, Marx had discovered the technology of human history—the forces and institutions that shaped and changed society. The dynamic role of social classes determined the course of history. Capitalism had made the workers into an alienated class. "What the bourgeoisie . . . produces, above all," he prophesied in the *Communist Manifesto,* "are its own gravediggers. Its fall and the victory of the proletariat are equally inevitable." He concluded the *Manifesto* by appealing to the proletariat to fulfill his scientific prophecy: "Workingmen of all countries, unite!" His was not a plea to fight against menacing odds, but rather an invitation to join the bandwagon of history, to move with the current.

Marx had developed his materialist scheme of history in articles and brief books, but finally elaborated it and provided the detailed, documented argument in the monumental *Das Kapital* (Vol. 1, 1867; Vols. 2 and 3, edited by Engels, 1885, 1894). The International Working Men's Association, which he had inaugurated, properly christened this work, with no intended irony, as "The Bible of the Working Class." Besides expounding the large historical frame for the future of society and to justify and explain the messianic role of the proletariat and the instability of the capitalist system, he offered a specific economic theory. This was the theory of surplus value, which Engels credited as Marx's second great "discovery." Based on David Ricardo's labor theory of value, the theory of surplus value explained how the capitalist expropriated the worker. If, as Ricardo had argued, all economic value was derived from human labor, then the capitalist prospered by paying workers less than the value that they had added and pocketing the difference. To secure the maximum profit, the capitalist paid the worker only enough for his subsistence. Surplus value, then, is the value produced by the worker beyond what he is compensated. Thus the capitalist's profit came from exploiting the worker. Although unequivocal in his dogmas of history and of economics, Marx's lively mind occasionally rebelled at hints of orthodoxy. And he more than once declared, "I am not a Marxist."

Karl Marx's sense of mission was strong enough to sustain him in years of misery and poverty. In 1849 he settled in London, but he was evicted from his house and his property was seized. Two of his four children died there, and his wife suffered breakdowns. All the while the Manchester industrialist, Engels, was supporting him. And Engels eulogized him as "the best-hated and most-slandered man of his age. Governments . . . vied with each other in campaigns of vilification against him. He brushed it all to one side like cobwebs. . . . And he died honoured, loved and mourned by millions of revolutionary workers from the Siberian mines over Europe and America to the coasts of California. . . . although he had many opponents he had hardly a personal enemy."

31

From Nations to Cultures:
Spengler and Toynbee

After 1870, European man at last had come to know all preceding societies. We had become "the inheritor of the whole planet," André Malraux observed. "The next step is obviously to conceive humanity as one." This momentous step in thinking about human history was signaled by the displacement of the idea of Nations by the idea of Culture. This innovation of modern social science would be a key to new ways of thinking about the meaning of history and the future. "Culture" would provide a concept far broader and more cosmopolitan than the idea of "Nations" that had spread across Europe after the fifteenth century. The founding prophet of this new idea was Edward Burnett Tylor (1832–1917), son of a prosperous English Quaker. As a Quaker, he could not enter a university and so began life in the family business. Seeking a climate to cure his tuberculosis, he went to America at the age of twenty-three. On a Havana bus he encountered a fellow Quaker, an archaeologist whom he impulsively joined in study of Toltec remains in Mexico. So began Tylor's lifelong study of strange and ancient societies and their relation to modern life.

These studies in Mexico put him on the path that produced *Primitive Culture* (1871) and made Tylor a founder of cultural anthropology. From the Toltec clues he saw all cultures as parts of a single history of human thought. The "savage," he saw, was not a mere brute but rather was on the first stage of development toward a higher, civilized state. He noted "animism," for example, as only the first form of what would become developed religious belief. The evolution that Darwin had described in biology, Tylor, too, now saw in society. "It is wonderful," Darwin wrote to Tylor, "how you trace animism from the lower races up to the religious beliefs of the highest races. . . . How curious, also, are the survivals or rudiments of old customs." "Culture" was not merely the arts and spiritual ideas but "all those habits and capabilities acquired by man as a member of society."

For Tylor, then, there was only one human history, which in this new breadth could be called anthropology. "The past," he wrote, "is contin-

ually needed to explain the present, and the whole to explain the part."
"There seems to be no human thought so primitive as to have lost its
bearing on our own thought, nor so ancient as to have lost its bearing on
our own thought." In 1896 Tylor would become the first professor of anthropology at Oxford. And "culture" would soon be liberated from uni-
linear evolutionary dogma. And from Victorian condescension to
"inferior" peoples.

The unfamiliar American scene, whose peoples had no place in the
European classical scheme, once again freed social scientists from the
provincialism of the Western European perspective on humankind.
Franz Boas (1858–1942)—a Seeker of the meaning of life to primitive
peoples—did more than any other single thinker to liberate Western social scientists from simplistic dogmas of racial superiority and from absolute hierarchies of cultural achievement. It was no accident, then, that
cultural relativism, the idea of the uniqueness of all cultures and opposition to Old World dogmas of racial superiority, developed in the
United States—and in the new social science of anthropology. Boas,
born in Germany in 1858 to a merchant family, had a precocious interest in natural science, studied in German universities, and earned a
Ph.D. in physics and geography from Kiel. At twenty-five he joined a
scientific expedition to Baffin Island, of the Canadian Arctic Archipel-
ago. There the Eskimo peoples awakened his interest in the variety of
culture. On returning, he became attached to the ethnological museum
in Berlin. Then in 1886, on his way back from a study of the Indians of
Vancouver Island, he stopped in New York, where he remained. Boas
helped prepare the anthropological exhibits in the 1893 Columbian exposition in Chicago, and became professor of anthropology at Colum-
bia University. He then directed and edited reports on the native peoples
of Siberia and North America. Along the way he became versatile and
comprehensive in studying strange and remote societies, including details of linguistics, demography, statistics, physical anthropology, and
folklore. For Boas, like Tylor, saw "culture" including all the ways of a
society.

The acknowledged American leader of the new science of anthropology, Boas was a scrupulous master of detail drawn from his field experience. Boas's *The Mind of Primitive Man* (1911; revised and
enlarged in 1938) demonstrated that "there is no fundamental differ-

ence in the ways of thinking of primitive and civilized man." He attacked simplistic racial stereotypes and insisted that "A close connection between race and personality has never been established." His conclusions were firmly based on facts gathered in the field. Boas argued that all surviving societies show equally the capacity to develop culture. They have evolved equally but differently. So he diverted the social scientists' focus from biology (the realism of evolution) to anthropology. And he received the accolade of the German Nazis when they burned his books and rescinded his German Ph.D.

In the Germany that was burning books by Boas (and many others) there had appeared a quite antithetic view of culture of breathtaking breadth, boldness, nuance, and aesthetic sensitivity. Oswald Spengler (1880–1936) surveyed world history with a cosmic pessimism. At the outbreak of World War I he had completed *Der Untergang des Abendlandes,* and soon thereafter *Outlines of a Morphology of World History* was published. The two volumes were translated into English under the title *The Decline of the West* (1918–22, revised ed. 1922). In a Preface Spengler explained that he owed "practically everything" to Goethe and Nietzsche. "Goethe gave me the method, Nietzsche the questioning faculty." "And therefore, that which has at last . . . taken shape in my hands I am able to regard and, despite the misery and disgust of these years, proud to call *a German philosophy.*" Despite this obeisance to the national spirit, Spengler's scheme broke free of the narrow units of nations and states into his own rich cosmopolitan world-encompassing symbolism—based on the idea of cultures.

Spengler sees eight distinct cultures: Egypt, India, Babylon, China, classical antiquity (Greece and Rome), Islam, the West (Faustian), and Mexico. Each culture has its own spirit, which cannot be transferred to another, and each has its own life cycle. He gave Giovanni Battista Vico's idea of cycles and the uniqueness of human history a rich new meaning. While the world of nature is governed by intelligible causes and effects, human history is ruled by destiny. So, Spengler explained, he offered "a new outlook on *history and the philosophy of destiny* (italics in original)—the first indeed of its kind." Drawing on the products of modern social science, Spengler would offer a new mystic historicism. "Morphology" was the right word for what he offered—not a linear account of social evolution but a dynamic inventory of forms that human efforts had taken across the earth, and so might take in the future. He naturally despises the simplistic division of world history into ancient, medieval, and modern and the imprisonment of thought into narrow Western categories. Instead he sees world history as a composite of cultures, each having its own character and life cycle.

In depicting each culture he offers intriguing and unforgettable suggestions, by a method that he says he owes to Goethe, relating science to the arts and everything to everything else:

> The Apollinian [classical Greek] Culture recognized as actual only that which was immediately present in time and place—and thus it repudiated the background as pictorial element. The Faustian [modern Western] strove through all sensuous barriers towards infinity—and it projected the centre of gravity of the pictorial idea into the distance by means of perspective. The Magian [Byzantine-Arabian] felt all happening as an expression of mysterious powers that filled the world-cavern with their spiritual substance—and it shut off the depicted scene with a gold background, that is, by something that stood beyond and outside all nature-colours. Gold is not a colour.

Spengler's book is rich in these "morphological relationships" between dissimilar activities that prove the coherent spirit of each culture and epoch. So there was a common spirit in the ancient Greek polis and in Euclidian geometry, as there was also between the differential calculus and the state of Louis XIV. Chronological "contemporaneity" was misleading. It should be replaced by an understanding of how different events play similar roles in expressing the culture spirit. Thus he sees his own kind of "contemporaneity" in the Trojan War and the Crusades, in Homer and the songs of the Nibelungs.

"*Cultures are organisms,*" Spengler explains, "and world-history is their collective biography." Like any other vital organism, then, each culture goes through the stages of youth, maturity, and decline. "Culture is the *prime phenomenon* of all past and future world-history." "Every Culture has *its own* Civilization. . . . The Civilization is the inevitable *destiny* of the Culture. . . . Civilizations are the most external and artificial states of which a species of developed humanity is capable. They are a conclusion, the thing-become succeeding the thing-becoming, death following life, rigidity following expansion, intellectual age and the stone-built, petrifying world-city following mother-earth and the spiritual childhood of Doric and Gothic. They are an end, irrevocable, yet by inward necessity reached again and again." Thus, while the culture is a period of ebullient creativity, the civilization that inevitably follows is a period of reflection, organization, and search for material comfort and convenience. For example, classical Greece was the culture; imperial Rome was the civilization. From the beauties of Greek poetry to the imperialism of Roman law, we now live in the civilization of Western ("Faustian") culture and cannot avoid the consequences. Among these Spengler foresaw the "megalopolis," the city of faceless masses, the omnipotence of money, and a new Caesarism.

"Decline" had for Spengler, then, a quite different meaning than had been popularized by Edward Gibbon's *Decline and Fall of the Roman Empire.* Gibbon's "Decline" was a phenomenon in time and space, could be traced on a map and was promoted or delayed by the forces he described. But for Spengler, decline was spiritual, even mystical—Destiny-governed.

The Decline of the West was enormously popular in Germany of the 1920s. The Nazis claimed Spengler as one of their prophets. In pamphlets after World War I he made pleas for the heroic Prussian spirit, but he several times explicitly repudiated the Nazis. And his cultural view of history was opposed to their crude racism. After the Nazis came to power they disavowed him. He died in obscurity in 1936, but was destined to have a posthumous revival in the United States.

It is not easy to explain the vogue of universal history in a world torn by the most destructive war of nations yet recorded on this earth. Perhaps the carnage of trench warfare in western Europe (six hundred thousand dead at Verdun, February–July 1916), the introduction of poison gas by Germany in 1915, countless losses at sea, and atrocities inflicted on civilians awakened the West to the follies of the nation-state. And set historians in search of concepts that might give meaning to history despite the tragic spectacle of warring nations. Even the direst pessimist could not deny the grand achievements of the human race by the early twentieth century. Western culture and/or civilization had conquered land and seas and was beginning to conquer the air; productive laboratories were advancing the sciences, copious libraries were teeming with the world's expanding knowledge, and grand museums were displaying the arts; technology was burgeoning and standards of living were rising. Humanity had ample reason for pride and awe. Perhaps history, then, could be given meaning by surveying and assessing the range and rhythm of human achievement. Spengler had offered brilliant insights with his dynamic inventory of cultures. And even his pessimism was inspired by awe at human possibilities.

After Spengler, the next widely influential Seeker of the meaning of history was Arnold J. Toynbee (1889–1975). The Toynbee family had a tradition of grand ideas and social conscience. His uncle, Arnold Toynbee (1852–1883), had founded the first "settlement house" to offer education and uplift to the poor of east London, and before his death at the age of thirty had written the book which invented the "industrial revolution." Benjamin Jowett had given him a post as tutor in Balliol College, Oxford, and the nephew, Arnold J. Toynbee, had followed to Balliol and studied classics there. Then, studying at the British School in Athens, he originated his ideas on the decline of civilizations. He served as tutor in ancient history at Balliol, joined British Intelligence in World War I, and was a delegate to the Paris Peace Conference in 1919. After reporting as the *Manchester Guardian* correspondent during the Greco-Turkish War (1921–22), Arnold J. Toynbee was director of studies at the Royal Institute of International Affairs in London and director of research for the Foreign Office in World War II. A prodigiously productive scholar, Toynbee had a wide experience of international affairs in his time. His monumental work would be the twelve-volume *Study of History* (1934–61). His observation of small and large wars between nations and the maelstrom of "international" affairs seems to have confirmed his determination to seek meaning for history in some unit other than the nation-state.

Toynbee recalled twenty-eight years later how Spengler's book (which he read in German in 1920) set him on his path of world history. Some critics would later describe Toynbee's work as simply "a Spenglerian heresy." Toynbee had found Spengler's work "teeming with firefly flashes of historical insight. I wondered at first whether my whole inquiry had been disposed of by Spengler before even the questions, not to speak of the answers, had fully taken shape in my own mind. One of my cardinal points was that the smallest intelligible fields of historical study were whole societies and not arbitrarily insulated fragments of them like the nation-states of the modern West or the city-states of the

Graeco-Roman world." But when Toynbee looked for answers about "the geneses of civilization" he found Spengler "unilluminatingly dogmatic and deterministic." While Spengler believed that the spirit of one culture could not be transferred to another, Toynbee observed that cultures were usually "apparented" to older cultures. Toynbee would use "society" as his synonym for both culture and civilization in Spengler's vocabulary. Avoiding the Germanic panacea of "destiny," he focused his original mind on facts to explain the origin, rise, flourishing, and decline of societies. "I became aware," Toynbee recalled, "of a difference in national traditions. Where the German *a priori* method drew blank, let us see what could be done by English empiricism."

Focusing on the genesis and survival of societies, his original approach was eminently practical and fact-oriented. He started with an intriguing paradox. "The view that certain environments, presenting easy and comfortable conditions of life, provide the key to an explanation of the origin of civilizations is examined and rejected." Instead he "suggests the possibility that man achieves civilization, not as a result of superior biological endowment or geographical environment, but as a response to a challenge in a situation of special difficulty which rouses him to make a hitherto unprecedented effort." Both sides of the paradox are supported by facts from around the earth:

> The Sinic [Chinese] Civilization originated in the Yellow River Valley. The nature of the challenge which started it is unknown but it is clear that the conditions were severe rather than easy.
>
> The Mayan Civilization originated from the challenge of a tropical forest; the Andean from that of a bleak plateau. . . .
>
> The Indic Civilization in Ceylon flourished in the rainless half of the island. . . .
>
> New England, whose European colonists have played a predominant part in the history of North America, is one of the bleakest and most barren parts of the continent. . . .
>
> The natives of Nyasaland, where life is easy, remained primitive savages down to the advent of invaders from a distant and inclement Europe.

The elementary notion, what gave Toynbee's work its popular appeal, was readily capsuled in the ideas of "challenge" and "response."

Toynbee offers his own explanation of how and why societies survive and prosper. It is the leadership of "creative minorities" that keeps societies alive and flourishing. But when the "creative" minority becomes a "dominant" minority, imposing its will by force and oppression, then proletariats (internal and external) are created and the society disintegrates. Though fervent and profuse with the data of his "English empiricism," Toynbee still developed his own mystique to replace "destiny." The real progress of a civilization consists in what Toynbee calls "etherialization"—"an overcoming of material obstacles which releases the energy of the society to make responses to challenges which henceforth are internal rather than external, spiritual rather than material."

Religions played an increasingly dominant role in Toynbee's view as he grew older and advanced with his "Study of History." "The principal cause of war in our world today," he wrote on April 9, 1935, in the *Manchester Guardian,* "is the idolatrous worship which is paid by human beings to nations and communities of States. This tribe-worship is the oldest religion of mankind, and it has only been overcome in so far as human beings have been genuinely converted to Christianity or one of the other higher religions. . . . The spirit of man abhors a spiritual vacuum. . . . People will sacrifice themselves for the 'Third Reich' or whatever the Ersatz-Götzen may be, till they learn again to sacrifice themselves for the Kingdom of God." After 1937, Toynbee flirted with Catholicism and he came to believe that the meaning of history would be revealed only in the slow and painful clarification of the relation between God and man.

For Toynbee, finally, the "higher religions" displaced societies or civilizations as the units that gave meaning to history. While brashly insisting on his naively English empirical reliance on facts, which he amassed in prodigious quantity, still in his personal quest for salvation he had developed his own universal apocalyptic view. His reassurance of universal salvation had wide appeal in an age of two world wars. Scholars have objected less to Toynbee's vague definitions of society and civilization than to his tendency to simplify the study of history into a branch of theodicy—an answer to Job, a science of justifying God's ways to man.

32

A World in Revolution?

The grand scholarly schemes of universal history purporting to explain the plight and destiny of civilization in the early twentieth century had their counterparts in a flood of popular literature in the West. People had been taught history, H. G. Wells complained, "in nationalist blinkers, ignoring every country but their own, and now they were turned out into a blaze."

> There were many reasons to move a writer to attempt a World History in 1918. It was the last, the weariest, most disillusioned year of the first World War. Everywhere there were unwonted privations; everywhere there was mourning. The tale of the dead and mutilated had mounted to many millions. Men felt they had come to a crisis in the world affairs. They were too weary and heart-sick to consider complicated possibilities. They were not sure whether they were facing a disaster to civilization or the inauguration of a new phase of human association; they saw things with the simplicity of such flat alternatives, and they clung to hope.

H. G. Wells (1866–1946) widened the Western readers' vision by providing a wonderfully compact, readable, and comprehensive history of the world. He revealed the interconnectedness and uncertainty of human destiny in the twentieth century and the need to transcend national ambitions.

This Western search for hope took many forms. Wells was only one of a community of popular Seekers. The most optimistic saw the world in revolution, and were exhilarated by the remarkable coincidence of so many peoples across the world rising against entrenched forces of privilege and evil. John Reed (1887–1920) was one of the most romantic and most focused of these enthusiastic Seekers—the Western spectators of revolution. Born to a wealthy family in Portland, Oregon, to a father who was active in the Progressive movement, Reed went to Harvard. On graduation in 1910, he worked his way across the Atlantic on a cattle boat and hitchhiked across England, France, and Spain. Settling in New York he wrote poetry and short stories for *Poetry* and *The Masses* and joined the avant-garde of Greenwich Village who came to call him their Golden Boy.

Reed had his first view of the struggle for social justice when he covered the strike against the steel mills in Paterson, New Jersey, in 1913, and spent four days in jail with members of the International Workers of the World. Six months later he went to Mexico to cover the revolutionary exploits of Pancho Villa (1877–1923). Finding Pancho Villa and his army in Chihuahua, he traveled with them. He came to know them well, while other reporters were sitting in the El Paso bars, waiting word from refugees from battle. Reed's melodramatic stories for *Metropolitan Magazine* led Walter Lippmann to say that "with Jack Reed reporting begins. . . . incidentally, the stories are literature." Reed put the stories together in a book called *Insurgent Mexico* (1914). Now one of the highest-paid reporters in the United States at five hundred dollars a week, he was sent to Europe to cover the Western front, and then the Eastern front, of the new world war.

Suspecting that the revolution of February 1917 in Russia signaled greater events to come, he went to Petrograd in September and was there observing and recording the climactic October when the Bolsheviks took over. On Reed's return to the United States his papers were seized on suspicion of his being a Bolshevik agent. When they were given back to him a year later, he wrote *Ten Days That Shook the World* (1919). "Unreservedly," Lenin wrote in his introduction, "I recommend it to the workers of the world. . . . It gives a truthful and most vivid exposition of the events so significant to the comprehension of what really is the Proletarian Revolution and the Dictatorship of the Proletariat." Reed helped organize a Communist Party in the United States, then went to Russia as delegate to the Second Congress of the Communist International. When he was stricken by the typhus that was killing millions of Russians he could not be treated because of the Allied blockade on food and medical supplies to the Soviet Union, and so died at thirty-three.

Reed's carefully documented day-to-day account of how the Bolsheviks seized power came to be called a Bible for revolutionaries in this century—a magic mirror to inspire young revolutionaries around the world. "Now there was all great Russia to win—and then the world! Would Russia follow and rise? And the world—what of it?

Would the peoples answer and rise, a red world-tide?" After describing the funeral ceremony and the playing of the *Internationale* in Red Square for five hundred proletarian martyrs of the revolution, Reed concluded:

> The poor love each other so! . . . I suddenly realized that the devout Russian people no longer needed priests to pray them into heaven. On earth they were building a kingdom more bright than any heaven had to offer, and for which it was a glory to die.

The promise and the threat signaled by the Russian Revolution of 1917 and its aftermaths were expressed in myriad ways across the West. There was hardly a writer who did not find his own way of depicting the world crisis. Lincoln Steffens (1866–1936), the leading muckraker journalist and Reed's mentor, went to the Soviet Union and returned with an unforgettable apocalyptic phrase: "I have been over into the future, and it works." Arthur Koestler (1905–1983) in his novel *Darkness at Noon* (1940) offered a parable of the evils of Stalin's regime and the "so-called Moscow trials." John Steinbeck (1902–1968) toured the Soviet Union and published an "affectionate account" in his *Russian Journal* (1948) concluding "that Russian people are like all other people in the world . . . by far the greater number are very good." *For Whom the Bell Tolls* (1940), the longest novel written by Ernest Hemingway (1899–1961), preached the universality of revolutionary hope. "I have fought for what I believed in for a year now," Robert Jordan, the heroic American who had joined the fight against the fascists, says. "If we win here we will win everywhere." For some years this was a surprisingly widespread view among Western intellectuals.

The frustration of Seekers who hoped to find salvation in Communism was summed up in *The God That Failed* (1950). The witnesses were a stellar group of intellectuals, including Arthur Koestler, Ignazio Silone, André Gide, Richard Wright, Louis Fischer, and Stephen Spender, who had been attracted to Communism in the time between the October Revolution and the Stalin-Hitler pact. As the editor, Richard Crossman, explains:

> In this book six intellectuals describe the journey into Communism, and the return. They saw it at first from a long way off—just as their predeces-

sors 130 years ago saw the French Revolution—as a vision of 'the Kingdom of God on earth' and, like Wordsworth and Shelley, they dedicated their talents to working humbly for its coming. They were not discouraged by the rebuffs of the professional revolutionaries, or by the jeers of their opponents, until each discovered the gap between his own vision of God and the reality of the Communist State—and the conflict of conscience reached breaking point.

PART SEVEN

SANCTUARIES OF DOUBT

There are no whole truths;
all truths are half-truths.
It is trying to treat them as
whole truths that plays the devil.
—ALFRED NORTH WHITEHEAD, *DIALOGUES* (1953)

33

"All History Is Biography":
Carlyle and Emerson

The dogmas of science and destiny would not remain long unchallenged. Man the restless Seeker would not be satisfied by such simplicities. The slaughter on Tiananmen Square in China and the dissolving of the Soviet empire were only climaxes of Western refusals to rest on the couch of dogma. The West had seen again and again the encompassing of the world in dogma, the embodiment of dogma in institutions, with the usual consequences of inquisition and persecution. The twentieth century, even more than ever before, saw the horrors of ideology enforced by institutions, whole nations organized for the slaughter of innocents. But seeking had never ceased. The centuries following the French Revolution of 1789 saw thinkers in the West questioning the certitudes of science and the very concepts that social scientists had devised to make experience amenable to dogma. Again, Western thought was stirred and enriched by champions of human autonomy, of the free individual, of the courage to doubt—rebels against grand simplicities. These dissolvers of ideology were prophets and the vanguard of a new cycle of seeking. They saw uncertainty in the mystery of existence, in the challenge to individual decision, in the vagaries of biography, in the elusive stream of consciousness, in the unpredictable diversity of nature, in the unknowable future of knowledge. Some even were awed by the absurdity of experience. Yet the seeking has never ceased.

The desperate search for the true past and its clues to the future led ingenious thinkers to turn from the unintelligible to the unknowable. In the early nineteenth century there was overwhelming evidence of the power of groups and impersonal forces. The community of French Enlightenment philosophers revealed what seemed the inevitable march of civilization. The baffling momentum of the Paris mob in the French Revolution of 1789 and what Carlyle called "the new omnipotence of the Steam-engine" led believers in the power of the human spirit to seek reassurance in the autonomy of the individual person.

For centuries, Plutarch's *Lives of the Noble Grecians and Romans* had shone in the classical canon. A lively style and vivid detail had made Plutarch (c. 46–c. 120) the popular interpreter of the ancient past. His "lives of the greatest men," Plutarch explained, marked the farthest reach of our knowledge of the past. "Beyond these there is nothing but prodigies and fictions, the only inhabitants are the poets and inventors of fables; there is no credit, or certainty any farther." "Let us hope that Fable may, in what shall follow, so submit to the purifying processes of Reason as to take the character of exact history." A latter-day Greek, troubled by what he saw as Roman decadence, Plutarch was less interested in how men shaped history than in their moral strength or weakness. They would provide lessons for an age when faith in old gods was declining.

In the early nineteenth century, two antithetic personalities were challenged by the threats of impersonal forces to give a role to the individual person. Thomas Carlyle (1795–1881) from Scotland and Ralph Waldo Emerson (1803–1882) from America drew quite opposite historical lessons from their views of past and present. Each saw a different kind of charisma or divine favor in the "great man," who seemed to dominate history. The overshadowing historical figure in their time was Napoleon (1769–1821). He was Carlyle's "last great man." Emerson, too, found him among the eminent men of the nineteenth century, "far the best known and the most powerful."

Carlyle, who had a way of making a mystery of all experience, was not discouraged by translating the simplicities of history into the mysteries of biography. "History is the essence of innumerable Biographies," he wrote, "but if one Biography, nay our own Biography, study and recapitulate it as we may, remains in so many points unintelligible to us; how much more must these million, the very facts of which, to say nothing of the purport of them, we know not, and cannot know!" Emerson in his own way would agree that "there is properly no history, only biography." And Thoreau, the American individualist, went on to the logical extreme: "Biography, too, is liable to the same objection; it should be autobiography."

Carlyle's own early life in Ecclefechan, a village in southern Scotland, was a parable of his view of the focus of history. The family was governed by his father, James Carlyle, a stonemason and small farmer. "I call him a natural man; singularly free from all manner of affectation; he was among the last of the true men, which Scotland (on the old sys-

tem) produced, or can produce; a man healthy in body and in mind. . . .
He was never visited with Doubt; the old Theorem of the Universe was
sufficient for him, and he worked well in it, and in all senses successfully and wisely as few now can do." "He was irascible, choleric, and
we all dreaded his wrath. Yet passion never mastered him; it rather inspired him with new vehemence of insight, and more piercing emphasis
of wisdom."

Perhaps then and there young Thomas Carlyle learned "that a man's
religion is the chief fact with regard to him." For his father was a committed and explicit Calvinist. "Man's chief end, my father could have
answered from the depths of his soul, 'is to glorify God and *enjoy Him*
for ever.' By this light he walked, choosing his path, fitting prudence to
principle with wonderful skill and manliness—through 'the ruins of a
falling Era; not once missing his footing.' " "This great maxim of Philosophy he had gathered by the teaching of nature alone: that man was
created to work, not to speculate, or feel, or dream."

It was no wonder, then, that Carlyle was impatient with parliaments
and detested democracy: "Man is sent hither not to question, but to
work: 'The end of men,' it was long ago written 'is an Action, not a
Thought.' " Nor surprising that he saw the world shaped by Heroes who
saved their worshippers the pains of reflection. In society and individuals, he insisted, "the sign of health is Unconsciousness. . . . Never since
the beginning of Time was there . . . so intensely self-conscious a Society." In Carlyle's time, the "dyspepsia" of self-consciousness appeared
everywhere. For example, in the "diseased self-conscious state of Literature disclosed in . . . the prevalence of Reviewing. . . . All Literature
has become one boundless self-devouring Review. . . . Thus does Literature also, like a sick thing, superabundantly 'listen to itself.' " Unre-
flective worship of the Hero could cure all. So, against the American
antislavery writer Elizur Wright he insisted that "men ought to be
thankful to get themselves governed, if it is only done in a strong and
resolute way."

Carlyle gave his views classic explosive statement in a series of popular lectures (published 1841), *Heroes, Hero Worship and the Heroic in
History.* Worship of a hero, he said, was the test of human nobility. "I
say there is, at bottom, nothing else admirable! No nobler feeling than
this of Admiration for one higher than himself dwells in the breast of

man. It is to this hour, and at all hours, the vivifying influence in man's life." Carlyle's hero had many shapes—Divinity (Odin), Prophet (Mahomet), Poet (Dante, Shakespeare), Priest (Luther, Reformation; Knox, Puritanism), Man of Letters (Johnson, Rousseau, Burns), King (Cromwell, Napoleon).

Before offering his dogma of the "Great Man," Carlyle had made his reputation with a work of history. His *French Revolution* (1837) also became a literary legend and an object lesson to authors. For comment and criticism he had lent the unique manuscript of the first volume to John Stuart Mill, in whose house it was accidentally destroyed. Doggedly, Carlyle simply rewrote it. When published in three volumes in 1837 it was an enormous success in the bookstores, ending his struggle for money and public notice. Lecture invitations now brought the financial support he sorely needed.

Though praised more often as poetry and rhetoric than as history, the work has its peculiar virtues. Perhaps it justifies G. M. Trevelyan's claim that Carlyle was "in his own strange way, a great historian." For Carlyle somehow captures the Paris mob, to whom he is surprisingly sympathetic. He also gives poignant insights into Danton, Robespierre, and other leaders. Finally, the book is an epic of the overwhelming power of grand forces. Carlyle sees the fate of the aristocracy as retribution for centuries of foolish misgoverning—another chapter in the text of Carlyle's "History as Divine Scripture."

Carlyle's later works documented his "Great Man" theory. Ever in his own strange way. For example, by impassioned editing of letters and speeches he offered "Elucidations" of his idol: "Poor Cromwell—great Cromwell! The inarticulate prophet; prophet who could not *speak*." He found Cromwell a "greater" man than Napoleon. Later, Carlyle's monumental six-volume life (1858–65) of another idol, Frederick the Great of Prussia, demonstrated the superiority of the decisive king over the "Anarchy (as I reckon it sadly to be) which is got by 'Parliamentary eloquence,' Free Press, and counting of heads." Wherever Carlyle looked into the past he found what he was seeking. Even in the medieval monastery (despite his anti-Catholic obsession), in *Past and Present* (1843), he saw the "magnanimous" leadership of the Abbot Samson, in stark contrast to the democratized confusions of his own age.

What is most surprising in this devotee of "greatness" is Carlyle's sympathy, grounded in his own early struggles, for the common people. This sympathy shows not only in his feeling for the abused masses of Paris in his *French Revolution* and in his depiction of life in the Abbot Samson's monastery in the twelfth century. His clues to medieval craftsmanship were taken up by John Ruskin and William Morris and supplied their themes. And he offered a more realistic vision of medieval life than was found in Sir Walter Scott's recent *Ivanhoe* (1819). His explosive laments on "The-Condition-of-England question" depicted the miseries of the new industrial working classes and inveighed against laissez-faire and the translation of human relations into cash. He saw the new evils of his England, but offered no new remedies. Nor did his catalog of Heroes suggest anyone who could lead the people out of the industrial wilderness.

Carlyle's father intended him for the ministry, but Carlyle never felt the vocation for a particular church. His writings, it has been said, were all meant to be read aloud. He aimed somehow to make the world his congregation. The thirty volumes of his collected works—including even his Reminiscences—are, with few exceptions, written in a homiletic style, peppered with capital letters, question marks, and exclamation points. Inspired by Goethe and German idealist philosophy, dismayed by the English utilitarians' pleasure-and-pain and the "profit-and-loss" Philosophy, Carlyle complained that "loss of religion is loss of everything. . . . Soul is not synonymous with Stomach." Troubled by the pallor of the established Church in his time, he became the prophet of his own unorganized church. He preached from the text he himself composed from History—"the true epic poem and universal Divine Scripture, whose plenary inspiration no man out of Bedlam or in it shall bring in question." And in a time when man's inventive ingenuity had given a newly repetitive and mechanical cast to industry, he tried to make work itself a divine mission. Yeats called Carlyle "the chief inspirer of self-educated men in the 'eighties and early 'nineties." But since the rise of Nazism and Fascism, Carlyle's Hero has had an evil and ominous ring, from which he has been stigmatized as a prophet.

The same age carried a different message on the other side of the ocean. Ralph Waldo Emerson (1803–1882), like Carlyle, was originally destined for the ministry. His father, pastor of the Second Church of

Boston, descended from a long line of New England preachers, originating in the first minister of Concord in 1634. The young Emerson, after graduating from Harvard College, attended the Harvard Divinity School. While still a student he preached in pulpits around Boston. In 1829 he was ordained as assistant pastor of the church where his father had preached, and within a few weeks was put in full charge. His sermons were already freewheeling. He appealed to the younger members of the congregation by his plain untheological but ethical messages. Impatient with church dogmas, he wrote in his journal, "I have sometimes thought that in order to be a good minister it was necessary to leave the ministry. The profession is antiquated." In 1832 he announced that he could administer the Sacrament only if the bread and wine were left out, since he believed that Christ had not intended the ceremony be a regular observance. So he resigned his pulpit. But he never ceased to be a preacher, though he made his living as a lecturer.

The independence Emerson expressed by leaving his first pulpit was in the spirit of westward-moving America in his time. Like Carlyle, he was surrounded by piety in his early years. But not the dour Calvinism. His father, who died when Emerson was eight, had little influence on his life, and Emerson's thoughts were shaped by the women in his family. His mother believed in Christianity, not as a theological path to salvation, but as a consolation. She urged her children to be kind "to all animals and insects." His aunt, Mary Moody Emerson, the dominant influence on his early years, was an incurable optimist with a mystic affinity for nature. Young Emerson saw in her letters "the best writer in Massachusetts."

While Carlyle had made his debut with a grandiloquent saga of the turbulent Parisian mob, Emerson's first book was the placid *Nature* (1836). When his family moved to the country outside Boston where he felt near to nature, his poem began "Goodbye, proud world! I'm going home." His varied essays sought to describe that identity in the "Oversoul" that others concocted into a philosophic doctrine called Transcendentalism.

Emerson's feeling of unity with nature meant something, too, for the relations of men to one another and to history. "Standing on the bare ground—my head bathed by the blithe air and uplifted into infinite space—all mean egotism vanishes. I become a transparent eyeball; I am nothing; I see all; the currents of the Universal Being circulate through me; I am part or parcel of God." So the relentless American leveler, Emerson merged each into all. While Carlyle idealized inequality, and measured men by their ability to worship "one higher than himself," Emerson the Seeker saw "the uses of great men" in a series of "Representative Men." Like Carlyle, he found Napoleon the "great man" of the century, and the idea for his "pantheon" grew out of his immersion in books about Napoleon. But while Carlyle saw Napoleon shaping history by his heroic charisma, Emerson's Napoleon was "the Man of the World" who "owes his predominance to the fidelity with which he expresses the tone of thought and belief, the aims of the masses of active and cultivated men."

Emerson goes overboard, denying originality even in the arts. "No great men are original." "The greatest genius is the most indebted man. A poet is no rattle-brain . . . but a heart in unison with his time and country." So he asked, "What can Shakespeare tell in any way but to the Shakespeare in us?" And further to demonstrate that greatness is not a national but a common human quality, Emerson's pantheon includes Plato (philosopher), Swedenborg (mystic), Montaigne (skeptic), Shakespeare (poet), Napoleon (man of the world), and Goethe (writer)—but no American.

Emerson the Seeker is less interested in the process than in the moral of history. His Representative Men command our interest not because they shape events but because they embody the common spirit, and help us feel it. "I described Bonaparte as a representative of the popular external life and aims of the nineteenth century. Its other half, its poet, is Goethe, a man quite domesticated in the century, breathing its air, enjoying its fruits, impossible at any earlier time. . . . Goethe, coming into an over-civilized time and country, when original talent was oppressed under a load of books and mechanical auxiliaries and distracting variety of claims, taught man how to dispose of this mountainous miscellany and make it subservient." For Emerson the flow of experience embodies the common spirit that "great men" express eloquently. So Goethe merits his highest praise because he "teaches courage and the equivalence of all times; that the disadvantages of any epoch exist only to the faint-hearted. Genius hovers with his sunshine and music close by the darkest and deafest eras."

34

Kierkegaard Turns from History to Existence

Seekers would be slow to turn their quest for meaning from the group to the individual—from history to existence. The prophet of what would be called Existentialism would arise on the periphery of European civilization, in the vanguard of theology, philosophy, and literature for the mid-twentieth century. This anti-ideology insisted on the individual concrete nature of experience. And experience became a name for personal problems.

Søren Kierkegaard (1813–1855) was born in Copenhagen to a father who had risen from dire poverty as a tenant farmer to become rich enough to leave Søren a fortune to support him in a life of writing. Two traumatic personal experiences seemed to dominate his personal consciousness and infected him with an obsessive sense of guilt. Søren's father, as a boy, had been so outraged by his penury as a tenant farmer's helper that he had stood on a hill in western Jutland and cursed God. Father and son believed that this had brought a curse on the whole family, causing the death of Søren's mother and five of his six brothers and sisters. His other obsession was a sense of guilt he brought on himself. At the death of his father, when he was studying theology at the University of Copenhagen, he fell in love with the young Regine Olsen. He proposed marriage to her and she accepted. Then, realizing the gulf between her innocence and his guilt-ridden sophistication, he broke off the engagement. "I was a thousand years too old for her," he wrote in his diary. He fled to Berlin, where, at the age of thirty, he wrote his first and most important book, *Either/Or* (1843). A philosophic explanation of his withdrawal, it has been called the longest love letter ever written—and is also the most cryptic. Regine became engaged to someone else. And *Either/Or* became the Bible of modern Existentialism.

Kierkegaard went on to write many books, all somehow haunted by his sense of guilt and his search for subjectivity. In one of his later books (*Concluding Unscientific Postscript,* 1846), which might have been a manifesto for the Existentialists, he eloquently explained the reason—even the necessity—for his work:

The more the collective idea comes to dominate even the ordinary consciousness, the more forbidding seems the transition to becoming a particular existing human being instead of losing oneself in the race, and saying, "we, our age, the nineteenth century." That it is a little thing merely to be a particular existing human being is not to be denied; but for this very reason it requires considerable resignation not to make light of it. For what does a mere individual count for? Our age knows only too well how little it is, but here also lies the specific immorality of the age. Each age has its own characteristic depravity. Ours is perhaps not pleasure or indulgence of sensuality, but rather a dissolute pantheistic contempt for the individual man. . . . Everything must attach itself so as to be a part of some movement; men are determined to lose themselves in the totality of things, in world history, fascinated and deceived by a magic witchery; no one wants to be an individual human being.

The spiritual poison against which Kierkegaard would provide his Existentialist tonic and antidote was G. W. F. Hegel (1770–1831), whose philosophy of the absolute was dominating Western European thought in the early nineteenth century. Hegel's view of the world, of history, and the individual, as we have seen, had an appealing coherence and unity. He argued that only in the institutions, activities, and destiny of his people did the individual find a universal life, into which he incorporated himself. Hegel devoted his life to trying to prove that the universe was a systematic whole. And understandably Hegel's philosophy has appealed to many thinkers in their youth, as it did to young Kierkegaard, after he had given up Christianity. But Kierkegaard soon took an opposite view. And much of his writing became a polemic against Hegel's disregard of the individual and of the ethical.

Kierkegaard's subjectivity took bizarre forms. His numerous publications fell into two classes. Many, including those that were most characteristic and most cryptic, and that became most famous, were published under several different pseudonyms. His publications were as prodigious as they were ambiguous. On October 16, 1843, when he had just reached forty years of age, three of his books appeared, each by a different "author," but all really by Kierkegaard. In addition to his pseudonymous books, which have given him his historic character, many appeared under his own name in a series that he called *Edifying Discourses*. Dedicated to the memory of his father, these homilies take off from a biblical text, on familiar topics like "Man's Need of God" and

"The Unchangeableness of God." Kierkegaard insisted that these were "discourses" and not "sermons." For sermons had the stamp of authority, "that of Holy Writ and of Christ's Apostles." Kierkegaard was troubled by the erratic public response to his writings. "I held out *Either/Or* to the world in my left hand and in my right the *Two Edifying Discourses;* but all, or as good as all, grasped with their right what I held in my left."

Though Kierkegaard insisted on the distinctive individuality of each existing self, he remained curiously ambiguous about his own true self. Perhaps we do not take seriously enough Kierkegaard's sense of humor. In *Either/Or* he relates that he had been taken up into the seventh heaven where the assembled gods gave him the privilege of making any wish, which they would fulfill.

> For a moment I was at a loss. Then I addressed myself to the gods as follows: "Most honorable contemporaries, I choose this one thing, that I may always have the laugh on my side." Not one of the gods said a word; on the contrary, they all began to laugh. From that I concluded that my wish was granted, and found that the gods knew how to express themselves with taste; for it would hardly have been suitable for them to have answered gravely: "Thy wish is granted."

Kierkegaard's wit is easier to grasp than his message. Montaigne, also a forerunner of Existentialism, had explained the problem: "If my mind could gain a foothold, I would not write essays, I would make decisions: But it is always in apprenticeship and on trial."

Yet we need not be troubled by our inability to sum up and make Kierkegaard's message intelligible, for his anti-Hegelian argument is that it is not possible to understand existence intellectually. So there can never be a system for existence, because existence is always incomplete and developing. "There is no such thing as repetition," he insisted as he reached for the uniqueness of each individual and each moment of existence. Yet the illusion of repetition explains much.

The tedium of life requires the intervening acts of the arbitrary existing self, as he explained in *Either/Or:*

> What wonder, then, that the world goes from bad to worse, and that its evils increase more and more, as boredom increases, and boredom is the root of

all evil. The history of this can be traced from the very beginning of the world. The gods were bored, and so they created man. Adam was bored because he was alone, and so Eve was created. Thus boredom entered the world, and increased in proportion to the increase of population. Adam was bored alone; then Adam and Eve were bored together, then Adam and Eve and Cain and Abel were bored *en famille;* then the population of the world increased, and the peoples were bored *en masse.* To divert themselves they conceived the idea of constructing a tower high enough to reach the heavens. This idea is itself as boring as the tower was high, and constitutes a terrible proof of how boredom gained the upper hand.

But man is misled if he thinks he can relieve boredom by what he sees when he travels. The only relief is to stay home, where the existing individual bores itself into inventiveness. And the littlest circumstances control our existence—"For example: a man who is tired of life and wants to throw himself into the Thames and is stopped at the decisive moment by the sting of a gnat." But this does not deprive man of his humanity. "The task of the subjective thinker is to transform himself into an instrument that clearly and definitely expresses in existence whatever is essentially human."

This existential emphasis is wonderfully concrete. The classic parable of the terrifying responsibilities of existence is the story of God's command to Abraham to sacrifice his son Isaac to prove his faith. For God's demand violated all the accepted rules of morals and of religious, civil, and family law. Did God have a right to demand such an immoral act of Abraham? And if so, did Abraham have a right to obey the command? Abraham faced a dreadful choice, a personal responsibility. Was there a "higher law" that overrules the moral law? Is there such a thing as what theologians call "the teleological suspension of the ethical"? Abraham seemed ready to act as if he believed so. But God rescued Abraham from the awful choice by providing a ram in the thicket to replace the sacrifice of Isaac. This parable became embodied in the Hebrew conscience as a divine command against human sacrifice.

Kierkegaard viewed himself as a religious writer, a missionary aiming to bring Christianity back into Christendom. With his refined sensibility and subjectivity, it is no wonder that he found himself violently at odds with the established Church of Denmark, whose clergy had become mere civil servants, while the Danish Court Preacher was a champion of the Hegelian absolute. Against these false Christians, Kierkegaard led a crusade so passionate and strenuous that it wore him to death at forty-two. He finally spent his fortune on a polemical antiestablishment periodical, *The Moment,* to which he was the only contributor. And he left his few personal effects to the jilted Regine, who was by then the wife of the governor of the Danish West Indies.

Kierkegaard's vision of the dilemma of existence, which gave reality to human life, would enlist creative disciples in the century to follow— a stellar array including Nietzsche and Sartre. Those who would call themselves—or would be called—Existentialists were among the most probing and widely influential writers of the West. Their grand theme was carried in Kierkegaard's most important (and most voluminous) work, *Either/Or* (1843). This was his heartfelt cry against the optimism of the Romantics who had dominated Western literature in the early years of the century. The title of this book, it has been said, is more important than the book itself. Its two volumes were arcane and elusive, but the title carried the simple message that existence was the life of choice. And it was a plain challenge to the fashionable philosophy of Hegel, which saw history as an endless mediation—always somehow preserving "thesis" and "antithesis" in a synthesis that reconciled the opposites.

Kierkegaard the Seeker saw that the bland and cheerful affirmations of the Romantics did not touch the experience that alerted and awakened man to his existence—pain, sickness, frustration, and death. How far was all this from the encompassing Absolute simplicities of Hegel:

> If you marry, you will regret it; if you do not marry, you will also regret it; if you marry or do not marry, you will regret both. Laugh at the world's follies, you will regret it; weep over them, you will also regret that; laugh at the world's follies or weep over them, you will regret both; whether you laugh at the world's follies or weep over them, you will regret both. Believe a woman, you will regret it, believe her not, you will regret both; whether you believe a woman or believe her not, you will regret both. Hang yourself, you will regret it; do not hang yourself, you will regret both. This, gentlemen, is the sum and substance of all philosophy.

Kierkegaard found a characteristically original way of describing man's dilemma in what is sometimes called the first work of depth psychology. This was *The Concept of Dread* (1844), which concludes in a chapter declaring "Dread as a means of Salvation in conjunction with faith." So he saw the poignancy of existence as an array of possibilities.

35

From Truth to Streams of
Consciousness with William James

There would be relief from the anguish of existence. The challenge of individual life could produce something other than Kierkegaard's dread. The promise of experience found an eloquent and peculiarly American prophet in William James (1862–1910). A clue to the difference between existentialist dread and pragmatic hope was their ways of thinking about the current of daily experience, their ways of seeking the meaning of life.

Kierkegaard had noted with dismay that "Repetition is not possible." He recounts that this cosmic truth was impressed on him by the disappointing experience of returning to a theater in Berlin to enjoy once again a comedian he had seen there before.

> Beckmann was unable to make me laugh. I held out for half an hour and then left the theater. "There is no such thing as repetition," I thought. This made a profound impression upon me. . . . I still believed that the enjoyment I once had in that theater ought to be of a more durable kind, precisely for the reason that before one could really get a sense of what life is one must have learnt to put up with being disappointed by existence in many ways, and still be able to get along—but surely with this modest expectation life must be the more secure. Might existence be even more fraudulent than a bankrupt? After all, he pays back 50 per cent or 30 per cent, at least he pays something. The comical is after all the least one can demand—cannot even that be repeated?

For William James, on the contrary, this lack of repetition was the very spice of life.

James would give a name to this fluid, dynamic nature of experience. He would call it "the stream of consciousness." His suggestive metaphor would be fertile in philosophy, psychology, and literature in the following century. For James it would be a way of describing human freedom, the promise of experience—and his way of denying a static "block universe." "Reasoning" for James, unlike the scholastics, would not be a process for arriving at empyrean truths, but simply the "ability to deal with novel data." James's homely metaphor would rescue the processes of thought from the arcanum of theology and pedantry:

Consciousness, then, does not appear to itself chopped up in bits. Such words as "chain" or "train" do not describe it fitly as it presents itself in the first instance. It is nothing joined; it flows. A "river" or a "stream" are the metaphors by which it is most naturally described. *In talking of it hereafter, let us call it the stream of thought, of consciousness, or of subjective life.* (*Principles of Psychology*)

No life could have been better devised to open a lively mind to the many ways of seeking meaning in experience. William James was born in New York City into a family of rare talents and versatility. His father, Henry James, Sr., a prolific theological writer and disciple of the Swedish mystic theologian Emanuel Swedenborg, provided for young William a cosmopolitan atmosphere, wide travel, and schooling in France and Switzerland. Henry Senior's works included *Christianity the Logic of Creation* (1857) and *Society the Redeemed Form of Man, and the Earnest of God's Omnipotence in Human Nature* (1879). It was said that William acquired his openness to unfamiliar ideas at the family dinner table. The extraordinary family seminar included a philosophical sister, Alice, and Henry Junior (1843–1916), the leading American novelist of the later nineteenth century.

Returning from erratic schooling abroad, William studied painting briefly with William Morris Hunt, then sciences at Harvard before entering the Medical School. After joining the naturalist Louis Agassiz on an expedition to the Amazon, William went to Germany, where he studied with Hermann Helmholtz and Claude Bernard, the philosopher of experimental medicine, and became acquainted with the writings of the French relativist philosopher Charles Renouvier. After receiving his M.D. he taught physiology, which for him was to become an avenue to psychology. Departing from what Santayana called "the genteel tradition" in which psychology (or "mental science") was a branch of theology, he developed psychology into a laboratory science.

James's education had been a mini-encyclopedia in an age of burgeoning sciences. These revealed an ever-widening range of forces—biological, economic, sociological—that inhibited man's power to decide. As the spirited young William James was introduced to the spectrum of human possibilities, he was deeply troubled by the problem of personal freedom. This, with other ailments, had led him to a breakdown and thoughts of suicide when he was in Germany, and then to periods of panic and despair on his return. Looking back from the career of the sanguine, healthy-minded, mature William James, it is hard to imagine him ever incapacitated by existential despair. He himself offered a charmingly simple, if not quite convincing, explanation of how he came out of it. He wrote in his diary in April 1870:

> I think yesterday was a crisis in my life. I finished the first part of Renouvier's second *Essais* and see no reason why his definition of free will—'the sustaining of thought *because I choose to* when I might have other thoughts'—need be the definition of an illusion. At any rate, I will assume . . . that it is no illusion. My first act of free will shall be to believe in free will.

Openness to new ideas and belief in the incompleteness of the universe would be the leitmotif of his life. It explained his receptivity to many ideas—including Christian Science, mind cure, and spiritualism—that were suspect to his fellow scientists.

It must have troubled James that his openness was treated as a "system" by champions and critics. The closest he came to congealing these ideas was in his Lowell Lectures, which he characteristically entitled *Pragmatism: A New Name for Some Old Ways of Thinking, Popular Lectures on Philosophy* (1907). Of course, he could not prevent academics from treating his refreshing distrust of "systems" of philosophy as if it were a "system" of its own. James's appealing colloquial mind preferred "Ways of Thinking." He had adopted his distinctively American "Ways" from the works of the eminent astronomer and mathematician Charles Sanders Peirce (1839–1914), whose arcane articles had invented "pragmaticism." Peirce had said that word was "ugly enough to be safe from kidnappers," but it was not safe from James, who wrote philosophy for everybody, and translated it into simple "pragmatism."

Seeking escape from the private world of academic philosophers, James's *Pragmatism,* with the enthusiasm of the amateur, offered an instrumental definition of truth that could make sense to everybody.

> A pragmatist turns his back resolutely and once for all upon a lot of inveterate habits dear to professional philosophers. He turns away from abstraction and insufficiency, from verbal solutions, from bad *a priori* reasons, from fixed principles, closed systems, and pretended absolutes and origins. He

turns towards concreteness and adequacy, towards facts, towards action and towards power.

So James rescued Truth from the metaphysicians. "The true is the name of whatever proves itself to be good in the way of belief, and good, too, for definite, assignable reasons. . . . Theories thus become instruments, not answers to enigmas, in which we can rest. . . . The truth of an idea is not a stagnant property inherent in it. Truth *happens* to an idea. It *becomes* true, is made true by events. . . . The possession of truth, so far from being an end in itself, is only a preliminary means towards other vital satisfaction." Among these satisfactions he would include "the religious experience," which he surveyed with a brilliant tolerance and encompassing sympathy in his *Varieties of Religious Experience* (1902). He shows that religion, like other experience, is to be tested not by its origin but by its fruits.

36

The Solace and Wonder of Diversity

William James's flowing experience was only one of many escapes from the "block universe." Another was the feel for diversity in every moment—in ideas, in institutions, in nature. The revolt against static Absolutes found eloquent expression in two early-twentieth-century Seekers—prophets of diversity—one who sang the virtues of diversity in thought and institutions, another who celebrated diversity in nature.

Oliver Wendell Holmes, Jr. (1841–1935), all three of whose names tied him to eminent New England Brahmin ancestors, was a surprising advocate of diversity. He found his forum in the law, which is more commonly seen as the agent of stability, uniformity, and predictability. With his temperament for action, it is remarkable, too, that Holmes made the law his vocation. In his family tradition, he attended Harvard College and on the outbreak of the Civil War enlisted as a private in the Massachusetts infantry. He saw action, was three times seriously wounded, and was mustered out as captain in July 1864. The war experience left a mark on his thought and character. He never ceased to talk of the "fighting faith." "Through our great good fortune," he recalled on Memorial Day, 1884, "in our youth our hearts were touched with fire. It was given us to learn at the outset that life is a profound and passionate thing." He believed that a man "should share the passion and action of his time in peril of being judged never to have lived."

In his letters throughout his life he would note the anniversaries of the Civil War battles of Ball's Bluff and Antietam in which he had been wounded. He liked to call himself an "old soldier," and to describe the qualities needed to make a lawyer "a fighting success." Although no American jurist would be more reflective, Holmes seemed to find satisfaction in the study of law not so much because it was philosophical as because it dealt with conflicting interests. And he even expressed his theological doubts in the metaphor of battle. As he wrote to Sir Frederick Pollock in 1925:

I think the proper attitude is that we know nothing of cosmic values and bow our heads—seeing reason enough for doing all we can and not demanding the plan of campaign of the General—or even asking whether there is any general or any plan. It's enough for me that this universe can produce intelligence, ideals, etc.—*et superest ager.*

Despite his philosophic temperament, he always seemed to enjoy the battle more than the cause. "It is the merit of the common law," he wrote early in his career, "that it decides the case first and determines the principle afterwards." Nor would he ever be paralyzed by this conflict in his nature. "I am inclined to belittle the doings of the philosophers," he wrote as he approved Santayana's *Life of Reason,* "while I think philosophy the end of life."

With his active temperament it is doubly remarkable that Holmes never became a dogmatist and remained a lifelong champion of openness and diversity in our seeking. Paradoxically, he would make the law and the highest court in the land his forum for preaching his gospel of uncertainty. The federal system of the United States Constitution had conveniently made the Supreme Court an ideal pulpit for an advocate of diversity, for the Court had the power to encourage experimental variety in the laws of all the states of the union.

Instead of following medicine, the profession of his eminent father, Holmes entered Harvard Law School after leaving the army. His father is reported to have exclaimed in dismay, "What's the use of that? A Lawyer can't be a great man!" The traditional law curriculum did not inspire young Holmes. But he stayed with it, graduated, and then took the traditional grand tour of Europe. Holmes returned to practice law in Boston, but his real interest was in the theory, philosophy, and history of law. He edited a scholarly law review and Kent's classic *Commentaries on American Law* (1873). Then he produced a legal classic of his own in his Lowell Lectures that became *The Common Law* (1881).

That book made him the spokesman of a refreshing pragmatic view, bringing into the law the same seeking spirit that his friend William James had brought into philosophy. He opened with what would become the manifesto of a new American school of jurisprudence:

The life of the law has not been logic; it has been experience. The felt necessities of the time, the prevalent moral and political theories, intuitions of public policy avowed or unconscious, even the prejudices which judges share with their fellowmen, have had a good deal more to do than the syllogism in determining the rules by which men should be governed. The law embodies the story of a nation's development through many centuries and it cannot be dealt with as if it contained only the axioms and rules of a book of mathematics. In order to know what it is, we must know what it has been, and what it tends to become.

In this spirit throughout his life Holmes reviewed the hallowed abstractions of legal thought.

One of the most ancient and revered legal abstractions was the idea of "natural law," which he dissolved in a wholesome inquiring suspicion, and with his attractive colloquial eloquence. "It is not enough," he observed of the reverence for "natural law," "for the knight of romance that you agree that his lady is a very nice girl—if you do not admit that she is the best that God ever made or will make, you must fight." "Natural law," according to Holmes, was only another example of the paralyzing temptation to believe in changeless absolutes. "There is in all men a demand for the superlative, so much so that the poor devil who has no other way of reaching it attains it by getting drunk." But lawyers have no more right than philosophers to idolize their current beliefs. "Certitude is not the test of certainty. We have been cock-sure of many things that were not so."

Everything Holmes did he did copiously and with a passion. He served for twenty years on the Supreme Judicial Court of Massachusetts. Then President Theodore Roosevelt named him to the Supreme Court of the United States in 1902, where he served for thirty years, until he was ninety-one. On the Court he was a voice for judicial restraint, believing that the federal system was intended to allow different experiments by state legislatures within the limits of the Constitution. He became famous as the Great Dissenter, seizing opportunities to speak out for urgent views that differed from the majority opinion. And his eloquent opinions, whether for the Court or in dissent, produced ideas and aphorisms that enriched the American legal tradition. In case after case he spoke up for freedom of expression, even in wartime. He had a talent for the commonplace examples, which he would make classic: "the most stringent protection of free speech would not protect a man in falsely shouting fire in a theater and causing panic." His test was "whether the words used are in such circumstances and are of such a nature as to create a clear and present danger that they will bring about the substantive evil that Congress has the right to prevent."

Inspiring all Holmes's championship of free expression was his seeking spirit, his doubt that he or anyone had an avenue to the absolute. "The great act of faith," he wrote to his friend William James (who hardly needed the advice), "is when man decides that he is not God." On his ninetieth birthday he was still reminding young men that his "discovery I was not God" was his "secret of success." And in his dissenting opinions he gave unforgettable expression to his liberal faith:

> When men have realized that time has upset many fighting faiths, they may come to believe even more than they believe the very foundations of their own conduct that the ultimate good desired is better reached by free trade in ideas—that the best test of truth is in the power of the thought to get itself accepted in the competition of the market, and that truth is the only ground upon which their wishes safely can be carried out. That, at any rate, is the theory of our Constitution. It is an experiment, as all life is an experiment. (1919; dissent in *Abrams v. United States*)

What the Constitution had protected, he insisted, was "not free thought for those who agree with us but freedom for the thought that we hate" (1928; dissent in *United States v. Schwimmer*).

If there ever was an age that needed prophets of diversity and the open seeking spirit it was surely the first half of the twentieth century. Technology, mass production, and the mass media were homogenizing ways of living and thinking. Totalitarian governments—Italian Fascism, German Nazism, Soviet Communism, and Marxist China—were using their unprecedented powers to enslave peoples and enforce ideologies. In much of the world, diversity had become heresy. At the same time, and as a by-product of these same technologies—but much less conspicuously—the variety of nature was being dissolved. But while social conformity was publicly enforced by the concentration camp, by inquisition and persecution, and by mock trials, the forces that reduced the diversity of nature were silent. By-products of industrial progress, these homogenizing forces were seldom noticed. The enemies of diversity in nature were hidden. Champions of diversity in nature, therefore, had a double task: first to remind people of the uncelebrated infinite extent of nature's diversity, then to awaken them to the dissolving forces.

The boyhood exploration of Edward O. Wilson (born in 1929) in the swamps of Alabama introduced him vividly to the diversity of nature. The jellyfish, needlefish, stingrays and porpoises, medusas, and rays enticed him in his earliest memories. "The child is ready to grasp this archetype, to explore and learn. . . ." This, Wilson observed, is "how a naturalist is created . . . the core image stays intact. . . . Hands-on experience at the critical time, not systematic knowledge, is what counts in the making of a naturalist." What the Civil War experience was to Holmes, awakening him to the meaning of "fighting faiths," the diversity of nature in the prolific waters of Paradise Beach, Alabama, was to Edward O. Wilson.

But what sort of naturalist would he be? A hereditary defect limited his hearing in the upper registers, which led him away from the world of birds. And, then, when fishing at Paradise Beach his right eye had been pierced by the spine of a pinfish that he had carelessly jerked with his fishing line. He was left with full sight only in his left eye, which proved to be more acute than average at close range. So he felt himself "destined to become an entomologist, committed to minute crawling and flying insects. . . . The attention of my surviving eye turned to the ground. I would thereafter celebrate the little things of the world, the animals that can be picked up between thumb and forefinger and brought close for inspection." So Wilson the Seeker explained the origin of his lifelong venture as an entomologist. "Most children have a bug period, and I never grew out of mine." In his explorations across the world—from Mount Orizaba in Mexico to the rain forests of New Guinea—he found new species of ants. He came to call himself a "neophile"—"an inordinate lover of the new." He was persuaded that most of nature had still been undiscovered, that the earth was a little-known planet. Recent studies had estimated that between 10 and 100 million species of plants, animals, and microorganisms exist on Earth, but, Wilson observed, only about 1.4 million had been studied well enough to be given scientific names. And many of these known species are vanishing or in danger of extinction. Since the tropical rain forests are thought to contain most of the species on

Earth, the loss of tropical rain forests depletes the ancient storehouses of biological diversity.

Human activities are destroying the tropical rain forests, at a rate of a little under 1 percent per year—with the result that roughly one quarter of a percent of species is extinguished or doomed to early extinction each year. To preserve the diversity of life, therefore, required a worldwide effort, for which Wilson developed a vocabulary. He gave currency to "biodiversity" (first recorded in 1985) and invented "biophilia" to describe "the inborn affinity human beings have for other forms of life." Wilson the Seeker repeatedly insisted that he had no interest in ideology. His purpose was "to celebrate diversity and to demonstrate the intellectual power of evolutionary biology."

Wilson showed a dramatic flair for depicting the processes of biodiversity. "The most wonderful mystery of life," he observed, "may well be the means by which it created so much diversity from so little physical matter. The biosphere, all organisms combined, makes up only about one part in ten billion of the earth's mass." He opens his brilliant and readable book *The Diversity of Life* with the story of Krakatau, a volcanic island between Sumatra and Java. The eruption of the Krakatau volcano at 10:02 A.M. on August 27, 1883, killed some thirty thousand people in Java, destroyed all life on the island, and reverberated with tidal waves and atmospheric effects around the earth. Nine months after the explosions a French expedition visited the remnants and scoured them for sign of animal life. "I only discovered one microscopic spider," a French naturalist reported, "—only one; this strange pioneer of the renovation was busy spinning its web." To catch what, no one could imagine!

This reckless wingless creature, Wilson explains, had dared to invade the sterile island by "ballooning"—a process employed by many species of spiders. They release a thread of silk from the spinnerets at the posterior tip of their abdomen which then catches an air current and stretches downwind like the string of a kite. These bold microscopic spiders had no control over their descent but happened to land where there was no competition. This incursion was only the vanguard of a miscellaneous invasion—a rain of planktonic bacteria, fungus spores, small seeds, insects, other spiders, and other creatures. Thus began from all directions a colonization of the once sterile island. Large lizards and crabs were washed ashore, and many species of birds never known there before. For Wilson the Seeker this was a parable of life on Earth, the relentless increase, multiplication, and variety of life.

Wilson envied the naturalists who had observed the variety of life being re-created on what remained of Krakatau. In search of "more Krakataus," he found, or rather made, his opportunity close to home in the Florida Keys. There he devised a bold and novel experiment that would allow him, too, to follow the burgeoning of the diversity of life in a sterile environment. Wilson became the very model of the naturalist who, unlike the "scientist," is more interested in the promise than in the system of nature. From his early Alabama excursions, he was obsessed by the mystery and variety of life. The spectacle of nature awed and entranced him.

Wilson devised his own experiment in biodiversity by creating miniature Krakataus on islands of the Florida Keys. He would sterilize an island, with the aid of a local exterminating firm, then study the natural return of life and the increase of biodiversity. In this convenient laboratory he found the data for his study of the "equilibrium of species." And so in an age of decimating species his seeking spirit would open vistas of nature's pristine diversity. "Today visitors walk along trails where tree snails still decorate the gnarled old lignum vitae trees and dagger wings alight among their delicate blue flowers and petard-shaped yellow fruits. The public can in perpetuity, I trust, witness the Florida Keys as they were in prehistory."

From the worldwide census of animal and plant species, Wilson, seeking the diversity of nature, observed catastrophic consequences of the destruction of habitats. A 90 percent reduction of forest cover (or prairie or river course), he noted, eventually halves the number of species living there. Which only further reduced the proportion of nature that man would know: "The great majority of species of organisms—possibly in excess of 90 percent—remain unknown to science. They live out there somewhere, still untouched, lacking even a name, waiting for their Linnaeus, their Darwin, their Pasteur. The greatest numbers are in remote parts of the tropics, but many also exist close to the cities of industrialized countries. Earth, in the dazzling variety of its life, is still a little-known planet."

All of this led Wilson to sum up his lifelong studies in his latest synthesis—his "three truths" of biophilia. "First, humanity is ultimately the product of biological evolution; second, the diversity of life is the cradle and greatest natural heritage of the human species; and third, philosophy and religion make little sense without taking into account the first two conceptions." So Wilson's seeking led him to "the very heart of wonder"—the diversity of species that was created before humanity and has never been fathomed to its limits. "Our sense of wonder grows exponentially: the greater the knowledge, the deeper the mystery and the more we seek knowledge to create new mystery."

37

The Literature of Bewilderment

The first half of the twentieth century, an age of triumphal and accelerating science, produced a literature of bewilderment without precedent in our history. This will seem less odd when we observe the consequences of the rising tide of science for Seekers and the search for meaning. The new emptiness of meaning and purpose itself became a resource for literature. And nothing better reveals man's infinite capacity to seek something out of nothing and to make the best of his troubled lot.

The Portuguese poet Fernando Pessoa (1888–1935) saw the special challenge of his time, as he opened his unfinished magnum opus, *The Book of Disquietude:*

> I was born in a time when the majority of young people had lost faith in God, for the same reason their elders had it—without knowing why. And then, since the human spirit naturally tends towards judgments based on feeling instead of reason, most of these young people chose Humanity to replace God. I, however, am the sort of person who's always on the fringe of what he belongs to, seeing not only the multitude he's a part of but also the wide open spaces around it. That's why I didn't give up God as completely as they did, and I never accepted Humanity. I reasoned that God, while improbable, might exist, in which case he should be worshipped; whereas Humanity, being a mere biological idea and signifying nothing more than the animal species we belong to, was no more deserving of worship than any other animal species. The cult of Humanity, with its rites of Freedom and Equality, always struck me as a revival of those ancient cults in which gods were like animals or had animal heads.

So he described the "moral landscape" on which a new literature would flourish and reach across Western culture.

This spirit of disquietude, which Pessoa expressed in his final, unfinished work attracted a galaxy of writers some of whom rivaled the great Elizabethans or the Romantics of the Age of the French Revolution. Pessoa was aware, too, of the vast openness of the challenge of his time, which he expressed in a Litany:

> We never know self-realization.
> We are two abysses—a well staring at the Sky.

The galaxy included some of the most influential writers of the mid-century—Camus (Nobel Prize for Literature, 1957), Ionesco, Pinter, and Beckett (Nobel Prize, 1969). This was not a school of writers but a cluster of dissimilar personalities, each making his own contribution—in essay, poem, novel, or drama—to the literature of bewilderment. The core idea was expressed by Albert Camus in his *Myth of Sisyphus* (1942): "A world that can be explained even with bad reasons is a familiar world. But, on the other hand, in a universe suddenly divested of illusions and lights, man feels an alien, a stranger. His exile is without remedy since he is deprived of the memory of a lost home or the hope of a promised land. This divorce between man and his life, the actor and his setting is properly the feeling of absurdity." The most successful and most influential form of this literature was the drama. For while the essay and the novel aim to explain the human condition, the drama simply shows. And the theater of the absurd revealed at the same time the power and the limits of words in revealing an absurd world.

Perhaps the most powerful and enduring figure in the theater of the absurd is Samuel Beckett (1906–1989), who has been called the most uncompromising of the absurdists. Born near Dublin, like other Irish stars—Shaw, Wilde, and Yeats—he, too, came from a Protestant Anglo-Irish family. He studied Romance languages at Trinity College, Dublin, and taught school before going to Paris, which would become the center of his life in 1928.

He became a lifelong friend of James Joyce, and there was a wondrous unspoken rapport between them. "Beckett was addicted to silences," Richard Ellman recounts, "and so was Joyce; they engaged in conversations which consisted often in silences directed towards each other, both suffused with sadness, Beckett mostly for the world, Joyce mostly for himself." Joyce's unhappy daughter, Lucia, was infatuated with Beckett, who took her to restaurants and the theater. Finally Beckett had to tell her that when he came to Joyce's apartment it was mainly to see her father. He later apologized to Peggy Guggenheim for not having been able to fall in love with Lucia.

Beckett traveled about Europe, but when World War II came he settled in France, was active in the Resistance, and at the war's end remained in Paris. During these years he had produced an astonishing literary miscellany—essays, novels, poems, and plays. His turning to write in French, which was his second language, he described as an act of self-discipline. But he never explained this in a way that did not have the sound of the absurd. Perhaps there was some masochism in his choice of the difficult. He was afraid of English, he explained, "because you couldn't help writing poetry in it." But he did say that French "had the right weakening effect," and that "in French it is easier to write without style."

Beckett first attracted wide attention in 1953 with the performance in Paris of his *En Attendant Godot* (English translation, *Waiting for Godot*, 1954). Despite Beckett's warnings against overinterpretation, this work was taken to be a manifesto of the theater of the absurd. It was, too, a perfect example of the austerity and sparseness of Beckett's style. When the director of the first American production asked Beckett what was meant by Godot, he answered, "If I knew, I would have said so in the play." Two men, Vladimir and Estragon, appear on an empty stage furnished with nothing but a solitary tree. They assume that since they are rational beings, there must be some reason for their being where they are. They assume they must be waiting for someone, and they call that person "Godot." But they have no evidence that that person ever made an appointment to see them, nor even that such a person exists. Beckett contrasts their waiting with another pair, Pozzo and Lucky, master and slave, aimlessly wandering, whose aimlessness only reinforces that of Vladimir and Estragon. At the end of Act I, Vladimir and Estragon are told that Mr. Godot cannot come, but that he will surely come tomorrow. At the end of Act I:

> Estragon: Well, shall we go?
> Vladimir: Yes, let's go.
>   [They do not move.]

Act II repeats the pattern, and ends with the same lines of dialogue, by the same characters in reverse order. The play has no plot, tells no story, but presents a challenging unchanging situation. "Nothing happens, nobody comes, nobody goes, it's awful."

At a poignant moment when Pozzo falls and cannot rise, Vladimir and Estragon speculate on whether to rob him or help him. Then Vladimir says, "Let us do something while we have the chance! It is not every day that we are needed. Others would meet the case equally if not better. To all mankind they were addressed, those cries for help still ringing in our ears! But at this place, at this moment of time, all mankind is us, whether we like it or not."

The slapstick comedy of the early silent films was in the spirit of Beckett's absurd, which itself was in the tradition of the ancient mimes and medieval clowns and jesters. All these comic forms showed the dramatic power of wordless and purposeless action. Vladimir and Estragon reflect Laurel and Hardy; a version of Charlie Chaplin appears as Hamm in *Endgame* (1957); and Buster Keaton himself played in *Film* (1964). A feeling for the absurd allowed Beckett to see the comic where others saw only the meaningless. And so Beckett arrays the trivia of everyday life to entertain us with a patient depiction of the human condition. Which made Beckett's insights perfectly suited to the ancient cathartic role of the theater.

With his feeling for the absurd it is not surprising that Beckett was fascinated by the mystery of time. His first separately published work was on the subject. During his first stay in Paris a prize of ten pounds was offered by Nancy Cunard and Richard Aldington for the best poem on the subject of time. Beckett's prizewinning poem, which he piquantly titled "Whoroscope," focused on his favorite philosopher, Descartes, reflecting on time, hens' eggs, and other miscellany. It was published in 1930 in an edition of one hundred signed copies at five shillings and two hundred unsigned at a shilling. Beckett, then, was naturally fascinated by Proust, on whom he wrote one of the first full-length studies—a critical essay (published in 1931) focusing on Proust's exploration of time. Time, as he wrote in his essay on Proust, would somehow give Beckett a key to novelty in the absurd ocean of experiences. This suggested, too, a theme of *Waiting for Godot.* The subject of the play, as often observed, was not Godot, but *waiting,* a habitual encounter with time. According to Beckett:

Habit is the ballast that chains the dog to his vomit. Breathing is habit. Life is habit. Or rather life is a succession of habits, since the individual is a succession of individuals. . . . Habit then is the generic term for the countless treaties concluded between the countless subjects that constitute the individual and their countless correlative objects. The periods of transition that separate consecutive adaptations . . . represent the perilous zones in the life of the individual, dangerous, precarious, painful, mysterious, and fertile, when for a moment the boredom of living is replaced by the suffering of being.

PART EIGHT

A WORLD IN PROCESS: THE MEANING IN THE SEEKING

But he never fell into the error of arresting his intellectual development by any formal acceptance of creed or system, or of mistaking, for a house in which to live, an inn that is but suitable for the sojourn of a night, or for a few hours of a night in which there are no stars and the moon is in travail. . . . no theory of life seemed to him to be of any importance compared with life itself.
—OSCAR WILDE, *THE PICTURE OF DORIAN GRAY* (1891)

The most beautiful thing we can experience is the mysterious. It is the source of all true art and science.
—ALBERT EINSTEIN, *WHAT I BELIEVE* (1930)

38

Acton's "Madonna of the Future"

The eloquent prophet of the modern liberal spirit, Lord Acton (1834–1902), would poignantly refer to his unfinished lifework—a history of liberty—as "The Madonna of the Future." This was the title of Henry James's story of an artist who devoted his life to a single great painting, but at the artist's death the easel in his studio showed only a blank canvas. While this way of describing Acton's history was delightfully ironic, it was also wonderfully true to the liberal spirit to which he gave his life and his writing. His history of liberty has been described as "the greatest book that was never written." Yet Acton became one of the most influential and most often quoted of the historians of his age.

Acton's life and work (and nonwork) included numerous lectures, essays, and reviews on historical subjects, but he never wrote a book. It was significant, too, that while he authored unforgettable aphorisms (for example, "Power tends to corrupt, and absolute power corrupts absolutely"), which have attained the authority of cliché, he is not famous for his theories of history. One of the most vigorous and relentless Seekers, he remained vividly aware of the burden and the promise of his Western inheritance. There was no more strenuous, nor more frustrated effort to reconcile the ancient doctrines of Christianity with the modern doctrines of liberalism. And, although Acton saw the rise of liberty as the grand theme of human history, he was a divided soul, a Seeker who would not abandon either path of his quest.

Born into an age that was dissolving the certitudes of Christianity, Acton still dared not abandon them. His life, he once said, was "the story of a man who started in life believing himself a sincere Catholic and a sincere Liberal; who therefore renounced everything in Catholicism which was not compatible with Liberty and everything in Politics not compatible with Catholicism." He was the perfect embodiment of the Seeker—too Catholic to renounce the wisdom of the past and too searching not to follow the inquiring spirit of his age. But he never retreated into the comforting dogmas of either past or present. There was never a more devoted acolyte of ideas, nor a more scrupulous attender to "the little fact that makes the difference." As he once said of his mentor Döllinger, "He knew too much to write." Always discouraged by the imperfection of the material, he always delayed his unifying work by the promise of new facts and new ideas still to come.

Acton's life and inheritance were designed to make his mind a battleground. Born into a cosmopolitan, aristocratic family, he inherited his Catholicism. His family had been converted to Catholicism in the eighteenth century and they saw that his education was supervised by leading Catholics. Schooled at the English Catholic school of Oscott, which had been a center of the Catholic Revival, near Oxford, which was the center of the Anglo-Catholic Oxford Movement, he was refused admission by three Cambridge colleges that did not welcome Catholics. In 1850 he was sent to Munich, then noted for its Catholic scholarship. There he was privately tutored by Professor Johann Ignaz von Döllinger (1799–1890), an independent-minded priest and historian, whose disciple he remained for thirty years.

From Döllinger, Acton inherited the idea of "developmental" Christianity. To reconcile history and theology, Christianity was conceived not as a set of dogmas but as a historical growth. But for Catholics in Acton's generation the conflict between dogma and the seeking spirit—between orthodoxy and liberty—was not to be so easily dismissed. As editor of the liberal Catholic monthly *The Rambler,* Acton tried to apply the developmental idea, but soon met papal opposition and had to discontinue publication (1864).

The issue was posed more dramatically and more deliberately than Acton had imagined when the imperious Pope Pius IX (1792–1878; pope, 1846–78) called the first Vatican Council (1869–70) to confront the conflict between traditional doctrine and the rising currents of liberalism. His would be the longest pontificate in history, and one of the most contentious. Though dominated by the papal bureaucracy, it was only after heated opposition that the Vatican Council promulgated the dogma of papal infallibility. "The bishops entered the council shepherds," the historian William Lecky observed from Rome, "they came out of it sheep." When Döllinger protested and refused to accept the dogma, he was excommunicated. Acton himself persuaded the prime minister Gladstone to protest the new dogma, and published his own attack on infallibility. But when Archbishop Manning supported the doctrine and confronted Acton, he reconsidered, and so was not excommunicated.

It is no wonder that Acton's great work, his history of liberty, remained a "Madonna of the Future"—never finished, and never really begun. For he remained a passionate, always unfulfilled Seeker. His need for personal faith he satisfied in Catholic Christianity, but for the whole human experience he found no dogma adequate. His idea of liberty was a way of describing the endless quest. Faith in liberty as the human destiny made every event a chapter of the larger history he never wrote. All his lectures and essays became part of that story.

Believing in the right to unbelief, he saw liberal faith as a bulwark against persecution, while religion was not. Though he detested persecution, yet he was unwilling to abandon his Catholic faith. Instead, he used his agile mind and historical detail to defend his personal faith while condemning Catholic acts of persecution throughout history. Acton's inward conflicts have been sensitively described by Gertrude Himmelfarb, who recounts the dynamics of his compromise. With a tortured historical argument, he elaborated in his essays his distinction between the Catholic and the Protestant theories of persecution—in which the Protestant theory came off much the worse. "The principle on which the Protestants oppressed the Catholics was new. . . . Catholic intolerance is handed down from an age when unity subsisted, and when its preservation, being essential to that of society, became a necessity of State as well as a result of circumstances. Protestant intolerance, on the contrary, was the peculiar fruit of a dogmatic system in contradiction with the facts and principles on which the intolerance actually existing among Catholics was founded. Spanish intolerance has been infinitely more sanguinary than Swedish; but in Spain, independently of the interests of religion, there were strong political and social reasons to justify persecution without seeking any theory to prop it up. . . ."

Catholic persecution, he argued, was no more than the enforcement of public morality, while Protestant persecution was the pure inhibition of freedom of religious thought, illustrated by the case of Servetus, whom Calvin had burned at the stake: "Servetus was not a party leader. He had no followers who threatened to upset the peace and unity of the Church. His doctrine was speculative, without power or attraction for the masses, like Lutheranism; and without consequences subversive of morality, or affecting in any direct way the existence of society, like Ana-baptism." Thus, as Himmelfarb observes, while Catholic persecution was more bloody as the instrument of prevailing morality, Acton argued that "the Protestant persecution was more soul-corrupting."

Obsessed by the need to find coherence, order, and unity in all human history, Acton imagined that unity might be found in a history of liberty. Yet all he could achieve was a bouquet of brilliant insights into epochal movements and revolutions. He offered these in his *Lectures on the French Revolution,* his *Lectures on Modern History,* his "Inaugural Lecture on the Study of History," and miscellaneous essays. His in-sights were diffuse, atomistic, and inconsistent.

Acton was hostile to the American abolitionists, who championed "an abstract idea" even at the cost of disrupting society. The American abolitionists, he argued, were the real enemies of the Constitution. They appealed to an abstraction and the passing whim of the majority against established institutions. "The influence of these habits of ab-stract reasoning, to which we owe the revolution in Europe, is to make all things questions of principle and of abstract law . . . and the conse-quence is that a false and arbitrary political system produces an arbi-trary code of ethics, and the theory of abolition is as erroneous as the theory of freedom."

So Acton saw uncontrolled democracy, too, like absolute monarchy, as the enemy of liberty. "The true democratic principle, that none shall have power over the people, is taken to mean that none shall be able to restrain or to elude its power. . . . The true democratic principle, that every man's free will shall be as unfettered as possible, is taken to mean that the free will of the collective people shall be fettered in nothing." But there was a higher law, which was not the mere will of the majority. This was the faith of "the Stoics who emancipated mankind from its subjugation to despotic rule, and whose enlightened and elevated views of life bridged the chasm that separates the ancient from the Christian state, and led the way to freedom. Their test of good government is its conformity to principles that can be traced to a higher legislator. That which we must obey, that to which we are bound to reduce all civil au-thorities, and to sacrifice every earthly interest, is that immutable law which is perfect and eternal as God Himself, which proceeds from His nature, and reigns over heaven and earth and over all the nations."

The historian's function, Acton insisted in his Inaugural Lecture as Regius Professor, is "to keep in view and to command the movement of ideas, which are not the effect but the cause of public events." Yet Acton's own history was a tale of concrete human experience, of human weakness and human hopes, which he noted:

> Use of history—no surprises. He [the historian] has seen all this before. He knows what constant and invariable forces will resist the truth and the Higher Purpose. What weakness, division, excess, will damage the better cause. The splendid plausibility of error, the dazzling attractiveness of sin. And by what adjustment to inferior motives good causes succeed. . . . History is not a web woven with innocent hands. Among all the causes which degrade and demoralize men, power is the most constant and the most active.

Although Acton would be popularly known for his aphorisms about power and its perils, he saw an antidote to power. The dynamic in history—a tireless struggle against the power of original sin—came from communal seeking for the modern mode of progress. Acton gave it the name of revolution.

"Liberalism," Acton insisted, "wishes for what ought to be, irrespective of what is," and is "essentially revolutionary. . . . Facts must yield to ideas. Peaceably and patiently if possible. Violently if not." "The supreme conquests of society are won more often by violence than by lenient arts. . . . If the world owes religious liberty to the Dutch Revolution, constitutional government to the English, federal republicanism to the American, political equality to the French and its successors, what is to become of us, docile and attentive students of the absorbing Past? The triumph of the Revolutionist annuls the historian."

Yet the historian must remember that "the modern ages did not proceed from the medieval by normal succession" but "Unheralded, it founded a new order of things under a law of innovation." Modern history was born in revolution, in the revolutions of Columbus, Machiavelli, Erasmus, Luther, and Copernicus—each of whom "broke the chain of authority and tradition." So the long continuity of history, for Acton, was a process of permanent revolution. This was his name for progress, and justified his optimism for humanity despite the evils of the self-serving power of individuals.

But how justify the existence of evil under a beneficent God? Acton, faced with Job's problem, was seeking his own solution. Which he found ingeniously, not in the omnipotence of God but in his own sacred theme of liberty. "Liberty is so holy a thing," Acton observed, "that God was forced to permit Evil, that it might exist."

So, after all, still not achieving his own great work, Acton brought together the best historians of his day to collaborate on the *Cambridge Modern History.* Advancing beyond "conventional history," they would not be confined in the history of nations, but would chronicle the grand leading ideas that unified humankind:

> By Universal History I understand that which is distinct from the combined history of all countries, which is not a rope of sand, but a continuous development, and is not a burden to the memory, but an illumination of the soul. It moves in a succession to which the nations are subsidiary. Their story will be told, not for their own sake, but in reference and subordination to a higher series, according to the time and the degree in which they contribute to the common fortunes of mankind.

It was significant that, while Acton left a rich miscellaneous legacy of his own essays, lectures, and ideas, his monument of scholarship was the collaboration of other historians of his age, seeking in a work of surprising objectivity.

Despite Acton's optimism about the long-term future of humankind, he raised the alarm against ideas and institutions of his time that menaced the liberty that was the proper human destiny. The most serious was the racism recently advanced by the French Orientalist Joseph Gobineau. Acton attacked racism as "one of the many schemes to deny free will, responsibility, and guilt, and to supplant moral by physical forces." "Nationality," newly flourishing in Europe in Acton's day, was a similar diversion of the great current of human liberty. "The progress of civilization depends on transcending Nationality. . . . Influences which are accidental yield to those which are rational. . . . The nations aim at power, and the world at freedom." And the State (as in Bismarck's Prussia)—the modern fellow conspirator of Nationalism—was "a vast abstraction above all other things" (invented, he said, by Machiavelli), which oppressed all its subjects and consumed their lives.

39

Malraux's Charms of Anti-Destiny

Marx had sought his clues to destiny in the industrial Manchester of his friend Friedrich Engels, in the plight of the oppressed surrounding him in Western Europe, and in the arcane science of economics. André Malraux (1901–1976) set out to find his meaning for history in the artwork of the buried past halfway around the world in Indochina. Yet he would risk his life in revolutionary movements foreshadowed by Marx's science, and would write enduring sagas of the adventure of revolution in his time. Malraux saw human fulfillment in the kinship of past and present everywhere and in individual acts of heroism, in war or art. "Art," he insisted, "is an anti-destiny," the fulfillment of man's unique and universal spirit. Obsessed by the passion and drama of history in his time, he found elegant refuge in his *Voices of Silence,* in the legacy of artists of all times and places.

Malraux was born in 1901 to a wealthy family in Paris. His father's heroes were the pioneers of technology—de Lesseps, Eiffel, Citroen, Blériot. He attended the lycée but never completed the program, and grew up in Paris where he worked for rare-book dealers. He read widely and especially admired Dumas. His father was a tank officer in World War I, which André considered "very romantic." The boy André glimpsed the carnage of battle in trains returning with heavy casualties. Never attending university, he acquired an amazing grasp of world art, history, and literature on his own. At eighteen his first publication, *The Origins of Cubist Poetry,* gave a clue to his lifelong interest in the surprising and the marginal. Stimulated by the effervescent community of Paris intellectuals, the impressionable Malraux explored mystical experiences, sought out works of erotica and exotica for publishers, and acquired a taste for Dostoyevsky and Nietzsche, which he never lost.

When he was twenty-one, Malraux enlisted his new bride, Clara Goldschmidt, on an expedition to Indochina in search of the ancient Khmer ruins about which he had read in an archaeological review. In the jungle he hoped to find the abandoned ruins of a temple that might rival the famous Angkor Wat. He had already given his own explanation of the special value of individual works recovered from the past—in his theory of confrontation, which he would develop thirty years later in his *Voices of Silence.* "The Greek genius," he had written, "is better understood by opposing one Greek statue to an Egyptian or Asian statue than by getting to know a hundred Greek statues." He secured a letter from the Minister of Colonies for French Indochina authorizing him to explore the site of the Khmer temples, his only obligation being to give an account on his return.

After a month's sea voyage from Marseilles, André and Clara briefly savored the exotic life of Saigon and of Hanoi, administrative capital of French Indochina. A riverboat took them to Siem Reap, the port for Angkor Wat, where they equipped themselves with tropical helmets, drinking water, and a local guide. After a two-day trek into the jungle with four bullock carts of supplies they found a neglected trail that led to the ruins mentioned in the archaeological review. In *The Royal Way,* Malraux would describe their finds—"bas reliefs of the best period, marked by Indian influence . . . but very beautiful." Still embedded in the walls were huge blocks of the treasured sculptures, which Malraux and his crew spent two days and several broken saws hacking loose. They estimated that the blocks would bring $100,000 on delivery in New York. The pieces they had cut out formed four blocks of bas-relief of dancing goddesses and men seated in lotus position. Their thousand pounds of treasure was loaded on a river steamer to a forwarding agent in Saigon. When the boat tied up at Phnom Penh, André and Clara stayed on board. They were awakened before midnight and placed under arrest.

The ruins that André and his crew had exploited had been among the "discovered and undiscovered" sites protected by the governor general's regulations and recent Paris decrees. During the six months before their trial, "the Angkor Wat robbers" became a cause célèbre in Paris and New York. Clara feigned suicide, was stricken by a tropical fever, and began a hunger strike. Despite uncertainty whether these Banteai Srey ruins had really been legally classified and protected as historical monuments, the judge convicted Malraux, sentencing him to three years in prison and five years' banishment from residence in Indochina. After months of pressure, petitions from eminent Europeans, and lengthy appeals, Malraux's sentence was reduced and he never had to go to prison. Malraux still wanted to appeal again, because, he said, he wanted his statues. But they were not to be his. In 1925 the statues were replaced in the temple wall, where they stayed until the whole area was leveled in a North Vietnamese–Khmer Rouge attack in 1970.

On his twenty-third birthday Malraux sailed for Marseilles. For him, seeking was never a purely aesthetic experience. Finding his very own way to every idea, he drew some surprising conclusions from his archaeological misadventure. "My revolutionary commitment," he would later explain, "was in reaction to colonialism. Until then I had never taken sides and Indochina was the touchstone to my becoming aware of—let's simplify 'social justice.' I became involved when I realized that for the peoples of Southeast Asia only a revolutionary movement would bring them a liberal status." After a brief stay in Paris to finance his next Indochina adventure, Malraux and Clara returned to Saigon in 1925. There they founded a "free" anticolonialist newspaper, *L'Indochine*. This put Malraux in touch with the left wing of the Kuomintang, the Nationalist Party in China. Meanwhile an enterprising Paris publisher had given him an advance and a contract for three novels.

The government in Saigon made trouble for him. He found it hard even to secure type to print his "free" newspaper, and it folded after a few months. Malraux gave new expression to his anticolonialist passion by founding *L'Indochine enchainée* (Indochina in Chains). Then he played a legendary role in the brewing revolution in China, perhaps as a "people's commissar" in the Canton uprising of 1925 and in the Shanghai insurrection of 1927. But his new publishing venture also folded, and Malraux was soon back in Paris in the brilliant circle of writers and artists that included Gide, Valéry, and Joyce. In the next few years he wrote three novels of revolution—*The Conquerors* (1928) and *Man's Fate* (1933) on China, and *Man's Hope* (1937) on Spain. The fame of these works made him a spokesman for Communist intellectuals in the West. He wrote other novels, too, and some cryptic impressionistic pieces on the future of civilization and the relation between East and West.

Malraux's quixotic passion for archaeology remained alive, and the sale of his novels supplied the means for new expeditions. Intrigued by the tales of the Queen of Sheba, he went in search of her ancient capital. Enlisting a friendly aviator, Malraux directed an air survey of the

Arabian desert, where he found a site that he impetuously declared to be the Queen of Sheba's mythical capital. Confirmation on the ground was still to come. And these frolics were interrupted again by his revolutionary passion. In 1934 at the All-Soviet Writers Congress in Leningrad, Malraux played a leading and slightly defiant role in the very year when Stalin's purge would begin. "The fundamental adventure for a writer," Malraux the Seeker told Maksim Gorky, "is his own astonishment in the face of life. . . . behind every artist you find the question, 'What is life, what does it mean?' " He titled his challenging speech "Art Is a Conquest," and he explained:

> Art is not an act of submission but a conquest. A conquest of what? Nearly always of the unconscious and quite often of logic. Your classic writers give a richer and more complex picture of the inner life than the Soviet novelists, and so it sometimes happens that a reader will feel that Tolstoy is more real to them than many of the novelists attending this congress.

The outbreak of the Spanish Civil War again summoned the revolutionary in Malraux. In 1936 he arrived in Madrid in a private plane piloted by the friend who had discovered the capital of Sheba three years before. No longer a mere journalist, he soon commanded the España Squadron in the air. He was risking his life in battle for the Republican cause, which now included the Communists. When Malraux toured the United States to arouse support for the Republican cause in Spain, he was lionized in New York and Hollywood. Asked why he had risked his life in Spain when he could have relaxed in his fame as an author in France, he responded, "Because I do not like myself." And when asked why he found fighting more important than writing, he answered, "Because death is a greater triumph." And he defended Stalin. "Just as the Inquisition didn't detract from the fundamental dignity of Christianity," he declared at a dinner given by *The Nation* in New York, "so the Moscow trials didn't detract from the fundamental dignity of communism."

Still, in his novels of the Chinese Revolution and the Spanish Civil War, Malraux was anything but the ideologue. He found the meaning of these struggles in individual acts of heroism, just as he had found the meaning of art in the individual work confronted by others. At the outbreak of World War II, he returned to France and joined the French army as a private. Captured by the Germans, he escaped from prison camp, and was active in organizing the Resistance. After the war he served de Gaulle as minister of information, then for ten years as minister of culture. This was a time when Malraux felt his country and the world needed "a new idea of man," and he saw the arts as the vehicle of that idea.

In 1951 Malraux finally offered his new view of man in his *Voices of Silence,* which he said he had worked on all his life. Every work of art, he believed, was "an encounter with time." And since about 1870, Western man had the new opportunity to envision all that humanity had known and accomplished.

> The difference between ours and other civilizations is quite obviously the machine and the fact that we are without precedent. Other cultures rarely knew the societies preceding them—the Renaissance knew Antiquity, yes; but Rome wasn't the inheritor of Egypt, much less of the Celts—whereas we are the sum of all the others, the first planetary civilization. This is something momentous that started around 1870 when so-called cultivated humanity realized that it was the inheritor of the whole planet. The next step is obviously to conceive humanity as one. . . .
>
> Culturally, this means there are no more secrets. We don't know what hasn't been discovered, of course—ruins never unearthed, but we know everything that exists and has been. (From Malraux's Foreword to the French translation of T. E. Lawrence, *Seven Pillars of Wisdom*)

Malraux now dared to inventory and assess this whole inheritance. His *Voices of Silence,* copiously illustrated, began with the history of museums, recounting how by making reproduction possible, modern technology had created the "Museum Without Walls," where a viewer anywhere could confront the whole heritage of art. And so ended the unchallenged sovereignty of Italy.

Our heritage is the product of a vast metamorphosis, where Greek statues have turned white and all the remote past reaches us colorless. So styles have replaced schools and the film has liberated individualist painting from movement and narration. Then "The Metamorphosis of Apollo," in the Medieval Retrogression and Byzantium, brought a Christian art that, unlike Greek art, individualized human destinies and was based on specific events. "The Creative Process" explained how the artist's eyesight was put to the service of his style, and how art was a process of reduction—"Every great style a reduction of the Cosmos to Man's measure."

And finally how modern art consummates in the "Aftermath of the Absolute." In the seventeenth century the sense of the absolute disappears from Western civilization, Christianity declines and is threatened by science and reason. "Our art," then, is "a questioning of the scheme of things. . . . A new all-embracing conception of art . . . The past seen steadily and whole for the first time. . . . History aims at transposing destiny on to the plane of awareness; art at transmuting it into freedom." Malraux the Seeker illustrates the power of individual vision by his adoration of the artists of the last four centuries who struggled against the newly secular world. They revealed the power of the artist to "transform a bouquet of flowers into a burning bush." These heroes are Rembrandt, El Greco, Goya, and Van Gogh. And they prove that art needs no ideology, but is itself sacred. "The human power to which art testifies is man's eternal revenge on a hostile universe . . . a revolt against man's fate."

So Malraux concludes that "humanism does not consist in saying: 'No animal could have done what we have done,' but in declaring: 'We have refused to do what the beast within us willed to do,' and we wish to rediscover Man wherever we discover that which seeks to crush him to the dust." The sweep and boldness and universality of Malraux's view is breathtaking. He reveals to us again and again what we had often looked at but never seen. If one reads no other book on the history of art, Malraux's *Voices of Silence* would awaken us to the grandeur, range, and subtlety of our inheritance—the scope of man's quest.

40

Rediscovering Time:
Bergson's Creative Evolution

Just as Job made problems for himself by his faith in one omnipotent, omnibenevolent God, so, as Malraux observed, the modern faith in science and technology created its own new problems. A quantified world was a homogeneous world, oriented toward seeking causes. Not toward the Why but the How. The best thinkers would offer explanations, but no justifications. Technology multiplied data in cataclysmic quantity before meaning could be found or even imagined—opening vast new realms of terra incognita. Never before had Western man known so much about the world or understood so little of his purpose.

By the early twentieth century a galaxy of minds, challenged by this intractable universe, sought new meaning in the very processes of change. Abandoning the breathless quest for absolutes, exhilarated by the flux of the unexpected, they learned to enjoy the mystery in the flow of experience. They justified their doubts of a predictable historic destiny by the new ways of biology, psychology, sociology, and the varieties of religious experience. In place of eternal ideas, they would adore the vitality of an ever-changing world.

The vitalizing spirit of this new way of seeking was the French philosopher and man of letters Henri Bergson (1859–1941), who found the fertile source of this dynamism in a new way of seeing time. To open the European mind to the promise of a world of change—Acton's "revolution in permanence"—thinkers had to be freed from the narrow channels in which the ways of science had confined them. Western science, making reason and experience their resources for mastering nature, had devised an interpretation that was increasingly mechanistic and materialistic. Francis Bacon, Isaac Newton, and their disciples had sought the laws of physical forces. And Darwin's *Origin of Species* appeared in the year of Bergson's birth. "As Darwin discovered the law of evolution in organic nature," we have heard Friedrich Engels declare at the graveside of his hero in 1883, "so Marx discovered the law of evolution in human history." Both Marx and Darwin saw the conflict of physical forces in history. For Marx, historic destiny was charted by the conflict of economic classes; for Darwin the rise and decline of species was charted by the conflict of organisms, by natural selection and the survival of the fittest. Evolution, the emergence of higher species (and finally man), was said to be the by-product of physical processes in nature over geologic millennia.

This explanation, somehow, did not satisfy Henri Bergson, a Seeker of the meaning of life. Not because it challenged the Bible and the dogmas of orthodox religion, but rather because it failed to provide a satisfactory explanation of evolution itself, and did not account for human consciousness and the lived experience. Some other force—not merely mechanical—must have been at work.

Creative Evolution (1911; French edition, *L'Évolution Créatrice,* 1907) offered the product of Bergson's dissatisfaction with the prevailing mechanistic and materialist views of evolution and outlined eloquently his own vitalist view. The book does not evade the technical problems but develops his argument in lively style with commonplace examples to persuade the lay reader. He succeeded in reaching the whole Western world of letters and in 1928 received the Nobel Prize for literature. "Oh, my Bergson," William James exclaimed when he read the book, "you are a magician and your book is a marvel, a real wonder. . . . But, unlike the works of genius of the Transcendentalist movement (which are so obscure and abominably and inaccessibly written), a pure classic in point of form . . . such a flavor of persistent euphony, as of a rich river that never foamed or ran thin, but steadily and firmly proceeded with its banks full to the brim." When the book appeared, Bergson had already earned acclaim across the literate West with the three brief seminal books that offered the essence of the ideas that would make him one of the most influential writers of the century.

To explain the processes and products of evolution, Bergson argued, there must have been something more than mindless physical forces. The process of natural selection operating on random variations could not explain the evolution of a complex organ like the eye of vertebrates. Evolution supposes that at each stage of development all the parts of an animal and of its organs are varying contemporaneously, for they must function together in order to ensure the survival of the species. Bergson found it implausible to suppose that the coadapted variations in the countless parts of the eye could have been random. What was maintaining the continuity of functions while the various forms were altering? Surely, he proposes, there must have been a vital impulse (*élan vital*) directing the growth of these complex parts and the organism as a whole.

Bergson was led to this suggestion by certain large features in the processes and products of evolution. "Two points are equally striking in an organ like the eye: the complexity of its structure and the simplicity of its function. . . . Just because the act is simple, the slightest negligence on the part of nature in the building of the infinitely complex machine would have made vision impossible." This suggested, then, that there must have been some other channeling force at work. Bergson called it an impulse—the vital impulse.

The same probability appeared from the fact that evolution advanced from relatively simple organisms to the complex. The earliest living things were unicellular entities well adapted to their environment. Why did not evolution stop at that stage, as pure mechanism would have dictated? Instead, life continued to complicate itself "more and more dangerously." Does this not make some vital impulse plausible or even necessary to explain the elaboration and multiplication of species? Something must have impelled life, in spite of the risks, to ever-higher levels of organization.

Bergson's master-insight reached beyond the millennial processes of evolution to describe the uniqueness of current lived experience. He found the meaning of life and its essential character in the lived experience of time. Which also provided his conclusive argument against mechanistic and materialistic dogmas. The prime effort from which the mechanistic view of time sprang was itself a by-product of technology—the idea of clock time, the notion that time could be ticked off and measured in homogeneous units. On the contrary, Bergson insisted that lived time was *duration*. This simple idea, which appeared in his earliest publications, would dominate and guide his thought and his worldwide influence. Time, he insisted, is just "the stuff" our physical life is made of.

There is . . . no stuff more resistant nor more substantial. For our duration is not merely one instant replacing another; if it were, there would never be anything but the present—no prolonging of the past into the actual, no evolution, no concrete duration. Duration is the continuous progress of the past which gnaws into the future and which swells as it advances. And as the past grows without ceasing, so there is no limit to its preservation. Memory . . . is not a faculty of putting away recollections in a drawer, or of inscribing them in a register. . . . In reality, the past is preserved by itself, automatically. In its entirety, probably, it follows us at every instant. . . .

His elementary idea—the uniqueness of time in the lived experience—was the basis of Bergson's ideas of memory, freedom, and change. "For an ego which does not change does not *endure*. . . ." "Things do not endure like ourselves." And *our* enduring is what makes freedom possible. Our freedom, then, is real, but indefinable "just because we *are* free." Which recalls William James's observation that "my first act of free will shall be to believe in free will." "Finally," Bergson concluded, "consciousness is essentially free; it is freedom itself." "For consciousness," he wrote, "corresponds exactly to the living being's power of choice; it is coextensive with the fringe of possible action that surrounds the real action; consciousness is synonymous with invention and with freedom."

With his flair for the unforgettable metaphor, which made him a literary prophet, he drew on the temptations of the latest technology for his account of human consciousness as "The Cinematographical Mechanism of Thought." The word "cinema" had entered English only a decade before. "Reality," he observed, "has appeared to us as a perpetual becoming. It makes itself or unmakes itself, but it is never something made. Such is the intuition that we have of mind when we draw aside the veil which is interposed between our consciousness and ourselves." So for Bergson the metaphor of the cinema—a succession of changed images seen in rapid succession—explains both the making of "the mechanistic illusion" and the need for the idea of duration.

Bergson's role in an age of rising faith in science was thus to liberate Seekers from the search for system and dogma, and to justify their joy in the search. His idea of duration—of lived time—had disposed of the mechanistic view. And he then broadened the sources of knowledge in a way to delight both pragmatists and mystics. For he had "put duration and free choice at the base of things." He pursued his favorite distinction between the paralyzing static expressed in clock time—the mecha-nistic spatial view of time—and the fertile dynamic expressed in the flow of lived duration. In *The Two Sources of Morality and Religion* (1935; in French, 1932) he developed the difference between the "closed society" dominated by codes of laws and customs and the "open society" expressed in the aspirations of heroes, saints, and mys-tics. The two sources were intelligence, expressed in science and the static spatial view of experience; and intuition, expressed in duration, lived time, freedom, and creativity, in the works of poets, artists, and mystics. Life could be known only by "bathing in the full stream of ex-perience."

When Bergson published his *Creative Evolution,* it seemed that the menace to free-flowing thought was a rigid reliance on science and its iron laws, what William James called "the beast, Intellectualism." So, while some attacked Bergson as "anti-intellectual" he was widely ap-plauded for his vitalism. His ingenious similes and his vivid poetic style had brought him the Nobel Prize for *literature* in 1928. But by 1939 the menace to liberated thought was a belligerent Axis anti-intellectualism, founded on fantasies of blood and race. Bergson, though desperately ailing, seized the opportunity to express his contempt for that bar-barism. A few weeks before his death, despite the exemption offered him, at the age of eighty-one he left his sickbed to stand in a queue in order to register as a Jew and so shame the German-inspired Vichy gov-ernment that had barred Jews from holding educational posts in France. And he renounced all the honors whose retention might have been taken for his approval of the government. He made his position clear in a pas-sage in his will (February 8, 1937):

> My reflections have led me closer and closer to Catholicism, in which I see the complete fulfillment of Judaism. I would have become a convert, had I not foreseen for years a formidable wave of anti-Semitism about to break upon the world. I wanted to remain among those who tomorrow were to be persecuted.

It is not surprising, either, that, impatient as he was with the prosaic rigidities of expanding science, he turned to the faith and insights of re-ligion.

"Our reason, incorrigibly presumptuous," Bergson had warned in *Creative Evolution,* "imagines itself possessed, by right of birth or by right of conquest, innate or acquired, of all the essential elements of the knowledge of truth. . . . it believes that its ignorance consists only in not knowing which one of its time-honored categories suits the new object. In what drawer, ready to open, shall we put it? . . . The idea that for a new object we might have to create a new concept, perhaps a new method of thinking, is deeply repugnant to us. . . . Plato was the first to set up the theory that to know the real consists in finding its idea, that is to say, in forcing it into a pre-existing frame already at our disposal."

We can, perhaps, save ourselves from this imprisoning of our thought by the other source, intuition. While intellect turns away from the vision of time, "It dislikes what is fluid, and solidifies everything it touches. We do not *think* real time. But we *live* it, because life transcends intellect." So, "to grasp the true nature of vital activity . . . we shall probably be aided . . . by the fringe of vague intuition that surrounds our distinct—that is, intellectual—representation." In contrast to intellect, intuition is a form of instinct. "By intuition," he observed, "I mean instinct that has become disinterested, self-conscious, capable of reflecting upon its object and of enlarging it indefinitely."

With his poetic genius, Bergson was adept at using simile or metaphor to give subtler meaning to the dogmas of science or theology. So he adds an original theological note to his *élan vital.* Evolution is God's "undertaking to create creators, that He may have, besides Himself, beings worthy of His love." Or, in a metaphor borrowed from the mechanistic world he distrusted, he concludes his *Two Sources,* "The universe . . . is a machine for the making of God."

Bergson insisted that he "had no system." And he said he deserved no great credit, for he had "only got rid of a certain number of ready-made ideas. I have tried to develop a taste for introspection." But perhaps because he was not competing with philosophic systems, he had a wide and permeating influence. He came to be considered the prophet of a "process philosophy." He was the most widely read and perhaps most influential of the exponents of a new dynamism in philosophy and literature in the twentieth century. William James adored him and found him a guiding kindred spirit, George Santayana felt his influence, and Alfred North Whitehead shared his approach to nature. His sense of real duration was shared and elegantly developed in Marcel Proust's *Remembrance of Things Past* (1913–27; English translation 1922–31). Bergson had justified James's judgment of his magical power to draw together the conflicting currents of the search for meaning in the twentieth century.

41

Defining the Mystery:
Einstein's Search for Unity

While technology had fragmented experience with its mechanical clock and distracted man from the unity of the lived experience, science in its way was fragmenting the physical world into separate universes of explanation. What Bergson did for biology and evolution, Einstein would do for physics. Both Seekers started with time and both would seek unity. Einstein saw the small and the large, the atomic and the cosmic, as a single puzzle. To find the whole explained by law and reason inspired what he called his "cosmic religious feeling." "The individual feels the futility of human desires and aims and the sublimity and marvelous order which reveal themselves both in nature and in the world of thought," Einstein explained. "Individual experience impresses him as a sort of prison and he wants to experience the universe as a single significant whole." Search for that whole became his lifework. His was the modern search for meaning.

At the end of the nineteenth century when Einstein came to physics, the works of the great scientists had produced two convincing—grand but incompatible—schemes to describe the movements of the physical world. Sir Isaac Newton's mechanics (since publication of his *Principia Mathematica* in 1687) had long dominated the world of science. Newton was elected president of the Royal Society in 1703 (and for the next twenty-five years); he was buried in Westminster Abbey, and celebrated by Wordsworth as "a mind forever / Voyaging through strange seas of thought alone." The other, more recent explanatory scheme was expressed in the equations of James Clerk Maxwell (1831–1879) for electricity and magnetism.

But the two schemes did not fit together. Newton's mechanics and his theory of gravity depended on the powers of forces-at-a-distance, while the new Maxwellian world of electromagnetism depended on the attractions of forces in a "field." Could they be brought together? "We must not be surprised," Einstein observed in his "Autobiographical Notes," "that . . . , so to speak, all physicists of the last century saw in classical mechanics a firm and final foundation for all physics, yes, indeed, for all natural science, and that they never grew tired in their attempts to base Maxwell's theory of electromagnetism, which, in the meantime, was slowly beginning to win out, upon mechanics as well." Reading Ernst Mach's *History of Mechanics* as a young man shook Einstein's "dogmatic faith" in the Newtonian base: "The incorporation of wave-optics into the mechanical picture of the world was bound to arouse serious misgivings. If light was to be interpreted as undulatory motion in an elastic body (ether), this had to be a medium which permeates everything. . . . This ether had to lead a ghostly existence alongside the rest of matter. . . ." The electrodynamics of Faraday and Maxwell had brought physicists "slowly around to giving up the faith in the possibility that all of physics could be founded upon Newton's mechanics."

Newton had introduced the idea of "absolute space"—uninfluenced by masses and their motion. But, prepared by Faraday, Maxwell, and Hertz, physicists turned away from Newton's theory of distant forces. And it was Maxwell's theory, when Einstein was a student, that was "the transition from forces-at-a-distance to 'fields' as fundamental variables." To Einstein, "The incorporation of optics into the theory of electromagnetism . . . was like a revelation." The next revelation was Max Planck's investigations (1900) into heat radiation, out of which Planck had succeeded in proving the "reality" of the atom and furnishing "exactly the correct size of the atom." Which led Einstein into his studies of the Brownian movement and with new clues to the electromagnetic foundations of physics.

All of which led Einstein to "the conviction that only the discovery of a universal formal principle could lead us to assured results." He noted the example of thermodynamics, with its general principle: the laws of nature are such that it is impossible to construct a *perpetuum mobile* [perpetual motion machine]. "How then, could such a universal principle be found? After ten years of reflection such a principle resulted from a paradox upon which I had already hit at the age of sixteen: If I pursue a beam of light with the velocity c (velocity of light in a vacuum), I should observe such a beam of light as a spatially oscillatory electromagnetic field at rest. However, there seems to be no such thing, whether on the basis of experience or according to Maxwell's equations. From the very beginning it appeared to me intuitively clear that, judged from the standpoint of such an observer, everything would have to happen according to the same laws as for an observer who, relative to the earth, was at rest. For how, otherwise, should the first observer know, i.e., be able to determine, that he is in a state of fast uniform motion?" "One sees," Einstein concluded, "that in this paradox the germ of the special relativity theory is already contained." In a footnote to his article he offered the essential idea—the equivalence of mass and energy—contained in his famous simplifying formula: $E = MC^2$. In 1916 he went on to his general theory based on the idea that gravitation was not a force but a curved field in a space-time continuum.

Einstein never gave up his quest for "a universal formal principle." And in the last years of his life, at the Institute for Advanced Study in Princeton, he was still seeking a "unified field theory." How was he first set on the path of the relentless Seeker?

We know a great deal about the youth of Einstein, and his biographies were written by intimate collaborators. Still, the sources of his seeking impulses remain as much a mystery as the order that he would find in the universe. And his fame would itself be a paradox in the history of science. Sir Isaac Newton, his predecessor in the pantheon of modern physics, was widely acclaimed in his own time. "Nature and Nature's law lay hid in night," Alexander Pope (1688–1744) proclaimed in the epitaph he prepared. "God said, Let Newton be! and all was light." Newton's laws were expounded in popular lectures and books. Einstein, too, in his turn, became a symbol of the most modern science—but at the same time a symbol of the unintelligible. Even while a tobacco company sought his permission to use his picture on their box of "Relativity Cigars," a colloquial expression of bewilderment was "It's all Einstein to me!"

Born in 1879 in Ulm, Germany, a manufacturing town, to an unsuccessful businessman, as a child he was moved with his family in his father's quest for prosperity to Munich, then to Milan. His parents were Jewish, but did not attend synagogue or observe the dietary laws. In his autobiography (which he called his obituary) that he wrote at the age of sixty-seven he recalled his childhood:

Even while I was a fairly precocious young man the nothingness of the hopes and strivings which chases most men restlessly through life came to my consciousness with considerable vitality. Moreover, I soon discovered the cruelty of that chase. . . . By the mere existence of his stomach everyone was condemned to participate in that chase. Moreover, it was possible to satisfy the stomach by such participation, but not man in so far as he is a thinking and feeling being. As the first way out there was religion, which is implanted in every child by way of the traditional education-machine. Thus I came— despite the fact that I was the son of entirely irreligious (Jewish) parents—to a deep religiosity, which, however, found an abrupt ending at the age of 12. Through the reading of popular scientific books I soon reached the conviction that much in the stories of the Bible could not be true. The consequence was a positively fanatic [orgy] of freethinking coupled with the impression that youth is intentionally being deceived by the state through lies; it was a crushing impression.

In his doubtless idealized account of how he became the historic Seeker of his generation, Einstein recounts that this "religious paradise of youth, which was thus lost, was a first attempt to free myself from the chains of the 'merely personal,' from an existence which is dominated by wishes, hopes and primitive feelings."

Where would he do his seeking? How would he find meaning? Surely not in any Descartian self-obsession, nor any island within. "Out yonder there was this huge world, which exists independently of us human beings and which stands before us like a great, eternal riddle, at least partially accessible to our inspection and thinking. The contemplation of this world beckoned like a liberation, and I soon noticed that many a man whom I had learned to esteem and to admire had found inner freedom and security in devoted occupation with it. The mental grasp of this extra-personal world within the frame of the given possibilities swam as highest aim half consciously and half unconsciously before my mind's eye." Ironically, his historic cosmic quest would reveal the inescapable contradiction between the "huge world" out there and the revelations to the senses of the human observer. He had found the path of his seeking. "The road to this paradise was not as comfortable and alluring as the road to the religious paradise; but it has proved itself as trustworthy, and I have never regretted having chosen it."

He recounted two early inspirations of his sense of "wonder" at the world. One was at the age of four or five when his father showed him a compass, with its needle that behaved in a strangely "determined" way. The other, at the age of twelve, came when a book of Euclidean geometry showed how triangles behaved with such "lucidity and certainty." His uncle Jacob stirred his interest in mathematics, and his mother encouraged an interest in music. He became an accomplished violinist and enjoyed playing as long as he was physically able. But he was not a promising student at school, and his teachers called him "Herr Langweil" (Mister Bore). After graduation from Catholic primary school, his father wanted him to train for a practical engineering career. But the young Einstein's interests were more academic and theoretical. On his second attempt he passed the entrance examination for the rigorous Polytechnic Academy in Zurich, where he would pursue physics for four years. Graduating in 1900, he became a Swiss citizen, and decided to pursue a career as a physics teacher, doing theoretical physics on the side. A young physics teacher in those days was said to "earn too little to live, and too much to die." After an unsuccessful stint of teaching, when he was fired for being "too informal," he found a job as examiner in the Swiss Patent Office. He enjoyed his scientific friends and colleagues, married Mileva Maric, a fellow student, and kept alive his interest in music.

Then at the age of twenty-six he began his spectacular career as a productive physicist. And then, too, he began to puzzle over the problems that led him to the theory of relativity. Pursuing the suggestions of Max Planck's quantum theory that radiation did not come in waves but in packets of corpuscles ("quanta"), he applied the theory to light and invented the word "photon" for those packets of energy that were light. But all the while Einstein remained the Seeker—in quest of "a universal formal principle." His first statement of what came to be called "relativity" appeared in 1905 in an article in the German scientific journal *Annalen der Physik,* "On the Electrodynamics of Bodies in Motion." There he provided a new way of mediating between the disparate worlds of mechanics (Newtonian) and of electrodynamics (Faraday-Maxwell). But the article was slow to make a stir. And was not easy for the lay mind to comprehend. The thirty-page article was unorthodox in form, for it did not cite authorities or offer footnotes. In this and other related articles the young Einstein proposed a new scheme of physics, revising some of Newton's basic assumptions. Newton's comfortingly simple scheme of forces-at-a-distance in a world of absolute space and time would no longer satisfy. Any explanation of the physical world after Faraday and Maxwell and the forces of electrodynamics would have to be more subtle and complex, barely intelligible to the literate layman but of cosmic significance.

The basic idea of what came to be called the Special Theory of Relativity was a denial of Newton's notions of absolute space and time. This was demonstrated by the fact that for all frames of reference the speed of light is constant (and could not be increased by applying more energy), and if all natural laws remain the same, then space and time are relative to the observer. The "ghostly" hypothetical "ether" was no longer needed. This meant, too, that there was no absolute simultaneity in nature. And Newton's laws were valid, then, only in circumstances limited by our physical senses. For space and time were relatively different in stationary and in moving systems. Clocks in motion moved more slowly than stationary clocks, and objects in motion contracted in relation to the observer. But these changes of objects in motion were so small at speeds less than the speed of light that they were hardly perceptible to the human senses. Yet they plainly contradicted the notions of absolute space and time. "The theory of relativity," Einstein once observed, "was nothing more than a further consequential development of the field theory." But he resisted the suggestion that his theory was not consistent with observed facts. He insisted, in 1921, "that this theory is not speculative in origin; it owes its invention entirely to the desire to make physical theory fit observed fact as well as possible."

Einstein was well aware that he had bridged the worlds of mechanics and of electrodynamics. "The relativity principle in connection with the Maxwell equations," he observed in 1905, "demands that the mass is a direct measure for the energy contained in the bodies; light transfers mass. A remarkable decrease of the mass must result in radium. This thought is amusing and infectious but I cannot possibly know whether the good Lord does not laugh at it and has led me up the garden path." All these ideas had brought Einstein to his misleadingly simple equation, $E = MC^2$, in one of his early articles. This was scientific shorthand for his momentous suggestion of the equivalence of mass and energy. What it said was that the energy contained in matter is equal in ergs to its mass in grams multiplied by the square of the velocity of light in centimeters per second. Which meant, of course, in view of the velocity of light (186,000 miles per second) that a small amount of mass is equivalent to a vast amount of energy. And which was horrendously demonstrated (with no participation by Einstein) at Hiroshima on August 6, 1945, when that city became the target of the first military use of an atomic bomb, with some seventy-five thousand people killed or fatally injured.

Moving on to a wider exploration of the relation of masses to one another, Einstein reexamined the meaning of gravity in the new electrodynamic world. His observation of "photons" suggested that light, too, consisted of "quanta," which, like everything else, might be affected by "gravity." If light was affected by some form of gravity, then time and space would have two different configurations—one when viewed from within the gravitational field and another when viewed from without. This brought Einstein to the foundation of his General Theory of Relativity—that gravitation was not a "force" (in Newton's terms), but a curved "field" in a space-time continuum, created by the presence of mass. Then, as Ronald Clark puts it, looking from the earth into outer space is looking through distorting spectacles. These were the suggestions of Einstein's article in 1916. Just as "special" relativity described events in a frame of reference moving uniformly in relation to the observer, so general relativity would explain events when the frame of reference was moving at accelerating speeds, and so might also describe events in a gravitational field.

Einstein became famous to the lay public not from the essential truth in his theories, but from a dramatic event, publicized throughout the world, that confirmed his arcane theories. On May 29, 1919, a British astronomical expedition, which included the famous physicist Arthur S. Eddington, was at Principe Island in the Gulf of Guinea in Africa to photograph an eclipse of the sun. For physicists it would be a dramatic and suspenseful occasion. It offered a rare opportunity for plain and visible confirmation of one of Einstein's basic postulates about the nature of mass and of gravitation. If, pursuant to Einstein's ideas, light was a form of energy and so had mass, light would be affected, like any other mass, by a gravitational field. And a beam of light would be deflected (curved) by the influence of a mass in its path. Einstein suggested that his theory could be tested and confirmed by observing the path of starlight in the gravitational field of the sun. But since stars are invisible by daylight, the only time when the sun and stars could be seen together in the sky was during an eclipse of the sun. Would starlight be deflected by the gravitational field of the sun? Here, in full view, physicists could confirm Einstein's theory of the physical world.

Despite heavy rain at Principe Island, Eddington and other eminent astronomers on the spot managed to make six photographs of the eclipsed sun with the rays of stars passing by its edge. Einstein had proposed that photographs be taken of the stars whose rays seemed to border the darkened face of the eclipsed sun, in order to compare them with photographs of the same stars at another time. By Einstein's theory, the rays of light from the stars around the sun should be bent inward, toward the sun, as the rays of light passed through the sun's gravitational field. Then the effect seen by observers on the earth should be to shift the images of those stars outward from their usual apparent position in the sky.

Einstein had predicted that for the stars closest to the sun the deviation would be about 1.75 seconds of an arc. The photographs taken by Eddington's group showed that the deflection of starlight in the gravitational field of the sun actually averaged 1.64 seconds of an arc. This was as close to perfect agreement with Einstein's prediction as the margin of error of the instruments allowed. Eddington later called this—observing the confirmation of Einstein's theory—the greatest moment of his life. When Einstein saw a letter from Eddington with the exact theoretical value of the light diffraction, he responded exuberantly, and with a characteristically cosmic perspective. "It is a gift from Fate," he wrote to Planck on October 23, 1919, "that I have been allowed to experience this."

When the findings of the eclipse expedition were publicized by journalists across the world, Einstein became an instant celebrity for a bewildered public. Even in Berlin, where the puzzling news had to compete with menacing political disorders, Einstein complained that the publicity was "so bad that I can hardly breathe, let alone get down to sensible work." And *The Times* of London published an article entitled "The Fabric of the Universe" that described for the layman the cosmic revision that was now required.

On November 28, 1919, *The Times* published Einstein's own answer to "What is the Theory of Relativity?" Which he concluded with his customary wit, "Here is yet another application of the principle of relativity for the delectation of the reader." He observed, "Today I am described in Germany as a 'German savant' and in England as a 'Swiss Jew.' Should it ever be my fate to be represented as a *bête noire,* I should, on the contrary, become a 'Swiss Jew' for the Germans and a 'German savant' for the English."

In his *Times* summary Einstein himself gave some clues to his momentous revision. Time and space were no longer absolute. "In the general theory of relativity the doctrine of space and time, or kinematics, no longer figures as a fundamental independent of the rest of physics. The geometrical behavior of bodies and the motion of clocks rather depend on gravitational fields, which in their turn are produced by matter." This "new theory of gravitation," he noted, "diverges considerably as regards principles, from Newton's theory." But its practical results, he observed, agreed so closely to Newton's that it was hard to find data in experience to distinguish and confirm the new theory.

He noted three examples of data "accessible to experience," all of which were—or soon would be—confirmed by experience. One was in the eccentric behavior of the planet Mercury, whose elliptical orbit around the sun deviated slightly each year in a way not explained by Newton's laws. Einstein explained this deviation was due to the fact that the planet Mercury (lying closest to the sun) was small and traveled with great speed. By Einstein's theory the intensity of the sun's gravitational field and Mercury's speed caused the ellipse of Mercury's orbit itself to swing slowly around the sun (at a rate of one revolution every three million years), and this agreed with Mercury's actual course. The second confirmation of Einstein's theory was the effect of gravitation on light, shown by the photographs of the British eclipse expedition. His third prediction was "a displacement of the spectral lines toward the red end of the spectrum in the case of light transmitted to us from stars of considerable magnitude (unconfirmed so far)." This, too, was soon to be confirmed.

The results of the British eclipse expedition, when they were reported to the Royal Astronomical Societies on November 9, 1919, had a dramatic impact on the world of scientists. "The whole atmosphere," Alfred North Whitehead reported, "was exactly that of the Greek drama." "We were the chorus commenting on the decree of destiny as disclosed in the development of a supreme incident. There was dramatic quality in the very staging . . . and in the background the picture of Newton to remind us that the greatest of scientific generalizations was now, after more than two centuries, to receive its first modification. . . . a great adventure in thought had at length come safe to shore."

While the public did not quite understand, they were ready to share the enthusiasm of journalists and famous scientists who acclaimed Einstein as prophet of a new view of the universe. "Lights all askew in the Heavens, Einstein Theory triumphs," headlined *The New York Times* on November 10, 1919. Which the London *Times* matched by declaring, "Revolution in Science, New Theories of the Universe. Newtonian ideas overthrown." When Einstein came to the United States on a lecture tour in 1921, at the request of Chaim Weizmann to raise money for the Palestine Fund, he was given the full celebrity treatment and was expected to speak wisely on all world affairs. Some irreverently called him "the P. T. Barnum of Physics." That year he was awarded the Nobel Prize for Physics. In January 1933, when Hitler became chancellor of Germany, Einstein renounced his German citizenship, and in October he immigrated to Princeton, where he became the star of the new Institute for Advanced Study. And he soon became an American citizen. He was mildly amused by his celebrity, which he called "psychopathological" and shrugged off as being out of proportion to his achievement. But he took advantage of his prominence to rally support for peace and world government, which excited the ire of leading members of the Soviet Academy of Science. He spoke out against Hitler, and even gave up his pacifism when he saw the rising tide of fascist power. As late as 1952 he wrote a correspondent telling him to "condemn the military mentality of our time. . . . I have been a pacifist all my life and regard Gandhi as the only truly great political figure of our age." He had reason to fear assassination by the German Nazis, who attacked him and his science simply because he was a Jew, and he needed the protection of bodyguards.

In 1939, when he learned of successful European experiments in splitting atoms of the uranium isotope 235, he saw the possibilities of German production of an atom bomb and learned of German efforts to control the supply of uranium. So he was persuaded to sign a letter to President Roosevelt alerting him to the atomic peril. He urged the president to use federal funds to secure a supply of uranium and speed up American experiments in this area. Although his theories had provided a scientific foundation for atomic fission, he never took part in the work of Los Alamos. When he learned of the dropping of the first atomic bomb on Hiroshima in August 1945, he exclaimed, *"Oh weh!"*—Oh, woe! But he remained somehow an incurable optimist about the human race and man's capacities for a world of peace. "Since I do not foresee that atomic energy will prove to be a boon in the near future," he wrote near the end of his life, "I have to say that, for the present, it is a menace. Perhaps it is well that it should be. It may intimidate the human race into bringing order to its international affairs, which, without the pressure of fear, undoubtedly would not happen."

The relentless Seeker, Einstein never abandoned his quest for meaning, for an intelligible unity in the universe. Back in 1930 he had described his quest as rooted in what he called "cosmic religious feeling. It is very difficult to elucidate this feeling to anyone who is entirely without it, especially as there is no anthropomorphic conception of God corresponding to it." And he had explained why he would never be wholly satisfied. "The individual feels the futility of human desires and aims and the sublimity and marvelous order which reveal themselves both in nature and in the world of thought. Individual existence impresses him as a sort of prison and he wants to experience the universe as a single significant whole." Einstein remained troubled by the indeterminacy that quantum mechanics had seemed to introduce into physics. And which led him to believe that such a view must be only a transitional stage in man's quest for cosmic understanding. In 1948 he explained his deep problem. "I still work indefatigably at science but I have become an evil renegade who does not wish physics to be based on probabilities." He expressed his simple faith in many ways, summarized in his most quoted aphorism: "God does not play dice with the world." And he amplified this by noting that "God is subtle, but he is not malicious." He had faith that the God who created rational man must have created an intelligible universe. All of which seemed part of the cosmic mystery that he never ceased to admire and to reach for.

It was fortunate for the world of science that Einstein had lived when he did, just when the new physics of electrodynamics—Faraday and Maxwell—came to challenge the mechanistic physics of Newton. With his passion for unity—for "a single significant whole"—he had his task temptingly set before him. And he was the man for that season. "I am truly a 'lone traveler,' " he confessed, "and have never belonged to my country, my house, my friends, or even my immediate family, with my whole heart; in the face of all these ties, I have never lost a sense of distance and a need for solitude—feelings which increase with the years."

He was equal to the challenge of conflicting grand theories of the physical world. He saw it his task to bridge the gap between the old physics and the new—to draw on them both to reveal a newly significant unity. He had the patience, "the holy spirit of inquiry," the sense of humor, and the faith that he was treading an endless path. For the last decades of his life he remained in quest of a unified field theory that would somehow combine the Newtonian gravitational field with the recently discovered electromagnetic fields.

He never ceased his seeking. On April 17, 1955, doctors had given up efforts to save him by operations to stop his internal bleeding, and he must have known he was at the point of death. He asked to see his equations and his unfinished statement declining the presidency of Israel. He reportedly picked up his equations first and complained to his son at his bedside, "If only I had more mathematics."

Some Reference Notes

These notes will help the reader walk some of the paths in the search for meaning that I have found most rewarding. At the same time they will indicate the sources for these chapters and my heaviest debts to other scholars. I have selected here, for the most part, works likely to be found in a good public library or college library. For each book the date of the most recent publication is given, and I have tried to note works still in print and in paperback editions. I have omitted many of the specialized monographs and articles in learned journals. The reader should be reminded that in humanist studies, unlike the sciences, the latest works are not necessarily the best. Earlier works can retain remarkable insights and a classic quality. Where subjects in this volume overlap or touch on those in the companion volumes, *The Discoverers* and *The Creators,* the reader should consult their Reference Notes. In treating works from languages other than English, I have tried, where the quoted passage is lengthy and of literary interest, either in the text or in these Reference Notes, to credit the translator, who is all too seldom adequately recognized. Passages quoted from the Bible are in the translation of *Today's English Version (TEV) Bible* (American Bible Society, 1976).

The search for meaning is so vast a subject that I have focused my chapters (and these Reference Notes) on those Seekers—persons and institutions—who have spoken most eloquently and suggestively to me of Western man's search, his dilemmas, and his rewards. Other aspects of the search, not a subject of this book, would, for example, include cosmology, explored in Edward Harrison's *Masks of the Universe* (1985), psychology (and "logotherapy"), in Viktor E. Frankl, *Man's Search for Meaning* (1963), and semantics, as in the classic C. K. Ogden and I. A. Richards, *The Meaning of Meaning* (3d ed., 1930), and still others. For this book I have selected some Seekers who have expressed and shaped the great changes in Western culture. As a longtime aficionado of dictionaries, reference books, and general treatises, I have enjoyed their ways of leading me to questions I had never thought of asking. High on this list are *The Encyclopaedia Britannica* (latest edition), the *Dictionary of Scientific Biography* (C. C.

Gillispie, ed., 16 vols., 1970–80), the *International Encyclopedia of the Social Sciences* (David L. Sills, ed., 17 vols., 1968), and its still helpful predecessor, *The Encyclopaedia of the Social Sciences* (Edwin R. A. Seligman, ed., 15 vols., 1930–34). Articles especially useful for the subject of this book are found in the admirable *Encyclopedia of Religion* (Mircea Eliade, ed., 16 vols., 1987), and its predecessor *Encyclopaedia of Religion and Ethics* (James Hastings, ed., n.d.), and in *Dictionary of the History of Ideas* (Philip P. Wiener, ed., 4 vols., 1974). Many of the texts by the Seekers whom I treat are found in the handsome and convenient volumes of *Great Books of the Western World* (Robert M. Hutchins, ed., 54 vols., 1952 and later editions).

BOOK ONE:
AN ANCIENT HERITAGE

Part I. The Way of Prophets: A Higher Authority

The prophets and the role of prophecy have invited a vast literature, which is sometimes as cryptic as the utterances of the prophets themselves. But there is an admirable introduction to the ideas and institutions of prophecy in Mircea Eliade, *A History of Religious Ideas,* Vol. I: *From the Stone Age to the Eleusinian Mysteries* (1978). Eliade has further illuminated the subject with his lively style and vivid examples in his *Patterns in Comparative Religion* (1972) and *Cosmos and History: The Myth of the Eternal Return* (1959). For the social context of early prophets, see A. Leo Oppenheim, *Ancient Mesopotamia* (1964), and Klaus Koch, *The Prophets* (Vol. I, 1983); and for the world of the Hebrew prophets, J. Lindblom, *Prophecy in Ancient Israel* (1962), and Joseph Blenkinsopp, *Prophecy and Canon* (1970); Martin Buber's classic *Moses* (1946) and *The Prophetic Faith* (1985); and see David E. Aisne, *Prophecy in Early Christianity and the Ancient Mediterranean World* (1983). Job has continued to inspire a literature on the problems of justifying God's ways to man, and the virtue of protest, recently in William Safire's *The First Dissident: The Book of Job in Today's Politics* (1992). To see how various are the explanations and justifications of the existence of evil in the different world religions a good introduction is John Bowker, *Problems of Suffering in Religions of the World* (1970). And this spectrum is illustrated in Alan Watts, *The Spirit of Zen* (1955); Wendy D. O'Flaherty, *The Origins of Evil in Hindu Mythology* (1976); K. Cragg, *The House of Islam* (2d ed., 1975); and Martin Buber, *Tales of the Hasidim,* Vol. I: *The Early Masters* (1947).

Part II. The Way of Philosophers: A Wondrous Instrument Within

Ancient Greece has continued to invite a rich and readable literature of history and interpretation. C. M. Bowra, *The Greek Experience* (1957), and M. I. Finley, *The Ancient Greeks* (1964), are an attractive scholarly beginning, to follow popular interpretations like Edith Hamilton, *The Greek Way* (1961), and G. Lowes Dickinson, *The Greek View of Life* (1958). Standard views of the social and political context are found in J. B. Bury, *History of Greece* (1907); M. Rostovtzeff, *Greece* (1972); and Robin Lane Fox, *Alexander the Great* (1974). For ancient Greek thought and institutions we are fortunate to have Werner Jaeger's elegant and lively *Paideia: The Ideals of Greek Culture* (3 vols., 1967–71) and E. R. Dodds's subtle *The Greeks and the Irrational* (1951). To relate ancient political thought to later movements, see: C. H. McIlwain, *The Growth of Political Thought in the West* (1932); Christopher Morris, *Western Political Thought*, Vol. I: *Plato to Augustine* (1967); and Karl Popper's polemical *The Open Society and Its Enemies* (2 vols., 1966–72). Each of the ancient Greek philosophers has stimulated a library of biography and interpretation. Convenient resources are Bernard Knox (ed.), *The Norton Book of Classical Literature* (1993), with a brilliant introduction and illuminating notes, and W. H. Auden (ed.), *The Portable Greek Reader* (1948). The best place to begin, of course, is with each of their own writings or reported utterances. Selected dialogues of Plato (in the Jowett translation) are available in Vol. 7 and works of Aristotle in Vols. 8 and 9 of *Great Books of the Western World*. A convenient edition of the dialogues of Plato is the Random House edition (Jowett trans.), 2 vols. Plato's *Symposium* is in Modern Library (rev. Jowett trans.). For the works of Aristotle, see the Modern Library volume, Richard McKeon (ed.), *Introduction to Aristotle* (1992). A scholarly general history, readable and balanced, is W. K. C. Guthrie, *The Greek Philosophers* (6 vols., 1962–81), and see F. M. Cornford, *Before and After Socrates* (1960). A. E. Taylor has provided basic scholarly biographies in *Socrates* (1932) and *Plato, the Man and His Works* (1936). Our legacy from pioneer nineteenth-century classical scholarship is George Grote, *Plato and the Other Companions of Sokrates* (new ed., 4 vols., 1974). For modern reverberations, see Paul Elmer More, *Platonism* (1917).

It has often been remarked that all Western philosophy is a footnote to Plato. When we study Plato, then, we are examining the foundations of our philosophic tradition. See, for example, G. M. A. Grube, *Plato's Thought* (1980); David Ross, *Plato's Theory of Ideas* (1976). Aristotle also left a fertile legacy, which we explore briefly in Part III below. For a study of Aristotle and what he meant in his own time, see I. During, *Aristotle in the Ancient Biographical Tradition* (1957), and *Aristotle* (1966); David Ross, *Aristotle* (1964); Werner Jaeger, *Aristotle* (1948).

Part III. The Christian Way: Experiments in Community

We are fortunate in the literature that links Christianity to ancient thought, notably C. N. Cochrane, *Christianity and Classical Culture* (1944), and J. Pelikan, *Christianity and Classical Culture* (1993). But for this perspective there have been few equals of Edward Gibbon's ever-lively *Decline and Fall of the Roman Empire,* available in many editions, and especially attractive in the Modern Library edition (3 vols., 1995), with the Piranesi illustrations. For the medieval background we can begin with H. O. Taylor, *The Medieval Mind* (2 vols., 1930); E. K. Rand's compact *Founders of the Middle Ages* (1957); C. G. Crump and E. F. Jacob, *The Legacy of the Middle Ages* (1932); and the insightful Morris Bishop, *The Middle Ages* (1970). And for reference J. R. Strayer (ed.), *The Dictionary of the Middle Ages* (13 vols., 1989). To place the Seekers in the long history of Christianity we can not do better than the chapters in Jaroslav Pelikan, *The Christian Tradition* (5 vols., 1971–89), and *Jesus Through the Centuries* (1985). A stirring perspective of medieval institutions is J. Huizinga, *The Waning of the Middle Ages* (1924), new translation by Rodney J. Payton and Ulrich Mammitzsch, *The Autumn of the Middle Ages* (1996).

For the rise of the Church a classic introduction is J. Burckhardt, *The Age of Constantine the Great* (1949). And see Arnoldo Momigliano, *The Conflict Between Paganism and Christianity in the Fourth Century* (1963). Monasteries and monasticism, not amply chronicled in most general histories, have stimulated a literature of their own, especially fascinating to the modern secular mind. A good introduction is Cuthbert Butler, *Benedictine Monachism* (2d ed., 1924), supplemented by Alban Butler, *Butler's Lives of the Saints* (ed. H. Thurston and D. Attwater, 4 vols., 1956–62), and Gregorius I the Great, *Life and Miracles of St. Benedict* (1980); and for the context, J. M. Hussey, *The Byzantine World* (1957). Daniel Rees, *Consider Your Call* (1978), suggests a theology of monastic life today.

Medieval universities offer striking contrasts to their modern descendants and are portrayed for us by scholars with a literary flair. See, for example, the cogent C. H. Haskins, *The Rise of Universities* (1923), and *The Renaissance of the Twelfth Century* (1957). A standard reference is Hastings Rashdall, *The Universities of Europe in the Middle Ages* (3 vols., rev. ed., 1936). And see G. G. Coulton, *Medieval Panorama* (1938). We are grateful to Étienne Gilson for his subtle essays: *The History of Christian Philosophy in the Middle Ages* (1955), *The Christian Philosophy of St. Thomas Aquinas*

(1983), and *The Spirit of Medieval Philosophy* (1991). For the life of the monumental Saint Thomas Aquinas, I have found most useful A. Walz, *St. Thomas Aquinas* (1951), and Vernon J. Bourke, *Aquinas' Search for Wisdom* (1965). Selections of Aquinas's works are in *Basic Writings* (Anton C. Degas, ed., 2 vols., 1944), and in *Great Books of the Western World* (Vols. 19 and 20).

The literature of Protestantism is naturally tendentious and often polemical, but the lives of the leaders have invited many sympathetic biographies. The attractive thinker Erasmus has elicited suggestive essays, notably Johan Huizinga, *Erasmus and the Age of Reformation* (1957), and Roland H. Bainton, *Erasmus of Christianity* (1982). Erasmus's *Praise of Folly* is available in numerous editions and translations—for example, in Penguin Classics (1986). For Martin Luther, a more prickly subject, we can turn to E. G. Rupp and B. Drewery (eds.), *Martin Luther* (1970), and R. H. Bainton, *Here I Stand: A Life of Martin Luther* (1990). We must explore John Calvin's own *Institutes of the Christian Religion* (trans. John Allen, B. B. Warfield ed., 7th ed., 2 vols., 1936) and can follow his checkered life in T. H. L. Parker, *John Calvin* (1975), or Williston Walker, *John Calvin, the Organiser of Reformed Protestantism, 1509–1564* (1969). Calvin's legacy in John T. McNeill, *The History and Character of Calvinism* (1954), is illuminated by studies of his Geneva—for example, Robert M. Kingdon's *Geneva and the Coming of the Wars of Religion in France 1555–1563* (1956) and *Geneva and the Consolidation of the French Protestant Movement, 1564–1572.* Roland H. Bainton has given us a concise and readable history of Protestant intolerance in *The Travail of Religious Liberty* (1958). For the career of Calvinism in New England, see S. E. Morison, *Builders of the Bay Colony* (1930), and for the ideas, Perry Miller, *The New England Mind* (2 vols., 1939, 1953).

BOOK TWO:
COMMUNAL SEARCH

Part IV. Ways of Discovery: In Search of Experience

Greek myths and the epics of Homer have become such commonplaces of Western education that we have tended to overlook their significance as expressions of ancient Greek culture and as shaping elements in the Western tradition. The best starting point, of course, is Homer, accessible in the *Iliad* and the *Odyssey* in classic English translations (for example, by John Dryden and Alexander Pope and in recent translations by Richmond Lattimore [1961] and Robert Fitzgerald [1961, 1974]). Edith Sitwell recounts the career of one of these in *Alexander Pope* (1948). A delightful recent translation is by Robert Fagles (with an introduction by Bernard Knox). For the place of Homer in the oral traditions: A. J. P. Wace and F. H. Stubbings, *A Companion to Homer* (1962), and a shorter version, *Homer and Epic* (1965). And on the limits of the oral tradition, Henri-Jean Martin, *The History and Power of Writing* (1944). I have found especially helpful M. I. Finley, *The World of Odysseus* (2d ed., 1977). An admirable anthology is Bernard Knox's *Norton Book of Classical Literature* (1993), with his brilliant introduction. For the wider social context, see G. S. Kirk, *Myth: Its Meaning and Functions in Ancient and Other Cultures* (1973). For a scholarly response to the question we all ask, see Paul Veyne, *Did the Greeks Believe Their Myths?* (1988).

For an incisive essay on how the Greeks related their myths to their history, see Bernard Knox, *Backing into the Future* (1994). To help us place the ancient Greek historian in our tradition, see R. G. Collingwood, *The Idea of History* (1961), M. I. Finley, *The Use and Abuse of History* (1975), *The Ancient Greeks* (1963). For scholarly assessment of the ancient historians, see Arnoldo Momigliano, *Essays in Ancient and Modern Historiography* (1977) or *The Classical Foundations of Modern Historiography* (1990). The standard introductory work is J. B. Bury, *The Ancient Greek Historians* (1909). The historians have been widely and variously translated, and have invited the best talents. Herodotus and Thucydides are both available in *Great Books of the Western World*, Vol. 6. M. I. Finley offers an attractive brief selection in *The Greek Historians* (1959). The George Rawlinson translation of Herodotus is most widely relied on, and often edited and reprinted. Thucydides is most often read in the Benjamin Jowett or Richard Crawley translation. The Thomas Hobbes translation (David Grene, ed., 2 vols., 1959) has a special interest because of the eminent translator's boasted sympathy with the author. An illuminating original view is F. M. Cornford, *Thucydides Mythistoricus* (1971). A rewarding selection from ancient Greek literature is found in *The Norton Anthology of World Masterpieces* (Bernard Knox, ed., Vol. 1, 4th ed., 1979).

For Virgil, an excellent introduction is the essay by Jasper Griffin in *The Oxford History of the Classical World* (1988), Ch. 15 or, more extensively, Jasper Griffin, *Virgil* (1986). Virgil's *Eclogues, Georgics,* and the *Aeneid* are in *Great Books of the Western World* (trans. James Rhoades), Vol. 13. Virgil, like Homer, has challenged the talents of translators in every generation. John Dryden's free translation of the *Aeneid* in 1697 was long standard. We now can read Virgil in C. Day Lewis's modern verse (1966), and Robert Fitzgerald's among others. The most widely used translation of Virgil is that of R. A. B. Mynors in the Oxford Classical Texts Series. T. S. Eliot's essay "What Is a Classic?" in his *On Poets and Poetry* (1951) helps us place Virgil in the tradition.

Sir Frederick Pollock dismisses Thomas More from his respected *History of the Science of Politics* (1923) as "a Platonic or ultra-Platonic fancy, bred of the Platonism of the Renaissance. Even more than the *Republic* of Plato it belongs to the poetry as distinguished from the philosophy of politics." Still, the appealing "poetry of politics" has often had more influence than the "philosophy." More's *Utopia,* often reprinted, is accessible in an Everyman Library edition (1928) and selections are in *The Norton Anthology of English Literature* (Vol. I, 4th ed., 1979), with helpful notes. For Bacon and the rise of Western science, see Reference Notes to *The Discoverers,* Bk. III, esp. Parts X and XI. A readable scholarly biography is Fulton H. Anderson, *Francis Bacon* (1962). *The Advancement of Learning* and *The New Atlantis* are in a Bacon volume in World's Classics (Oxford University Press). A useful selection of major works is E. A. Burtt (ed.), *English Philosophers from Bacon to Mill* (Modern Library, 1997). For a wider view, see the suggestive John Hale, *The Civilization of Europe in the Renaissance* (1994).

For Descartes, readable biographies are Elizabeth Haldane, *Descartes: Life and Times* (1905), and J. R. Vrooman, *René Descartes* (1970). For the legacy of Descartes, Jacques Maritain offers stimulating suggestions in *The Dream of Descartes* (1946) and *Three Reformers: Luther, Descartes, Rousseau* (1970), as does

Albert B. Balz, *Descartes and the Modern Mind* (1952). A selection of Descartes's works is found in *Great Books of the Western World,* Vol. 31 (trans. Elizabeth S. Haldane and G. R. T. Ross).

Part V. The Liberal Way

In the United States today, while "conservatism" has become an icon, the great tradition of liberalism, which for centuries has given meaning and purpose to people and societies in the West, lacks outspoken champions. We would do well to recall some of the Seekers in that tradition, who are suggested in this part. Spokesmen for the liberal spirit have been eloquent in our Western culture. Few have been as durable as John Stuart Mill (1806–1873), whose essays "On Liberty" and "Representative Government" though widely reprinted are too seldom read. The tradition encompasses a wide variety of Seekers who have hoped that the fulfillment of liberty in society will somehow add meaning and purpose to human life.

The writings of the surprising and widely misunderstood Niccolò Machiavelli suggest some of the roots of the communal search for meaning in the modern nation. *The Prince* is in *Great Books of the Western World* (Vol. 23); *The Prince and the Discourses* are in Modern Library (1940). The comprehensive biography is Pasquale Villari, *The Life and Times of Niccolò Machiavelli* (new ed., 1968). For a re-

cent view, see Sebastian de Grazia, *Machiavelli in Hell* (1989). A balanced brief introduction is Neal Wood's article in *The International Encyclopedia of the Social Sciences* (Vol. 9). John Locke's life is readable in Maurice Cranston, *John Locke* (1957), and his life and works are surveyed in Richard I. Aaron, *John Locke* (3d ed., 1971). A helpful interpretation is John W. Yolton, *John Locke and the Way of Ideas* (1963). For the basic writings, see E. A. Burtt (ed.), *English Philosophers from Bacon to Mill* (Modern Library) and *Great Books of the Western World* (Vol. 35), and *Of Civil Government* (Everyman). For an important recent reinterpretation, see Peter Laslett (ed.), *Two Treatises of Government* (1964).

Voltaire, one of the wittiest and most persuasive of the Seekers, was also one of the most versatile and productive. A convenient introduction is Ben Ray Redman (ed.), *The Portable Voltaire* (Penguin Books, 1977). For readable scholarly biography, see Theodore Besterman, *Voltaire* (1969), and Gustave Lanson (intro. by Peter Gay), *Voltaire* (1966). A stirring essay is John Morley, *Voltaire* (1973). For his life and works, see the comprehensive Ira O. Wade, *The Intellectual Development of Voltaire* (1969). And for special aspects, see: A. Owen Aldridge, *Voltaire and the Century of Light* (1975); Peter Gay, *Voltaire's Politics: The Poet as Realist* (1977); T. D. Kendrick, *The Lisbon Earthquake* (1956). Voltaire's wide acquaintance with leading thinkers of his day gives his letters a wider than biographical significance, as in Theodore Besterman (trans. and ed.), *Selected Letters* (1963). Besides the voluminous *Complete Works* (Theodore Besterman, ed.), individual works have been frequently translated and reprinted. *Candide* (trans. Richard Aldington) and *Philosophical Letters* are brought together in the Modern Library (1997). *The Age of Louis XIV* and *The History of Charles XII* are in the Everyman Library. For the range of Voltaire's thought, see *The Philosophy of History* (1965) and *Philosophical Dictionary* (2 vols., 1962). And for a suggestive sequel, John R. Saul, *Voltaire's Bastards: The Dictatorship of Reason in the West* (Vintage, 1993).

For a new perspective on Diderot and Encyclopedism, we owe much to Robert Darnton, *The Business of Enlightenment: A Publishing History of the Encyclopédie, 1775–1800* (1979), of wider significance than its title suggests. We can find new insights in P. N. Furbank, *Diderot: A Critical Biography* (1992). And see Lester G. Crocker (ed.), *Diderot, Selected Writings* (1966); and Jonathan Kemp (ed.), *Diderot, Interpreter of Nature: Selected Writings* (1979).

Rousseau has incited a copious, romantic, and polemical literature. We are therefore grateful to Maurice Cranston for his ample, balanced, and perceptive *Jean-Jacques Rousseau,* in progress: Vol. I, *Early Life: 1712–1754* (1982), and Vol. II, *Noble Savage: 1754–62* (1991). For a sense of Rousseau's idiosyncrasies we should all taste his *Confessions,* often reprinted, e.g., Everyman (2 vols., 1941) and in Penguin (1953). *The Social Contract* (trans. G. D. H. Cole) and *Émile* are in Everyman Library. *The Discourse on the Origin of Inequality* and *The Social Contract* are in *Great Books of the Western World* (Vol. 38). There are few historical polemics as stirring as Irving Babbitt, *Rousseau and Romanticism* (1919), which alerts us to the contemporary moral and immoral implications of Rousseau's ideas.

The whole literature on Thomas Jefferson, ranging from muckraking to hagiography, is vast. In it there is a rich resource of balanced and readable scholarly works. For a focused treatment of Jefferson and his fellow Seekers on the American scene, see Daniel J. Boorstin, *The Lost World of Thomas Jefferson* (new intro., 1993); and for the wider context, Boorstin, *The Ameri-*

cans: The Colonial Experience, Bk. II. A good starting point for the life is the article by Dumas Malone in *The Dictionary of American Biography* or Merrill D. Peterson, *Thomas Jefferson and the New Nation* (1970), amplified by Dumas Malone's definitive *Jefferson and His Time* (6 vols., 1948–81). For informed guidance into special topics, see Merrill D. Peterson, *Thomas Jefferson, a Reference Biography* (1986) and Silvio A. Bedini, *Thomas Jefferson Statesman of Science* (1990). Accessible editions of Jefferson's writings are in Modern Library, Adrienne Koch and William Peden (eds.), *The Life and Selected Writings of Thomas Jefferson;* Merrill D. Peterson (ed.), *The Portable Jefferson* (1975); or Saul K. Padover (ed.), *The Complete Jefferson* (1941). The definitive edition of Jefferson's writings is edited by Julian P. Boyd and successors (1950–). Jefferson's life and his vision continue to be an endless source of illuminating history, recently in Stephen E. Ambrose, *Undaunted Courage* (1996), an engrossing account of the Lewis and Clark expedition. For biographies of Jefferson's fellow Seekers on the American scene, see *The Dictionary of Scientific Biography.*

The copious literature on Hegel is, not surprisingly, dominated by polemics and influenced by Hegel's Germanic and Prussian chauvinist bias. For a balanced and sympathetic survey of his life and writings, see the brief article by the philosopher Morris R. Cohen in *Encyclopaedia of the Social Sciences* (1932), Vol. VII, or that by George Liehtheim in *International Encyclopedia of the Social Sciences* (1968), Vol. 6. For a cogent treatment of the founder of the idealist movement, see the article on Kant by Ernst Cassirer in *Encyclopaedia of the Social Sciences,* Vol. VIII. Less sympathetic is Bertrand Russell's lively treatment of Hegel (along with Kant) as part of the Idealist movement in Ch. XXII of his *History of Western Philosophy* (1945). For a readable introduction to that movement, see A. D. Lindsay, *Kant* (1934). An accessible selection of Hegel's writings, translated into English, is in the Modern Library, *The European Philosophers from Descartes to Nietzsche* (ed. Monroe C. Beardsley, 1992, with updated bibliography). The full text of Hegel's *Philosophy of History* is available in English (trans. J. Sibree, Bohn's Libraries, 1902).

BOOK THREE:
PATHS TO THE FUTURE

Part VI. The Momentum of History: Ways of Social Science

A striking witness to the resilience and energy of Western culture is the appearance in the same era—and almost simultaneously—of thinkers offering dogmas and ideologies proposing skeleton keys to experience and all history, while others equally eloquent and persuasive were seeking refuge in sanctuaries of doubt. Positivism and existentialism were symbols of the restless seeking spirit—demanding simple keys to experience and history, yet never quite satisfied with the latest answers. The earlier answers could be qualified, or discredited, and the Seeking spirit would remain alive and vigorous, somehow finding the meaning in the seeking.

For brief articles on leading figures in the social sciences a good source is still *The Encyclopaedia of the Social Sciences* (Edwin R. A. Seligman, ed., 8 vols., 1931–35), updated by the *International Encyclopedia of the Social Sciences* (David L. Sills, ed., 17 vols., 1968). For historical perspective on the rise of the social sciences, see Peter Gay, *The Enlightenment, an Interpretation; The Rise of Modern Paganism* (2 vols., 1966), and F. A. Hayek, *The Counterrevolution of Science: Studies in the Abuse of Reason* (1957). J. B. Bury, *The Idea of Progress . . . Its Origin and Growth* remains a useful starting point. Antoine-Nicolas de Condorcet, *Sketch for a Historical Picture of the Progress of the Human Mind* (trans. June Barraclough, 1955) is in the Noonday Press Library of Ideas. Works of Auguste Comte have been frequently reprinted and anthologized, but are not easily accessible. Basic is *Positive Philosophy* (3 vols., 1896). His *General View of Positivism* was reprinted in an official centenary edition by the International Comte Center Committee (1957). For the intellectual context of both Condorcet and Comte, see in the Modern Library, *European Philosophers from Descartes to Nietzsche* and G. P. Gooch, *History and Historians in the Nineteenth Century* (Beacon Press paperback, 1959). For a suggestive study of the relation of the Enlightenment to the romantic movement in literature, see Alfred Cobban, *Edmund Burke, and the Revolt Against the Eighteenth Century* (2d ed., 1960).

Karl Marx has, of course, inspired a vast literature—hagiographic and polemical. Franz Mehring, *Karl Marx* (trans. Edward Fitzgerald, 1926), is a readable sympathetic account by a follower, whose efforts were encouraged by Marx's daughter. See also Saul K. Padover, *Karl Marx, An Intimate Biography* (1978), and Isaiah Berlin, *Karl Marx: His Life and Environment* (3d ed., 1963). A selection of Marx's writings, not elsewhere so conveniently collected, is Emile Burns (ed.), *A Handbook of Marxism* (Gollancz, London, 1935). These are also brought together in the less accessible *Karl Marx: Selected Works* (Marx-Engels-Lenin Institute, Moscow, 2 vols., 1935). All readers should have a taste of *Das Kapital,* English trans. *Capital: A Critique of Political Economy,* Vol. I (trans. S. Moore and E. Aveling) (1886), Vols. 2 and 3, ed. F. Engels, first published posthumously in German; in English trans. E. Untermann (1908, 1909, rev. trans., 1952). One of Marx's basic essays, *Grundrisse; Foundations of the Critique of Political Economy* has appeared in Vintage paperback (trans. Martin Nicolaus, 1973). For a historical assessment of Marx and his critics, see F. A. Hayek, *Capitalism and the Historians* (1954).

To share some of the excitement of the invention (and discovery) of modern anthropology, read Edward B. Tylor, *Primitive Culture: Researches into the Development of Mythology, Philosophy, Religion, Language, Art, and Custom* (first ed., 1871; reprinted, 1929) and *Anthropology* (abridged with foreword by Leslie A. White, 1960), and share the seminal insights of Franz Boas, in *The Mind of Primitive Man* (1911; revised and enlarged, 1938) and *Anthropology and Modern Life* (1928). On Oswald Spengler, see H. Stuart Hughes, *Oswald Spengler: A Critical Estimate* (1952), and on his problems and the reception of his works, see Erich Heller, *The Disinherited Mind* (expanded ed., Harvest paperback, 1975), "Oswald Spengler and the Predicament of the Historical Imagination," and in Pitirim A. Sorokin, *Modern Historical and Social Philosophies* (1950). No student of history should miss the stimulus and poetic inspiration of Spengler's *Decline of the West* (trans. Charles F. Atkinson, 2 vols. in one, 1932), which sparkles with insights even for those who do not share the dogmas. And for a partial view, *Man and Technics: A Contribution to a Philosophy of Life* (1932). Arnold J. Toynbee, more accessible, more plausible, and less poetic than Spengler, is introduced by William H. McNeill, *Arnold J. Toynbee: A Life* (1989), who knew Toynbee and worked with him. Toynbee's major work, *A Study of History* (12 vols., 1935–61), was popularized in a one-volume edition (revised and abridged by the author and Jane Caplan, 1972), and in contrast to Spengler, was widely quoted and commented on. The one-volume edition is coherent and persuasive.

The story of revolutionary ideas and enthusiasms in this century would be a history of Western culture. H. G. Wells's wonderfully readable *Outline of History* in many editions (1920–71; new ed., Raymond Postgate and G. P. Wells) helps us share the excitement and the promise, and still rewards us with an unfashionably wide perspective. For a passionate personal view of the world in revolution, see the Modern Library volume *The Collected Works of John Reed,* which includes *Ten Days That Shook the World* and his writings on revolutions in Mexico. See also John Steinbeck, *A Russian Journal* (1948; Bantam paperback, 1970). The chronicle of the rise and fall of ideologies is brilliantly collected by Richard Crossman, *The God That Failed* (1950). The passions of the age are dramatized in Arther Koestler, *Darkness at Noon* (1940), and the writings of Ernest Hemingway, notably, *For Whom the Bell Tolls* (1940), and André Malraux (see Part VII below).

Part VII. Sanctuaries of Doubt

The certitudes of ideology, social science, and destiny have bred questions that themselves have become ways of finding meaning. These were doubts about wholesale units of history, about the nature of truth and philosophy, about the homogeneity of society and experience. Witty and ingenious authors even made a literature of the modern bewilderment. Carlyle and Emerson found a refuge in biography, which they popularized in essays and lectures. This tradition owed much to Plutarch, whose *Lives of the Noble Grecians and Romans* can be sampled in Modern Library (2 vols.). A representative selection of Carlyle's writings is G. M. Trevelyan (ed.), *Carlyle: An Anthology* (1953) or in *The Norton Anthology of English Literature,* Vol. II (44th ed., 1979). The classic biography is by Carlyle's literary executor James A. Froude (abridged and edited by John Clubbe, 1979), notorious for its frankness, *The Life of Carlyle.* And see Froude's suggestive *My Relations with Carlyle* (1971). The individual works have been often reprinted. For Carlyle's place in European historiography, see the useful anthology, Fritz Stern (ed.), *The Varieties of History: From Voltaire to the Present* (Vintage, 1973).

For a biographical introduction to Ralph Waldo Emerson, see Mark Van Doren's article in *Dictionary of American Biography.* For his place in the traditions of American literature, F. O. Matthiessen, *American Renaissance* (1941), and for detail, Robert D. Richardson, *Emerson: Mind on Fire*

(1955). Representative selections are Mark Van Doren (ed.), *The Portable Emerson* (1946) or *Selected Writings* (Modern Library) or its predecessor *Complete Essays and Other Writings* (Modern Library; Brooks Atkinson, ed., 1940).

The writings of William James have a captivating charm that encourages us to believe that we can all be (or at least can understand) philosophers. For his biography and his place in the phenomenal James family, see R. W. B. Lewis's admirable *The Jameses* (1991), and for a suggestive informal approach, Jacques Barzun, *A Stroll with William James* (1983). His copious writings have been often printed separately. A good selection is by John J. McDermott (ed.), *Writings of William James* (comprehensive ed., Modern Library, 1968) or *Writings (1902–1910)* (Library of America). And no one should fail to sample *The Varieties of Religious Experience* (Modern Library). James's lively spirit is so pervasive that almost any of his writings conveys the electrifying spirit of the man. His pioneering in psychology appears in his *Principles of Psychology* (2 vols., 1901) or the shorter version (ed. Gordon Allport, 1961; rpt. 1985), and his illuminating spirit, especially in *Pragmatism* (1907) and in *The Will to Believe and Other Essays in Popular Philosophy* (1979). Louis Menand (intro. and ed.) has provided an excellent anthology of the texts of pragmatism and its background (Vintage, 1997). For the biography, the best avenue is Ralph Barton Perry, *The Thought and Character of William James* (2 vols., 1935), supplemented by *The Letters of William James,* edited by his son, Henry James (2 vols., 1920), and Linda Simon, *Genuine Reality: A Life of William James* (1998).

Justice Oliver Wendell Holmes, Jr., known to lawyers as the Great Dissenter, should be more widely read by students of American culture. An admirable, if slightly hagiographic, biography by his disciple Justice Felix Frankfurter is found in the *Dictionary of American Biography,* Supp. I. For representative essays and opinions, see Max Lerner (ed.), *The Mind and Faith of Justice Holmes* (1948; Modern Library, 1954). His classic *The Common Law* (1881), which should be read by all American law students at the beginning of their studies, has much to tell the layman about the lawyer as Seeker, as does his *Collected Legal Papers* (1920). A subtle and readable account of the shaping years is Mark DeWolfe Howe, *Justice Oliver Wendell Holmes* (2 vols., 1957–63). A popular biography that usefully attracted the attention of students of American culture is Catherine Drinker Bowen, *Yankee from Olympus* (1944). For a suggestive Anglo-American dialogue, see Mark De Wolfe Howe (ed.), *The Holmes Pollock Letters* (2d ed., 2 vols., 1961).

The best introduction to Edward O. Wilson is his own readable books. His vivid autobiography is *The Naturalist* (1995). All his books reward the layman with intimate insight into the naturalist as Seeker: *On Human Nature* (1978), *Biophilia* (1984), and especially *The Diversity of Life* (1992).

An admirable introduction to the literature of bewilderment is Martin Esslin, *The Theatre of the Absurd* (rev. ed., 1973) or Richard N. Coe, *Samuel Beckett* (1970). For the writings see John Calder (ed.), *A Samuel Beckett Reader* (1967). *Waiting for Godot* (1954) is in several reprints. For other authors and special topics, see Kenneth McLeish, *The Penguin Companion to* *Arts in the Twentieth Century* (1988). For the underlying ideas, see Albert Camus, *The Myth of Sisyphus* (1942). A creative and challenging Seeker whom I have only touched on is the tantalizing Portuguese poet Fernando Pessoa (1888–1935), accessible in José Blanco (ed.), *Fernando Pessoa, A Galaxy of Poets* (1985); *A Centenary Pessoa* (Eugenie Lisboa and L. C. Taylor, eds., 1995); or George Monteiro (ed.), *The Man Who Never Was: Essays on Fernando Pessoa* (1982). His English poems were collected in *Poemas Ingleses* (1935). One of his most piquant and puzzling works is his *Book of Disquietude* (trans. Richard Zenith, 1995).

Part VIII. A World in Process: The Meaning in the Seeking

The cheerful seeking spirit, finding "scientific" and materialist answers unsatisfying, ingeniously devised ways to see the meaning in the seeking. This way of seeking came to be known as "the process philosophy." Lord Acton opened this path for the liberal spirit in his appropriately uncompleted history of liberty, and in his other writings. An admirable, sympathetic biography is Gertrude Himmelfarb, *Lord Acton* (1952). Representative selections are Acton, *Essays in the Liberal Interpretation of History* (intro. William H. McNeill, 1967) and *Essays on Free-* *dom and Power* (G. Himmelfarb, ed., 1948). Acton's ideas are accessible in his *Lectures on Modern History* (J. N. Figgis and R. V. Laurence, eds., 1906) or *Lectures on the French Revolution* (J. N. Figgis and R. V. Laurence, eds., 1959).

André Malraux is one of the most versatile and eloquent of modern Seekers. He was a brilliant novelist, penetrating art historian and essayist, and effective political figure. For his biography, see Axel Madsen, *Malraux* (1976), or Malraux, *Anti-Memoirs* (trans. T. Kilmartin, 1968). For his view of East-West cultural relations, *The Temptation of the West* (trans. R. Hollander, Vintage, 1961). His writings, despite their political message, remain alive and readable: *The Conquerors* (1928); *The Royal Way* (1935; Vintage); *Man's Fate* (trans. H. M. Chevalier, Modern Library, 1934); *Man's Hope* (trans. S. Gilbert and A. MacDonald, 1938). And explore his illuminating *Voices of Silence* (trans. S. Gilbert, 1951).

For the process philosophy, most accessible to the layman are the writings of Henri Bergson or Alfred North Whitehead. See Bergson's *Creative Evolution* (Modern Library, 1911), *Time and Free Will* (1960), or *The Two Sources of Morality and Religion* (1935). Or see H. A. Larrabee (ed.), *Selections from Bergson* (1949). For a sharp critique: Bernard Russell, *The Philosophy of Bergson* (1914). Whitehead offers a cogent interpretation of the rise of modern science in *Science and the Modern World* (1931).

Albert Einstein himself was fluent and articulate in words as well as equations. An admirable selection of his writings on science, religion, and world affairs is his *Ideas and Opinions* (intro. Alan Lightman, Modern Library, 1994). His readable and revealing "Autobiographical Notes" can be found in *Albert Einstein: Philosopher-Scientist* (ed. Paul A. Schlipp, 2d. ed., 1951; in Library of Living Philoso-

phers), along with essays about him by philosophers and scientists and his own response. The comprehensive biography is Ronald W. Clark, *Albert Einstein: The Life and Times* (1971). And note Philipp Frank, *Einstein* (trans. G. Rosen, 1947), written from personal acquaintance. Of the many popular biographies the most helpful are: Jeremy Bernstein, *Einstein* (1973); Lincoln Barnett, *The Universe and Dr. Einstein* (foreword by Einstein, 1948); Peter Michelmore, *Einstein: Profile of the Man* (1962). Gerald Holton, on the editorial board of Einstein's collected papers, has given us several readable and suggestive essays: *Einstein, History and Other Passions* (1995); his Introduction, "Einstein and the Shaping of Our Imagination," in *Albert Einstein: The Centennial Symposium in Jerusalem* (ed. G. Holton and Yehuda Elkana, 1982). Especially related to my chapter is his "Einstein's Search for the *Weltbild*," in *Proceedings of the American Philosophical Society* (1981), with essays by Robert H. Dicke, Steven Weinberg, and John A. Wheeler. For Einstein's own statement of leading scientific ideas, see Albert Einstein, *Relativity* (1920); (with Leopold Infeld) *The Evolution of Physics* (1938). Serious students of physics and qualified mathematicians may wish to consult the essays on Einstein by Martin J. Klein and Nandor L. Balazs in *Dictionary of Scientific Biog-*

raphy (1971), Vol. IV. Einstein's wide influence beyond the world of physics, suggested by Holton's essays (above), is illustrated by José Ortega y Gasset, "The Historical Significance of the Theory of Einstein," in his *The Modern Theme* (Harper Torchbook, 1961), where he treats Einstein as the prophet of "finitism," the message that "now, all at once, the world has become limited." In the lay public Einstein has inspired wit as well as awe, for example in Alan Lightman's whimsical novella, *Einstein's Dreams* (1993), and the delightful "Documentary Comic Book," *Einstein for Beginners* (1979), by Joseph Schwartz and Michael McGuinness. Also revealed in the extensive illustrated exhibit $E = mc^2$ at the Centre Georges Pompidou (1979) in Paris, accompanied by a copiously illustrated catalog. Not to be overlooked are Harry Woolf (ed.), *Some Strangeness in the Proportion: Centennial Symposium to Celebrate the Achievements of Albert Einstein* (1980), and David Cassidy, *Einstein and Our World* (1995).

Acknowledgments

This is the most personal volume of the trilogy that began with *The Discoverers* and *The Creators,* as it concerns those Seekers in our Western past who have most helped me toward seeing meaning and purpose in history. The acknowledgments for this volume should include those noted in the earlier volumes, for my pursuit of discoverers and creators has led me into the paths to meaning that I explore here. This book would have been impossible without the incomparable collections of the Library of Congress.

It is a pleasure to thank friends and fellow scholars who have given me suggestions or read parts of the manuscript. They have saved me from errors of fact, have helped me on to new paths, but have often not shared my interpretations or my emphases. They include Gerald Holton, Mallinckrodt Professor of Physics and Professor of History of Science, Emeritus, Harvard University; Bernard Knox, Director Emeritus of Harvard's Center for Hellenic Studies in Washington, D.C.; Professor R. W. B. Lewis of Yale University; Professor Kenneth Lynn of Johns Hopkins University; Peter Marzio, Director, The Museum of Fine Arts, Houston; Professor Edmund S. Morgan of Yale University; Professor Jaroslav Pelikan of Yale University; Gerard Piel, former editor and publisher of *Scientific American;* and my sons, Paul Boorstin, Jonathan Boorstin, and David Boorstin.

Again, Robert D. Loomis, vice president and executive editor of Random House, has shown me how a publishing editor at his best can guide and encourage an author. Most important has been his guidance toward what this book should (and should not) try to be. And by his insistence on what I should omit he has helped me give focus to the book.

Ruth F. Boorstin, my wife and intellectual companion, has been as always my principal and most penetrating editor. Her poet's feeling for words and her impatience with vagueness and the cliché have made the book briefer and more readable. To dedicate this book to her is, once again, a conspicuous understatement, which is only one of the literary virtues she has tried to teach me.

Index

About the Author

Historian, public servant, and author, DANIEL J. BOORSTIN, the Librarian of Congress Emeritus, directed the Library from 1975 to 1987. He had previously been director of the National Museum of History and Technology, and senior historian of the Smithsonian Institution in Washington, D.C. Before that he was the Preston and Sterling Morton Distinguished Service Professor of History at the University of Chicago, where he taught for twenty-five years.

Born in Atlanta, Georgia, and raised in Tulsa, Oklahoma, Boorstin graduated with highest honors from Harvard College and received his doctorate from Yale University. As a Rhodes Scholar at Balliol College, Oxford, England, he won a coveted double first in two degrees in law and was admitted as a barrister-at-law of the Inner Temple, London. He is also a member of the Massachusetts bar. He has been visiting professor at the University of Rome, the University of Geneva, the University of Kyoto in Japan, and the University of Puerto Rico. In Paris he was the first incumbent of a chair in American history at the Sorbonne, and at Cambridge University, England, he was Pitt Professor of American History and Institutions and Fellow of Trinity College. Boorstin has lectured widely in the United States and all over the world. He has received numerous honorary degrees and has been decorated by the governments of France, Belgium, Portugal, and Japan. He is married to the former Ruth Frankel, the editor of all his works, and they have three sons and six grandchildren.

The Discoverers, Boorstin's history of man's search to know the world and himself, was published in 1983. A Book-of-the-Month Club Main Selection, *The Discoverers* was on the *New York Times* best-seller list for half a year and won the Watson Davis Prize of the History of Science Society. This and his other books have been translated into more than twenty languages.

Boorstin's many books include *The Americans: The Colonial Experience* (1958), which won the Bancroft Prize; *The Americans: The National Experience* (1965), which won the Parkman Prize; and *The Americans: The*

Democratic Experience (1973), which won the Pulitzer Prize for History and the Dexter Prize and was a Book-of-the-Month Club Main Selection. Among his other books are *The Mysterious Science of the Law* (1941), *The Lost World of Thomas Jefferson* (1948), *The Genius of American Politics* (1953), *The Image* (1962), *The Republic of Technology* (1978), and *The Daniel J. Boorstin Reader* (1995). For young people he has written the *Landmark History of the American People.* His textbook for high schools, *A History of the United States* (1980), written with Brooks M. Kelley, has been widely adopted. He is the editor of *An American Primer* (1966) and the thirty-volume series *The Chicago History of American Civilization,* among other works.